MW01124019

GETTING YOUR
SEX LIFE
OFF TO A
GREAT START

Other Books by Clifford and Joyce Penner

From Word Publishing:

The Gift of Sex
Counseling for Sexual Disorders
Sex Facts for the Family
Restoring the Pleasure

From Thomas Nelson Publishing:

52 Ways to Have Fun, Fantastic Sex

GETTING YOUR
SEX LIFE
OFF TO A
GREAT START

*A Guide for Engaged
and Newlywed Couples*

CLIFFORD L. PENNER, Ph.D.
JOYCE J. PENNER, R.N., M.N.

THOMAS NELSON
Since 1798

NASHVILLE   DALLAS   MEXICO CITY   RIO DE JANEIRO   BEIJING

© 1994 by Word Publishing. All rights reserved. No portion of this book may be reproduced, stored in retrieval system, or transmitted in any form or by any means—electronic, mechanical, photocopy, recording, or any other—except for brief quotations in reviews without prior permission of the publisher.

Published in Nashville, Tennessee, by Thomas Nelson. Thomas Nelson is a trademark of Thomas Nelson, Inc.

Thomas Nelson, Inc. titles may be purchased in bulk for educational, business, fundraising, or sales

Unless otherwise indicated, all Scripture references in this volume are from the New American Standard Version of the Bible © 1960, 1962, 1963, 1968, 1971, 1972, 1973, 1975, 1977 by The Lockman Foundation. Used by permission.

Scripture verses indicated KJV are from the King James Version of the Bible.

Verses indicated TM are from *The Message.* © 1993. Used by permission of NavPress Publishing Group.

Verses indicated NIV are from the New International Version of the Bible, © 1983 by the International Bible Society. Used by permission of Zondervan Bible Publishers.

Clients' stories included in this volume are composites of actual cases. Names and details have been changed to protect identities.

Library of Congress Cataloging-in-Publication Data

Penner, Clifford.
    Getting your sex life off to a great start : a guide for engaged and newlywed couples / Clifford L. Penner and Joyce J. Penner.
       p. cm.
    ISBN 10: 0-8499-3515-6
    ISBN 13: 978-0-8499-3515-2

    1. Sex instruction. 2. Sex in marriage. 3. Sex—Religious aspects—Christianity. I. Penner, Joyce. II. Title.
HQ31.P4463 1994
646.7'8—dc20   94-28374
                                                         CIP

Printed in the United States of America

07 08 09 10 11 12 RRD 28 27 26 25 24 23

To our son, Greg, and our soon-to-be daughter-in-law, Carrie, in celebration of your engagement and upcoming marriage. May your love mature with the same beauty with which it has budded and blossomed. May you learn to practice diligently the love that never gives up, that cares as much for each other as for yourselves, that doesn't place demands but freely gives, that ignores the other's weaknesses and delights in each other's strengths. May you continue to enjoy your childlike playfulness even as you pursue your passion for each other and your goals for your life together.

The authors welcome readers' comments and responses about the information in this book, but they regret that they cannot always answer individual letters. For further information regarding seminars or other speaking engagements, please write or call:

Dr. Clifford and Joyce Penner
300 North Lake Avenue, Suite 1111A
Pasadena, California 91101
626-449-2525

Contents

◆◆◆◆◆◆◆◆◆◆

Acknowledgments ix
Preface xi
So You've Found the Love of Your Life 1

Part I. Learning Together 13
    1. Dispelling Myths 15
    2. Getting to Know Yourself 28
    3. Getting to Know Each Other 43
    4. Clarifying Expectations 53
    5. Pursuing Biblical Passion 66
    6. Discovering and Enjoying Your Bodies 82
    7. Designing a Successful Honeymoon 112
    8. Preparing for Your First Time 124
    9. Choosing and Using Family-Planning
       Options 140

Part II. Behind Closed Doors 165
    10. Your Wedding Night 167
    11. Keeping Sex for Pleasure 182
    12. Getting Past Disappointments 203
    13. Keeping the Spark Alive 218

Epilogue: Two Become One: A Symbol of Christ and
    the Church 231
Notes 237
Additional References 241

Acknowledgments

◆◆◆◆◆◆◆◆◆◆

Our thanks to:

Four young couples whose interaction with the initial form of this manuscript gave us insight, clarification, and more accurate ways to communicate with premarital and newly married couples—

Greg Penner and Carrie Walton, our son and future daughter-in-law, who will be married next summer.

Phil Smith and Amy Schultheis, our friends, who will be married about the time this book arrives in the bookstores.

Scott and Denise Buhler Marble, our niece and her new husband, who received the final chapters the week before their wedding.

John and Julene Stellato, our son-in-law and daughter, who have been married for one year.

Thanks also to Kristine Penner, our youngest, who prepares to leave for her first year of college as we write this. Her quick eye and great wisdom have caught many an error and added spark to the way we express ourselves.

To Sue Ann Jones, our skillful and flexible editor, who has evidenced incredible patience with our need to attend to detail.

And to the many couples in our premarital classes who asked questions that sharpened our awareness of the need for the information in this book to aid others in *Getting Your Sex Life Off to a Great Start*.

Preface

◆◆◆◆◆◆◆◆◆◆

"I don't agree with what you are doing," Joyce's eighty-seven-year-old grandmother wrote us a number of years ago, referring to our work as sex educators. "Adam and Eve didn't need it; Abe and I didn't need it, and neither does anyone else."

Perhaps, like Joyce's dear grandmother, you don't think you need any help in preparing for your sexual relationship as husband and wife. Some of you may be right. Not everyone needs to prepare in order to have a happy sex life in marriage. Some couples really can "do what comes naturally" and have a delightful, fulfilling experience. But for the majority, lack of preparation leads to sharp disappointment, even despair.

We've written this book to help you prepare, not just for your wedding night, but for a lifetime of exhilarating, fulfilling, and nurturing sexual experiences.

To prepare when you don't need to is a happier mistake than to not prepare and find out you should have. Intelligent, deliberate preparation to sharing your lives together physically, emotionally, and spiritually will be a worthy investment you won't regret.

We were fortunate that our sex life in marriage got off to a great start and is a fulfilling, delightful part of our lives today. We are convinced that our successful beginning can be attributed to the knowledge and encouraging attitudes about sex in marriage that Joyce received during a Preparation for Marriage class she took right before we were married. Her eagerness to share that information with Cliff opened our communication about this vital dimension of our relationship. From our own positive experience and the changes we have observed in hundreds of couples' lives, we share the information in this book with an overwhelming conviction that accurate knowledge, healthy attitudes and expectations, and the ability for the two of you to talk openly about sex will give you the tools to get your sex life off to a great start!

So You've Found the Love of Your Life . . .

. . . and you're going to get married. Or perhaps you are newly-weds, and you're feeling all the newness and emotions created by joining your two families. For most of you these are very special days and months to remember. For all of you, they are exciting and life changing.

The two of you have made one of the most important decisions of your lives. This book is *not* about making that decision. It *is* about preparing for a great sex life in marriage once you have chosen each other as lifetime partners. A great sex life is based on commitment, love, trust, romance, intimacy, and passion. This introductory chapter will help you build these vital ingredients in your relationship.

Commitment

Deciding to get married is the first step of commitment. This commitment affects people differently. Ideally, your decision has brought you a sense of peace and excitement. Take time to examine the effect your decision to marry has had on each of you and on your relationship. How have your feelings about yourself changed? How have they changed toward your partner? What changes have you felt from your partner? Have you been relating more easily, or has there been an increase in tension and differences? Have insecurities arisen or been relieved? Has your physical desire for one another increased or decreased? A strong sex urge between two people who are attracted to each other is normal. If you are not yet married, how are you dealing with those urges? If you are married, has your lifetime commitment brought the freedom and delight you had hoped for sexually? We were designed so that physical desire increases with increased commitment and love.

Love

Love is the unconditional warmth that will keep you committed to one another and glowing even when it seems your sexual flame begins to fade. Sex without love is like a fire without warmth. Love is the commitment to hang in there when the fire of passion is no longer vibrant. Love is caring as much about your partner's well-being as you do yourself. It is deliberate.

In the musical *Fiddler on the Roof*, Tevia sings to Goldie, his wife, "Do you love me?"

Goldie is perplexed by his question and replies with a list of all she's done for him during their twenty-five years of marriage. He continues to ask, "But, . . . do you love me?"

She adds to the list and finally sings, "After twenty-five years, I suppose I do."

The question of love is one we hear frequently in our office. Couples wonder if they are still "in love," as if love is something magical that they have or do not have, something that is completely out of their control.

Love is not just a feeling. The intense emotions we associate with love will come and go. There are times in every good marriage when a husband and wife don't feel very loving toward each other. "Emotions are like that," wrote Dr. James Dobson in his book *Love for a Lifetime.* "They flatten out occasionally like an automobile tire with a nail in the tread. Riding on the rim is a pretty bumpy experience for everyone on board."[1]

It is at those bumpy times that you will need to practice the behaviors of love detailed in this passage from the Bible's "Love Chapter":

> Love never gives up.
> Love cares more for others than for self.
> Love doesn't want what it doesn't have.
> Love doesn't strut,
> Doesn't have a swelled head,
> Doesn't force itself on others,
> Isn't always "me first,"

Doesn't fly off the handle,
Doesn't keep score of the sins of others,
Doesn't revel when others grovel,
Takes pleasure in the flowering of truth,
Puts up with anything,
Trusts God always,
Always looks for the best,
Never looks back,
But keeps going to the end.
Love never dies.

(1 Cor. 13:4–8 TM)

It is this ability to love consistently that ensures a lasting marriage. The capacity to love and to be lovable was learned in your childhood home by how your parents interacted with each other. How did your parents show their affection for each other? How did they communicate love? What if you were raised in a single-parent home? What did that parent convey to you about commitment, respect, and love toward the opposite sex? How did your parents give their love to you and your siblings? How would you like your home to demonstrate love? How have the two of you demonstrated your commitment of love to each other? Take some time to share your responses to the Sharing Love form below.

Sharing Love

When I love you I show it by _____.

I know you love me when you _____.

I know you are reaching out to me when you _____.

When you reach out to me I feel _____.

I get insecure about your love for me when _____.

When I feel insecure about your love, it helps me if you _____
_____.

I have difficulty expressing my love for you when _____.

The biggest threat to our love that I have ever experienced was ____
_____.

The way I like to deal with conflict is _____.

I see our greatest strength as _____.

I see our greatest weakness as _____.

Even when I don't feel loving toward you, I commit myself to love you and will demonstrate my unconditional love by _____
_____.

Love must be freely given; it cannot be demanded. God loved us and gave Himself to us through His Son, Jesus Christ. He offers Himself to us but never demands that we receive His gift of love. That is the model of how a husband and wife are to love each other. If you delight in each other and give your love freely without keeping a balance sheet, you will both be incredibly happy. Being secure enough in yourself to reach out and love your partner without neediness will leave you deeply satisfied.

Love is life's most precious commodity. It is the gift of yourselves to each other. Nurture it! If giving love does not come easily, plan it into your lives. Discipline yourselves to give to each other in one small way each day. A telephone call from work, a love note on a pillow, a compliment, relieving the other of a responsibility by doing a task—all these actions are ways of saying, "I love you." Each week, plan a little more significant gift of yourself. You might prepare a special meal, have a dinner out, meet for lunch, or prepare a love nest by the fireplace. Monthly giving can be even bigger and more sacrificial. You might make a list for each other of what you would enjoy from the other. Make your yearly anniversary a time of reflection, recommitment, and a deliberate nurturing of your love.

Never violate your love for each other. In moments of anger, it is easy to make hurtful comments that devalue your spouse and your love. When that happens make a special effort to replenish that loss and restore your love.

As you nurture your love, it will steadily increase. When you are old and feeble and rocking together in a home for the elderly, you will glow with a rich love that will warm those who care for you.

Trust

Trust is built on the commitment of love. Putting your trust in the commitment to love may or may not come easily. If your trust was never violated, trusting your partner may be as automatic as the sunrise and the sunset. However, trust may have been broken between the two of you sometime during your dating history. Even though forgiveness and reconciliation have occurred, the possibility of a repeat of a previous violation may still linger in your heart.

Nancy and Jim's dating years were characterized by both intense passion and repeated violations of Nancy's trust by Jim's disregard of her and his inappropriate attention to other women. Eventually, however, Jim's commitment of trustworthiness to Nancy stabilized, and they decided to marry. Their relationship grew in the joy they shared. Nevertheless, Nancy continued to carry thoughts of Jim's past, and she had difficulty completely trusting his commitment to love her faithfully.

It is difficult to totally relinquish pain or hurt even after we have forgiven. When Christ forgave us, His forgiveness of us was complete and instant, but that is not so for us. Our forgiveness of others takes work. According to Dr. Lewis Smedes, professor of ethics at Fuller Theological Seminary, the work of forgiving requires that we give up the need to get even. It takes time and is helped by understanding.[2]

For Nancy to forgive Jim for his past behavior toward her required a commitment from both of them. She needed to recognize her anger and talk about the hurt she had suffered. Jim needed to care about Nancy's pain and accept responsibility for his inappropriate actions. With the help of a therapist, he learned the reasons for his unreliability and shared these with Nancy. Nancy's understanding of Jim, and Jim's commitment to make himself accountable to love her faithfully, led to healing and the building of their trust.

You may have difficulty trusting even if trust has never been violated in your relationship. Trust may have been broken in your childhood family. Talk about your difficulty with your partner and have him or her help you establish trust. On the other hand, if it is difficult for your partner to trust you, first make certain you are trustworthy. Then try to understand and empathize with your spouse's lack of trust. The more consistently you demonstrate loving commitment, the more quickly you will create trust. Be patient.

A fun way to test the trust within your relationship is to guide each other on a trust walk. Take turns being the one who has to trust the other to lead. First, blindfold your partner so there is no way he or she can see. The one who is not blindfolded then takes the other one on a walking-talking tour of the house or yard. Then reverse roles. The leader must be highly trustworthy. This is not the time to play tricks on one another; it is the time to build trust. When it is your turn to be the leader, describe exactly where you are, where you are going, and how to proceed so there will be no surprises. Behave as if your blindfolded partner is literally blind and you are lovingly teaching him or her how to get around your home or yard.

The trust walk was very helpful to Nancy and Jim. But Nancy expressed a need for an ongoing reminder of the need for trustworthiness that the blindfold had provided on their walk. They decided they would practice using their wedding rings as a symbol of their trust by placing their ringed hands on top of each other when they prayed at mealtimes.

You may find a creative approach to the issue of trust as Nancy and Jim did. Once trust, based on commitment and love, has been well established between the two of you, you are ready to pursue romance.

Romance

Romance is the breeze that fans the sexual flame to keep the warmth of your love glowing. Romance is the imaginative, adventurous, picturesque, and expressive dimension of your relationship. Paying attention to the romance can be fun. That may come more easily for one of you than it does for the other. If romantic ideas come easily for you, enjoy being the aggressor. If not, you may need to be more deliberate in expressing romance in any way that is possible for you.

Just this week we got a letter from a woman complaining that she had to initiate all the romance in their marriage. Her husband was shy and found it difficult to express himself romantically. For her, initiating the romantic connection was easy, but she did not want to be the aggressive one in their relationship for the rest of her life. Being solely responsible for any aspect of your marriage will become burdensome. Yet remember, each of you comes to your marriage with unique gifts. Enjoy those differences and *learn* how to be romantic if that doesn't come easily.

To learn to be romantic, first, emphasize and practice beautiful virtues such as kindness and gentleness. Second, be aware of the external conditions that heighten your senses. What did you do to win each other initially? What are the necessary ingredients of a romantic experience for you? Cleanliness, beauty, nature, scents, music, waves, art, dance, play, touch, language, being well-groomed, intense expression of positive feelings, and creating together are all expressions of romance. Finally, plan specific romantic events for just the two of you. You may find that the traditional candlelight dinner or going out for a dinner together is your favorite way of being romantic. Or you might prefer a picnic, a hike in the woods, a stroll along the beach, a walk in your neighborhood, a bike ride, watching the rain, sitting by the fire, reading your old love letters or your journal entries, serving coffee in bed, or cooking a meal together. The possibilities are unending; write your own list and refer to it when you both would like to do something romantic but neither of you has the energy or imagination to think of anything. If you run out of ideas, you might use Gregory J. P. Godek's book *1001 Ways to Be Romantic.*[3]

Intimacy

Sex without intimacy is like enjoying a fire by yourself. The fire will keep you warm, but the experience is a lonely one. Likewise, non-intimate sex will take care of your physical sexual need for arousal and release. It can temporarily meet your need for fusion with another person to relieve your anxieties of not being loved, but it does not permanently satisfy.

Women tend to need emotional intimacy as a prerequisite for physical intimacy. In general, men, more than women, have difficulty with intimacy. You may have to work at intimacy if your family was not intimate and did not allow you to develop your capacity for intimacy. This capacity was learned primarily during your first year of life by the bonding that occurred between you and your primary caretaker; usually that would have been your mother. If this person was not able or willing to give warmth through closeness and touch, you may have learned to survive without that deep sense of connection.

You obviously will not remember whether the process of bonding happened for you. It probably *did* if you desire emotional and physical closeness. If you are able to soak in bodily pleasure for yourself without worrying about your spouse or without focusing on sexual release, you have the capacity for intimacy. If you are able to reveal the information about yourself that is requested in the sharing exercises in this book, you have the capacity for intimacy.

Combining sex and intimacy requires a sense of yourself as a worthy separate person.[4] You can practice intimacy as you share with each other all the communication and touching exercises we recommend throughout this book. As you share yourselves, be aware of your internal worlds of thoughts and feelings. Reveal these to each other while being sensitive to and reflective of your partner's inner world of thoughts and feelings. Intimacy is the bond that will hold the two of you together and fulfill that sense of two separate, complete individuals uniting with one another.

Passion

Passion is the flame of your sexual relationship. It can manifest itself in intense expression of sexual feelings as well as feelings of anger or any other emotion. Relationships with a high quotient of passion are often both intensely sexual and conflictual. A newly married couple who live in a second-story apartment told us recently that their first-floor neighbors probably believe they have the world's greatest marriage because they likely hear the newlyweds' sexual activity while the neighbors who live beside them may think they are on the verge of divorce because they hear the intensity of their differences being expressed.

Passion ignites most intensely in a new relationship. It is similar to when you first light a fire. It takes a little while to kindle the flame, then it burns with intensity until all the wood is ignited and the red-hot logs are glowing and radiating warmth. Depending on the type of firewood, some fires ignite almost instantly. Others are very slow to get started. All fires eventually die down but can be revived if firewood is added before the last spark is out.

The same is true for your relationship. You may have been almost instantly attracted to each other with intense passion. Or you may have gradually grown to know each other so the passion in your relationship ignited rather slowly. You may have already made the transition from the intense passion of a new attraction to a warm, glowing, loving companionship. Or you may still be driven by that fervent excitement so common to new relationships. Eventually, the flame of your passion will fade, but it will not die out if you keep putting fuel on the fire. That is, if you keep commitment, love, trust, romance, and intimacy alive. Then you will always have a sexually fulfilling relationship that provides warmth, closeness, and spark long after the flames lessen.

Even though you will go through (or may have already experienced) a transition from the initial passion to a more intimate companionship, there are ways to keep low-level flames alive forever. Passion can be maintained at some level throughout a lifelong relationship.

When we talk about passion, we refer to a vigorous intensity, an excitement about being who you are and being together! It is the opposite of sameness, predictability, and boredom. To feel passionate you must be able to risk being vulnerable—letting go and being out of control. You must expand your capacity for feeling. You must be willing to stretch yourselves and live life to the fullest. Inhibitions stifle passion; surprises enhance passion. Insecurities, anxieties, distrust, guilt, hurt, disappointment, and all other emotions that keep you from being vulnerable with each other will inhibit your vitality and thus will limit your passion. Things that are new and unexpected keep passion alive. Elements of suspense and intrigue will spark passion.

Conclusion

Once you are certain of your choice of each other, you are ready to commit yourselves to build love, trust, romance, intimacy, and passion in your relationship. This book assumes you are secure in your choice of each other. If you are not, we would highly recommend Neil Clark Warren's book *Finding the Love of Your Life*. Dr. Warren discusses ten proven principles to help you choose or know you have chosen the person you can commit to love and live with happily for a lifetime.[5]

If you are looking forward to your marriage, you may so desperately desire each other right now that you cannot imagine your sexual relationship being anything but ecstatic. The fire of passion has been lit between you.

Your love for each other will mature as you grow in your knowledge of yourselves and each other. As your capacity to love increases, your intimacy will deepen and your romantic expressions will be more naturally integrated into your married life. You will experience more warmth, but not likely as much intense passion. As passion lessens, the deeper, quieter love will grow, making you friends and confidants forever. A decrease in passion is normal; it will not cause indifference. Indifference is a warning sign that the fire is about to die—if it hasn't already. When that happens, call for help!

Whether you begin your married sex life as virgins or one or both of you have been sexually active prior to your marriage, the transition from premarital passion to a married sexual relationship is a critical one. It can contribute to—or hinder—the positive adjustment that brings the highest peaks of happiness that married life offers. The information and processes described in this book will help you make that transition most effectively.

Working through the chapters that follow will give you the information and the tools you need to get your sexual relationship off to a great start. The knowledge you gain will help you establish sexual patterns to keep the warmth of the fire of your sex life glowing throughout your marriage.

Today the world is challenging couples to rediscover monogamy, *erotic* monogamy. On February 2, 1994, a headline in
the *Los Angeles Times* proclaimed, "Mad About Monogamy."
The article said, "Eager to push the erotic envelope? You may
not have to go very far. A wave of new books suggests that the
best hunting ground for great sex is right at home."[6] And that
is what we wish for you: great sex with your lifetime mate!

PART I

Learning Together

1

* * * * * *

Dispelling Myths

You already have clear opinions about sex. How tenaciously you hold to your beliefs has little to do with their accuracy. Myths are falsehoods that are generally accepted by a large segment of society as the truths. Many misconceptions about sexuality have been passed as truths from one generation to another.

Sometimes falsehoods begin during childhood as the child's way of trying to understand sexuality. This was evidenced to us by our son Greg when he was just five years old, the age most children become sexually aware and therefore begin to develop modesty. We were watching television as a family and having Greg and his older sister change into their pajamas while we watched. As Greg took off his pants and undershorts, he covered his genitals with his hand. This was a new expression of modesty for him, so Cliff asked him, "Greg, why are you covering yourself?"

Greg responded, "Because it pops up if it sees a girl!"

The myths in his response are clear: The penis acts independently of the person, and it responds visually to females (it can see—perhaps through the hole at the end!). There are adult men who continue to believe that these and other myths about the penis are facts.

It might be interesting for the two of you to compare your reactions to our list of myths and our countering facts. To do this, talk about what led you to accept a myth as truth, what experience contributed to your view of each myth, when you started believing a particular myth, and who influenced your belief in this false assumption.

Myth 1: Don't learn about sex; do what comes naturally!

If we lived in a primitive society and started experimenting sexually from the time we felt any sexual awareness, we might know what to do naturally. In primitive societies, we might also be "initiated" by an older person of the opposite sex. Because of our Christian and moral values, however, it is inappropriate that we practice such experimenting and initiation rituals. Nor do we watch others have intercourse unless we watch distorted sexual encounters on television and in movies.

Thus, the only way you can learn how to enjoy a satisfying sexual relationship in marriage is to educate yourselves, experiment with each other, teach each other, and practice with each other. Whether or not your childhood or dating experiences have prepared you to easily find sexual pleasure and satisfaction, you can *learn* to be a good lover!

Myth 2: You will automatically be interested in sex whenever your spouse is.

Unfortunately, sexual desire is not always "contagious"; just because one of you is in the mood for sex doesn't mean *both* of you are. It just doesn't work that way. Sexual drive is an appetite. Just as each of you will differ in your appetite for food—the amount you eat and when you eat—you will likely experience differences in your sexual appetites. And just as you work together to coordinate your eating habits you will also need to work out a way to coordinate your sexual differences to take care of each of your desires without "overfeeding" one of you. While you cannot survive without food, you *can* survive without sex. Therefore, it usually works best in the long term if the one with the higher desire does not put pressure on the one with lower desire. "Force feeding" kills the appetite totally.

Myth 3: Thanks to greater sexual freedom introduced by the sexual revolution you can now expect to be more comfortable with and find greater fulfillment during sex.

Not so! There may be more comfort with hearing and using sexual slang and observing explicit sexual activity today than in previous generations, but this has not contributed to our society's having more accurate knowledge, higher sexual satisfaction, or greater comfort with talking openly about sexual feelings or experiences or clinical information. You will have to make this freedom and openness happen in your relationship.

Myth 4: Sex must be spontaneous!

In movies and romantic novels, exhilarating sex is spontaneous. The couple's eyes meet across the room, and they are so drawn to each other that they slip away to some corner and make mad, passionate love before they hardly know each other's names. In real life, the more preparation, anticipation, talking, guiding, and scheduling you put into your sexual times with each other, the better they likely will be. If you wait for some mysterious erotic energy to grab you before you have sex, you may not be having sex very often. The most satisfying sexual encounters between you and your spouse will often be the ones you plan for and talk about. By anticipating this sexual encounter you set aside quality time for just the two of you.

Myth 5: Sex weakens you, so ration it out. Only engage in sex when you can afford to lose the energy, or do it the last thing at night.

Sex is great for your body! Believing otherwise is like believing that exercise weakens you so to stay strong and vibrant you shouldn't exercise too much. Sex is good for your heart; it improves circulation, releases tension, and generally enhances bodily systems.

Myth 6: Sex gets boring unless you keep changing partners.

As a matter of fact, the greatest sexual fulfillment comes for those who learn and grow together throughout a lifetime commitment to each other. Changing partners today is not only risky to your emotional health, it can have deadly consequences if one of your partners carries the HIV virus.

Myth 7: To be good at sex and have learned it all, you have to have had many sexual partners.

Wrong! You don't get a quality education by reading the first page of several different books. Likewise, you do not become a competent lover by repeating the same inadequate experience over and over. You become a competent lover by listening to each other's guidance and learning throughout a lifetime of intimate sharing with the same person.

Myth 8: Good sex should always be a ten. You should always feel the earth move!

Sex is like every other aspect of life. Some sexual times will be better than others. No cook prepares a perfect meal every time. Even if all the meals he or she prepares are satisfying and enjoyable and attractive, they will still vary. Some may even be ordinary. With meals, as with sex, it is great to have a ten every now and then, but a diet of tens would get too heavy.

Myth 9: To be normal, you should have sexual intercourse at least two or three times per week.

Normal frequency is what the two of you determine is right *for you.* That could be twice per day, twice per week, or twice per month. The key is to negotiate the best balance of your natural sexual desires.

Myth 10: You should not have sexual intercourse during menstruation and not very often during pregnancy.

False! Some women will have their highest interest and peak responsiveness during menstruation or pregnancy, possibly because they are not afraid of getting pregnant. You must discover for yourselves what is most comfortable and what brings the most enjoyment for both of you.

Myth 11: Since it is the woman who gets pregnant, she should take responsibility for birth control.

It is certainly true that the woman carries the baby and so needs to feel secure about the method of birth control used. But the responsibility for choosing a particular method needs to be a joint one because it will affect both the husband and the wife. The woman can easily feel alone in making this decision, so husband, don't desert your wife on this one.

Myth 12: Real men are supposed to be aggressive, rational, logical and nonexpressive. They shouldn't get into gooshy, romantic, talking and feeling stuff.

While there are typical gender differences between men and women, women can learn to be assertive and men can learn to be sensitive. Men do tend to be more competitive, assertive, and rational and are often not as aware of their feelings as women are. Women tend to be more gentle, nurturing, intuitive, emotionally responsive, and relationally oriented. All men and all women exhibit some portion of all of these qualities. Breaking away from these traditional role expectations is often beneficial to a couple's relationship.

If you develop your potential in the areas of expression that are not as natural for you, your sexual life will be enhanced. As men learn to know, share, and be sensitive to feelings and as women become more assertive in expressing their sexual desires, needs, and wishes their capacity for ecstasy is heightened.

Real men truly become "real men" as they discover and develop their romantic and intimacy capabilities. Sensitivity is a positive male attribute!

Myth 13: Women can flirt and tease but it is unladylike to directly express sexual interest.

Women have sexual urges and thoughts just as men do. In fact, women tend to fantasize even more than men. Men often need visual images while women create their own. When women learn to express their sexual urges directly and share their creative fantasies, their husbands are delighted and their sex life is sparked.

Myth 14: Men are always ready and willing and women should always be available.

This myth produces incredible demand! It demands that the husband behave as though he is interested even when he is not. It demands that the wife be responsive to her husband's arousal even when she is not interested. Even though both can decide to participate in a sexual time together when one is feeling the desire and the other is not, that should not be by demand. Sex should always be a choice. Demand is a killer to a healthy, long-term sexual relationship.

Myth 15: You have to feel "horny" before you initiate sex!

Not true! Two people with a deep love and commitment will often become sexually interested when they take time to connect, share, and pleasure each other. It is detrimental and decreases frequency to expect interest as a prerequisite to a positive sexual experience.

Myth 16: During sex, the man always takes the lead.

This may be a common cultural expectation, but it is neither true nor necessary. The opposite often works better. Since women tend to fluctuate more and be more particular about where, when, and how they want to be touched; it takes pressure off the husband and produces greater pleasure for the wife if she leads.

Myth 17: The stronger the person's faith, the less interested and less active he or she will be sexually.

This statement is not necessarily true. In fact, some studies confirm the exact opposite to be true! The Family Research Council conducted a poll that confirmed previous studies positively linking "religiosity" and sexual satisfaction. The poll was reported in the council's *Family Policy* bulletin in February 1994.

Myth 18: The better and more mature way for a woman to have an orgasm is during intercourse.

Although any woman can learn to be orgasmic during intercourse if she desires that, the majority of women do not have orgasms during intercourse. Most women respond orgasmically to manual and/or oral clitoral stimulation. There are other women who only respond during intercourse and still others who respond either way. Orgasmic response during intercourse can be stimulated by touching the clitoris or by stimulating the G-spot, an area in the vagina just beyond the pubococcygeus (PC) muscle toward the front of the woman's body (at the twelve o'clock position in the diagram, page 92). All variations are delightful ways of receiving sexual pleasure and release and have nothing to do with rightness or maturity. What is right is what works for you!

Myth 19: A real man produces an orgasm for his wife during penile thrusting.

Double-fault! First, it is not the man's responsibility to "produce" an orgasm for his wife. The woman's orgasm, just like the man's, is a reflex response to building arousal in the body as the result of intensely enjoying one another's bodies and each allowing the letting go of the buildup of that intensity. Second, the stimulation that triggers the orgasm in the woman has nothing to do with the man or his masculinity. The husband's sexual competence is only related to his ability to freely enjoy his wife's body for his own pleasure and to lovingly and caringly follow her guidance as to what is most pleasurable for her. As both listen to their inner desires and communicate those desires to each other and respond positively to each other's invitations, the automatic response of orgasm is likely to happen.

Myth 20: To be truly sexy and have a great sex life a woman must be multiorgasmic.

The number of orgasms a woman experiences during sex is not an indicator of her sexiness or her sexual satisfaction. Many women are totally satisfied after one release; others quickly get restimulated and desire more. The number of orgasms has no more to do with the quality of your sex life than the number of times you sneeze has to do with the quality of your respiratory system. It has to do with the need for release of pelvic (or, in the case of sneezing, nasal) congestion!

Myth 21: A man instinctively and intuitively knows how to make love to a woman and will show her his greatest love when he does what comes naturally.

This is a big error! William Masters and Virginia Johnson said it well in their book *Human Sexual Inadequacy*. "The most unfortunate misconception our culture has assigned to sexual functioning is the assumption, by both men and women, that men by divine guidance and infallible instinct are able to discern exactly what a women wants sexually and when she wants it."[1] This expectation leaves the man feeling inadequate and the woman feeling frustrated with his inadequacy. The myth also carries with it a number of other false assumptions: that the man is sexually all-knowing, that all women are sexually the same, and that a woman will respond the same from one day to the next.

The reality is that unless one partner is sexually more knowledgeable through past experience or study, a couple has to learn with each other through reading, talking, touching, and teaching each other what they enjoy. The woman is the best authority on her own body just as the man is on his. As you discover and share together, you will grow in the pleasure you enjoy.

Myth 22: Since men get turned on faster than women, the husband has to work on his wife to get her ready for intercourse more quickly.

There is some truth to this myth, so let us sort out the facts from the fiction. Physiologically, men and women both respond to effective sexual stimulation within seconds; the man has an erection and the woman has vaginal lubrication. But this does not mean either of them is ready for intercourse, especially the woman. Women tend to be more aware of their need for relational and emotional readiness than for physical readiness. So if a husband feels he needs to "work on" his wife to speed her along, the best approach he could take would be to connect with her emotionally and spend plenty of time pleasuring her body rather than trying to produce a result in her physically. As sex therapists, we spend our time helping men learn to connect, enjoy pleasure, and slow down rather than "work" at producing a result, especially not the result of making the women speed toward the goal of intercourse or orgasm.

Myth 23: The way to turn on a woman is to find the clitoris and "rub the heck out of it!" (or rub it until she responds).

Vigorous, direct rubbing of the clitoris drives women crazy with pain, frustration, and irritation, not with ecstasy! Most women enjoy closeness, cuddling, and total-body pleasuring. The genital stimulation that is usually most arousing for women is very general stroking of the shaft and the hood of the clitoris, not directly stimulating the head. Women will need to guide their husbands to teach them what is the most enjoyable clitoral stimulation. Just because your husband loves you does not mean he will know how to please you sexually!

Myth 24: A man can determine if a woman is ready for intercourse by checking to see if her vagina is moist.

This "dipstick" method of checking for readiness is based on two false assumptions. First, it assumes that the man is the best authority on when the woman is ready. Second, it assumes that the woman is ready when she is lubricated. As mentioned previously, a woman lubricates within seconds after stimulation but is not *emotionally* ready for entry for quite some time. It works best if the woman signals her husband when she is ready without placing any demand on him to also be ready at that moment.

Myth 25: A man's erection is a signal that he is going to need intercourse or ejaculation—and probably soon!

An erection for the man is no different than vaginal lubrication for the woman. It means the man is aroused, and that is all! An erection is not a demand for action, even though many men say they just cannot handle getting aroused and not having an ejaculation. The truth is that all men get erections every eighty to ninety minutes while they sleep, but these erections rarely lead to an ejaculation—and the man doesn't experience any physical discomfort. Most of these involuntary nighttime and sometimes daytime erections just come and go. It is equally possible to allow arousal to come and go during caressing or in response to seeing his wife's body. A woman should never allow an erect penis to become a sexual message of demand to her. Instead, enjoy it and let it give you pleasure as you desire.

Myth 26: Men are always interested and ready for sex!

Sexual desire in men, as in women, varies from one man to another and from one time to another. In our practice, we have many couples seeking help because the man lacks sexual interest, and we have couples seeking help because the woman lacks sexual desire. Some men go through stages when their desire is lessened because of outside pressures, emotional turmoil, or physical illness.

Myth 27: Once pleasurable physical touching has been initiated, it must lead to intercourse and orgasm.

Sex is so much more than intercourse and orgasm. The mind is the most powerful sex organ, and the total surface of the skin is a sexual receptor. We can have a complete sexual experience without either intercourse or orgasm. Deep satisfaction and delightful pleasure comes from cuddling, kissing, stroking, playing, talking, and just lying together. All of that is sex! The option to proceed to intercourse should only be pursued when both of you want it; proceed on to orgasm when that is desired and the spouse is willing. In his book *Rekindling Desire*, Dr. Warwick Williams states this well in what he calls his key sexual attitude. "Lovemaking means literally that—interacting physically and emotionally with someone you care about. Arousal, intercourse, and orgasm or ejaculation are nonessential, and simply possible lovemaking options."[2]

Myth 28: Once entry has occurred, the goal is to thrust to orgasm.

Entry is not the beginning of the end! A fulfilling sexual encounter includes ebb and flow, intensity and quiet glow, moving and rolling, thrusting and resting, withdrawal and re-entry, being silly and being serious, *and* moving intentionally to orgasm.

Myth 29: The normal position for sexual intercourse is with the man on top.

The man-on-top position is commonly used by many couples, but that does not make it *the* normal or right position. You will discover with experience which positions bring you the most pleasure. Often, to change negative habits in a couple's sexual relationship, having the woman of top is the most helpful. What is most important is that you feel free to try a variety of positions.

Myth 30: If you are great lovers, the house will shake, the china will rattle, and the dogs will howl when you reach orgasm.

An orgasm is a by-product of a wonderfully pleasurable sexual time together. Orgasms vary from one person to another and from one time to another. Orgasms are like sneezes: Some are loud and boisterous, and some you hardly hear; sometimes one is needed, and other times several are desired. Quiet intensity can be as powerful as loud expressive release. Enjoy your responses!

Myth 31: To reach ultimate sexual fulfillment, a couple should strive for simultaneous orgasms.

Simultaneous orgasms can be fun if that happens every now and then, but always having that as a goal is most often destructive and certainly not the measure of success. The demand for both spouses to have orgasms at the same time gets in the way of the pleasure of enjoying each other. Besides, many couples prefer separate orgasms so each one can experience the other's. During orgasm, you are so absorbed in your own sensations you are not aware of the other's response.

Myth 32: In marriage, you should be able to perform sexually. Normal people do not have sexual problems.

All men and women struggle sexually at some time in their marriages. There will be times when the husband is not interested, doesn't get an erection, loses his erection, ejaculates too quickly, or doesn't ejaculate at all. Likewise, the wife will have times of not being interested, not getting or feeling aroused, not being able to let go orgasmically, or experiencing pain. If you shift your focus off of performance and your bodily responses and back onto pleasure, these dilemmas will often correct themselves. If not, that is the time to go for help!

Myth 33: Penis size is associated with multiple myths: the larger the penis, the more of a man you are; the larger

the penis, the greater your sexual drive; the larger the penis, the more sexually desirable you are; the larger the penis, the better you are as a lover; the larger the penis, the greater satisfaction you will be able to bring to your wife.

Penis size has nothing to do with a man's sexuality, his attractiveness to a woman, his skill as a lover, or the satisfaction he can bring to a woman. The quality of sex is not in any way related to penis size. When erect, penises vary little in size from one to another. A smaller, flaccid penis enlarges proportionately more when erect than does a larger flaccid penis. Also, the vagina is an organ of accommodation. It adapts to the penis. And it is only in the outer third of the vagina that the woman responds to the penis. So all the man needs is one and a half to two inches. The penis myths perpetuated by locker-room jokes and pornographic writings have nothing to do with reality.

Myth 34: Sexual interest and ability diminish for both men and women with age.

Sexual changes occur as the result of aging, but lack of desire or inability to function sexually are not included in those changes. The physical changes for women are the lessening of vaginal lubrication and the thinning of the vaginal wall; these may require hormonal replacement therapy and/or the use of a vaginal lubricant. The changes for men include a reduced urgency in sexual desire. As a man ages, he may need direct stimulation of his penis to get an erection, his erections may not be as firm as they once were, an ejaculation may not be needed with every experience, and the ejaculations will not be as intense. These changes do not prevent couples from continuing to enjoy an active and satisfying sexual life well into their eighties and nineties and right up to the time of death.

Myth 35: The honeymoon will be one continuous sex orgy!

The honeymoon is often a time of sexual and personal adjustment. Whether or not there has been sexual activity before marriage, the stress and excitement of the wedding as well as the awareness of their now being husband and wife can cause a couple to change. In chapter 4, we assist you in setting realistic expectations for what your relationship will be like after you are married.

You may have discovered that you believed some of these myths as though they were truths. We hope that your reading our list of myths together will have opened discussion between the two of you about your beliefs. We encourage you to continue to discuss any additional myths you discover. You may find that some of your personal beliefs or misconceptions are actually myths in regard to your sexuality. Share these with each other. You will contribute to your own growing sensual reality as you do.

2
♦♦♦♦♦♦

Getting to
Know Yourself

We met in September of 1959 at the freshmen "get-acquainted" social at Grace College of the Bible in Omaha, Nebraska. Joyce was a hesitant Minnesotan, and Cliff a self-assured Canadian. We were both rather limited in our self-awareness and completely naive about our sexual selves.

Our years of dating, our education, and our interaction with peers after that introduction helped prepare us for our first complete sexual experience four years later. With great eagerness and excitement, we drove away from our wedding reception in our classic bronze-and-cream 1957 Chevrolet. That first night was a positive start to more than thirty years of a growing and fulfilling sexual relationship.

A great sex life requires that a husband and wife know themselves personally and sexually. True fulfillment is impossible until you have a sense of who you are and what you bring to your sexual relationship. One of the reasons it is detrimental for adolescents to be sexually active is because adolescence is the time of self-discovery—the time of learning who we are as persons separate from our families of origin. During intercourse we lose ourselves to another person, and it is emotionally unsettling to lose ourselves when we have not yet found ourselves!

In this chapter we will guide you through a self-analysis to help you know yourself a little better. It might be helpful to have paper and pencil handy to jot down your thoughts as you read through the sections because later on we'll ask you to share your responses with each other.

Who Are You?

Take some time to describe yourself. Set aside at least thirty minutes for a time of privacy when you will not be interrupted or feel pressured to do anything else. Imagine that you are introducing yourself to someone you will never meet in person who needs to know every detail about you. Use the following topics and questions to guide your self-analysis.

Your Personality

How do you see yourself? Are you quiet or talkative, reserved or outgoing, serious or flippant, free-spirited or set in your ways, distant or available, closed or open, organized or chaotic, independent or dependent, self-oriented or other-oriented . . . ? How do others see you? What feedback have you gotten from family, friends, teachers, bosses, coworkers, or past romantic relationships?

A helpful tool to give you accurate input on your personality is the Myers Briggs Type Indicator. It is available in the book *Please Understand Me: Character and Temperament Types* by David Keirsey and Marilyn Bates. We highly recommend that you take the inventory and then read about your characteristics; it is an affirming experience. The basic premise of Keirsey and Bates's book is that since people are different, it is beneficial to understand and utilize these differences. The indicator will rate you on four scales: extroversion versus introversion, intuition (more innovative) versus sensation (more practical), thinking versus feeling, and judging (liking closure) versus perceiving (liking open options). You can order the book by calling 619-632-1575.

Your Spiritual Self

If you charted a road map of your walk with God, what would it look like? Where and when did you first meet God? What were the significant nurturing stops along the way? Did you backtrack or take detours? Were there some tough mountains to climb? Did you feel a sense of exhausted exhilaration when you reached new peaks? Who were the support people who encouraged you? Who distracted you? What was your family's and church's influence? Was your sexuality connected with any noteworthy events along your pathway? Describe your current destination and where you hope to travel in your future spiritual journey.

Your Mind

How you use your intellect affects what you bring to your sexual relationship. Are you quick-witted or methodical? Do you love to create or learn new approaches, or would you rather stay with the familiar and what's already known? Are you the kind of person who takes in new information, digests it, and assimilates it into your life rather easily, or does it take repeated input to produce change? Does an intellectual challenge invigorate or intimidate you? Are you the person with the answers, or do you look to others for solutions? Are you threatened by others who seem to know it all? Do you try to win approval by pleasing others? Do you put high demands on yourself, or are you easygoing? If you are demanding does that produce results or immobilize you? Your mind is your largest sex organ. You can learn to use it to work for you, but only as you understand how it works.

Your Body

Describe your physical characteristics so the person you have never met can picture you clearly. You might start with the specifics: I'm _____ feet _____ inches tall. I weigh _____ pounds. I have _____ hair, _____ eyes, _____ eyebrows, a _____ nose, _____ shaped face, _____ lips, _____ ears, _____ neck. My skin color is _____. I would describe my build as _____. I have _____ shoulders, _____ arms, _____ hands, _____ chest, _____ waist, _____ abdomen, _____ buttocks, _____ thighs, _____ legs, _____ feet. I tend to look best when _____.

Now that you have described yourself factually, we have a more difficult task for you, a body-image mirror assignment. How you feel about your body, your body image, will greatly affect how openly you are able to share your body with your spouse. The view you have of your body developed during your childhood and adolescence by how you were touched, the messages you received from the significant people in your life, and the models you measured yourself against. The more closely your *ideal* body matches your view of your body, the higher your comfort level will be with your body. The more comfortable you are with your body, the freer you will be to share your body with your spouse visually and sexually.

If your early-childhood sensory experiences were physically affirming you will have developed a warm, soothing connection with your body. For example, if you were comforted by being held closely, rocked, stroked, and patted, that physical affirmation will have given you the desire for physical closeness. Your skin will be feel hungry for touch. You will be sensitive to textures as well as emotions communicated through touch. On the contrary, if you experienced physical pain, lack of touch, or jerky, anxious, or self-serving touch, you may have either blocked out the need for touch, react negatively to unexpected touch, or experience touch as a demand. Should you bring a lack of physical affirmation into your marriage, you will need to take responsibility for awakening those needs in your relationship. That may require you to take charge of touching by letting your spouse know when certain physical approaches startle you, asking for the affirming stroking you need before you feel comfortable sharing your body, and planning into your sexual lives an increased amount of nonsexual cuddling. Since you may not be aware of the natural urge to touch or to be touched, you will need to plan for touching by decision rather than waiting for the felt desire.

The input you got from your parents, teachers, and peers about your appearance will have left you with either a positive or a negative view of your body. It is amazing to us to hear some of the cruel messages adults still carry with them that they received as children. A mother, in all seriousness, told her daughter they would have to work on developing her personality to make up for her looks. A father consistently teased his adolescent daughter by referring to her small breasts as half-empty baskets. A teacher nicknamed a student Pinocchio because of his long, pointed nose. Children have often called each other "Fatty" or given each other even more derogatory labels. These messages linger long after a person no longer fits the label. The less-attractive little girl may develop into a physically beautiful young woman but still perceive her mother's negative view of her looks as accurate. A new bride may feel self-conscious undressing in front of her husband and block out positive sensation from breast stimulation because of her father's messages about her breasts even though her husband finds her breasts stimulating and attractive. An overweight child may grow into a well-proportioned adult but still perceive himself or herself as fat.

Confronting your body will help you differentiate between those messages you carried from childhood into adulthood and an accurate perception of how your body is now. To examine your view of your body you will need a full-length mirror. Before you face the mirror, however, take a warm shower or bath to relax yourself. While in the bath or shower, look at the various parts of your body. Describe what you see. How do you feel about what you see? What would you change? Now dry off and take some time to relax before you position yourself in front of the full-length mirror. This may be more difficult. You may have avoided full-length mirrors, especially when you were in the nude. If it helps you, start by wearing a towel wrapped around you. Lower the towel as you get to the parts of your body the towel is covering.

As you stand facing yourself in the mirror, how do you feel about what you see? Try to separate what you see from the feelings associated with your body. Objectively, how would you describe yourself? How is that description different from how you *feel* about your body? Once you have struggled with the general view and feelings you have about your body, have a look at your specific body parts from both a realistic perspective and a feeling viewpoint.

Start with your hair. Reflect on what you like about it now, how you felt about it growing up, what messages you got back then or get now from others, and how you would change it if you could. Proceed from your hair to your face and the various parts of your face, to your neck, chest or breasts, arms, hands, abdomen, genitals, thighs, legs, and feet. Then turn your back toward the mirror and look over your shoulder as you examine the back of your body and your feelings about that.

When you finish the body-image mirror exercise, take some time to reflect on how that felt. How comfortable or uncomfortable are you about facing your body? What things about your body are you hiding? What things about your body are you proud of? What parts of your body do you associate with pleasure? What parts of your body do you associate with pain? Do you believe people like or dislike you for your body? Do you believe that your appearance expresses who you are? What parts of your body did you leave out? Why? How closely does your view of your body match your ideal of how you would like your body to look? If there is a large gap between your real and your ideal body image, what can you do about that? How can you bring the two closer together?

If there are steps you can take to improve your body, you would help yourself and your marriage by starting those steps now. Write down what those steps would be. It may be a change in diet. If you are overweight, you may want to select three high-calorie foods to avoid. If you are an overeater or a "snacker," you might find it helpful to make a daily eating plan for six small meals per day. Emphasize fresh fruit and vegetables, whole grains, and low-fat proteins in your eating plan.

It might be exercise that would help you feel better about the shape or tone of your body. If that is the case, set up a realistic exercise routine that you will actually follow. For example, you may find you are most likely to follow your plan if you are committed to doing it with someone else. Or you may find it works best to do some form of exercise at home on your own time with the aid of an exercise video and/or equipment. On the contrary, you may be a person who needs to sign up for a regular exercise program at a fitness center. Your plan will need to fit your financial ability, your time schedule, and your personality.

Whatever it is that could improve your feelings about your body, pursue that improvement! At the same time, be realistic about what you cannot change, and begin a process of accepting those aspects of your body. The ultimate goal is to decrease the gap between your ideal and your actual body image.

The final factor that has influenced your view of your body is the model you have chosen as your ideal for yourself. When we grew up, our role models were the real people in our lives. We did not go to movies, nor did we have televisions in our homes. Today most people believe they should look like movie and television personalities. Those are unrealistic models. People selected for those roles often have bodies that represent only a very small percentage of the population. Those particular body types that we, as a society, have identified as ideal have nothing to do with personal, marital, or sexual satisfaction. Many times, the bodies we see on the screen have been created by the skillful hand of the plastic surgeon, not by the master Creator. So if you think of TV and movie stars as the ideal, reconsider your role models and readjust your ideal as another way to feel better about your body.

Your Habits

You may not have given much thought to how your personal habits affect your sexual relationship in marriage, but indeed they do.

A couple came to us for sexual therapy complaining of lack of sexual desire for the husband. They had been married only six months, and his decrease in sexual interest was a traumatic surprise to his new wife. As we met with each of them to gather data and do our detective work to ascertain the source of his desire problem, nothing seemed to surface. Finally, we were direct with him about the fact that we could not identify any history or obvious contributing factors to cause a decrease in his desire. Hesitantly, he shared with us that he had been raised in a home with extreme privacy for using the toilet. He was shocked and turned off by his wife using the toilet when he could see or hear her. Inside ourselves, we chuckled with a sigh of relief, then asked the young man if we could share this information with his wife. He consented. We did. She was happy to change her habits, and they lived happily ever after! No sexual therapy was needed.

To assess your personal habits, think about whether you are a high- or low-energy person, obsessively clean or a slob, easily cold or easily hot, a health-food nut or junk-food addict, a wine connoisseur or a teetotaler, exercise freak or couch potato, morning person or night person, require little sleep or much sleep, sleep with the window open or closed, and sleep in the nude or bundled up with your socks on. Are you a high- or low-maintenance person? Being aware of your habits and how they can affect your sexual relationship is helpful to a smooth sexual adjustment.

Your Health

Since sexual functioning is dependent on physical and emotional well-being, your health status is also critical to your sexual life in marriage. Consider developing a written health history that you keep current. First list all illnesses, accidents, and surgical operations you incurred from birth until now. Also describe any dilemmas you struggled with, such as bedwetting, and describe how those problems were handled. What illnesses or health problems have any of your family members had or now have?

Once you have a picture of your health history, write a description of your current health. Do you suffer from any of the following difficulties?

headaches	loss of appetite	sedative usage
dizziness	bowel disturbances	depression
fainting spells	fatigue	anxiousness or fears
palpitations	insomnia	suicidal thoughts
stomach trouble	nightmares	alcoholism

Do you have any allergies? Are you on a special diet? List all medications you are taking. Do you use alcohol, tobacco, non-prescription drugs, or other substances? If so, how frequently and how much of these do you use? What affect does the usage have on you? Have you ever had or do you have any difficulty with your breasts, genitals, rectum, prostate gland or uterus, hormonal balance, ejaculations or menstrual cycle or any other part of your body that may affect sexual functioning? Are you aware of having an active case of, having had, or carrying a sexually transmitted disease? If you are a woman, it would be helpful to have a clear sense of your menstrual history, your current pattern, and any difficulties such as problems with irregular menstrual cycles, menstrual cramps, premenstrual symptoms, pregnancies, abortions, miscarriages, and infertility struggles. If you have used contraceptives, what kind did you use and how did they affect you?

How would you describe your mental health? How do you usually feel emotionally? Have you struggled with anxiety, depression, panic disorders or phobias, or other mental health difficulties? How have these been treated? Are you currently being treated? If so, what is that treatment?

Your Sexual Self

Your view of yourself has been developing since the day you were born and will continue to evolve until the day you die. You were a sexual being from the time of your conception and will be until you take your last breath.

From hearing hundreds of case histories and reading many sexual autobiographies, we are convinced that there are critical stages of learning about ourselves as sexual persons that affect our sexual adjustment as adults. These stages are pictured in Table 2-1.

During *the first year of life* you learned the capacity for intimacy by the bonding that occurred with your mother or primary caretaker. You learned about yourself as a sexual person through the touch and holding you received. If it was warm, close, comforting, and giving, you will be able to give and receive touch with your spouse, and you will desire physical intimacy. If you were not given warmth through holding and touch, you may feel no need for physical closeness. Or you may want sexual release but not the intimacy of a caressing relationship, or you may be highly desirous of physical contact but have no capacity to freely give of yourself. If your intimacy needs were not developed, you will need to learn to give and receive pleasure through sensuous touch. The sexual retraining process detailed in our book *Restoring the Pleasure* would be most helpful for you and your spouse to practice together.

You formed your view of your genitals during the *toddlerhood* stage, when you were one to four years old. Ideally, your parents gave you the gift of accepting your genitals as part of God's perfect design for you. Unfortunately, for many children that does not happen. By the time you were four years of age you either felt

TABLE 2–1

States of Sexual Development

Stage	Critical Learning	Impact on Sexual Adjustment
Infancy	Bonding	Capacity for intimacy
Toddlerhood	Touching, naming, and controlling of genitals	Positive acceptance of genitals (user-friendly)
Preschool	Question-asking	Open communication regarding sexuality
School age	Exploration	Sexual awareness
Preadolescence	Erotic feelings and bumbling discovery	Self-acceptance and competence in relating to opposite sex
Adolescence	Decision making	Taking responsibility for own sexuality

comfortable and matter-of-fact about your genitals or you had learned that they were untouchable, unmentionable, and dirty.

It is natural that during diaper changing or bathing you touched your genitals and discovered that touching felt good. If your hand was slapped or moved away or you were told, "No, no," you learned that genitals are a dangerous part of the body, a part to be avoided much like a hot stove or an electrical outlet. If genital exploration was responded to like any other curiosity about your body—poking your finger up your nose, in your ear, and into your navel—you will have a sense of comfort with your genitals. For most toddlers, genital touching is soothing, much like sucking the thumb or rubbing a blanket. The touching increases when a toddler is lonely, sad, experiencing pain, or in need of more holding.

Toddlerhood is also the stage when you learned to talk. The names your family used to refer to genitals will have given you a message about your sexuality. Parents are usually proud when their children can name body parts—eyes, ears, nose, elbow—but when parents refer to genitals, they revert to such nicknames as "wa-wa" and "do-do." The toddler learns rather quickly that these are parts of the body parents are not proud of—in fact, they are unmentionable!

You learned control of elimination at this age. If that was mastered with pride, you will come to adulthood with a sense of mastery and control over your sexuality. If not, you will see sex as something that happens to you, not as actions you can choose to limit or pursue. Ideally, in the process of toilet training, the person teaching you was able to differentiate between your genitals as a clean part of your body and your anus as a highly contaminated area. If not, you may perceive your genitals as dirty and therefore think of sex as dirty. When the genitals are freshly washed and free of infection, they are free of germs—they are clean!

As you probably sense by now, the information you learned by age four has greatly affected your view of your sexual self. Since you probably do not remember this early period of your life, this would be a great time to talk with a family member about how your sexual development was handled during your infancy and toddlerhood. The process of gathering this information will be most beneficial.

Curiosity starts in *preschool* children with question asking. You may or may not remember asking your first question about sexuality. Usually the first questions relate to reproduction—how babies are made. How your early questions were responded to will have set the tone for the openness or caution that followed. If you still do not feel comfortable talking about sex, the process of reading through this book out loud as a couple will help break down those barriers.

Curiosity manifests itself during the *school-age* years through sexual awareness and modesty. Girls become aware and modest a year or so earlier than boys. Once you were aware of sexual differences, you may have engaged in some form of exploratory play. That may have been playing doctor, house, or "I'll show you mine if you'll show me yours." The desire to check out each other's genitals is a common expression of sexual curiosity during the early school-age years. When exploratory play occurs between same-age children who have not been sexually abused or exposed to sexually explicit materials, that discovery causes no harm but should be seen as an indication that teaching about sexual differences and boundaries is needed. However, if your innocent and age-appropriate search for answers regarding male-and-female differences was met with a punitive, demeaning, or explosive reaction from a parent or primary caregiver, you will have been left with incredible confusion about natural sexual feelings and interests. This may have been the event when you first connected guilt with sexual feelings.

Because of the new sense of yours and others' sexuality, this is also the age when nudity in the home becomes an issue. Once you were aware of sexual differences and your own sexuality, it was important that no adult body was exposed to you for the arousal it excited in the adult. *Never* should nudity in your home have been used to exploit you as a child. If confusion or sexual feelings were triggered in you in reaction to an adult's body or behavior, that was a violation that will have left you with an overprotective sense of modesty. Likewise, never having seen your parents or other older family members without clothing may have left you with a lack of freedom with your body, even with your spouse. Other times, extreme modesty in the home has triggered excessive curiosity in children. If that was the case for you, you may carry into adulthood guilt about the way you went about trying to make sense out of what you did not know about adult male and female bodies. What we have found is that school age is a critical period for learning about sexual differences and for establishing appropriate boundaries with bodily exposure so that as an adult you have a healthy balance of self-consciousness and freedom with bodily exposure. It is natural to feel self-conscious when sharing your body with your spouse for the first time, but comfort and freedom to be in the nude with one another will develop quickly if your school-age sexual curiosity was handled wisely.

Preadolescence was probably an awkward stage of your sexual development. This was the time when your body was changing and so were your peers'. You may have changed faster or slower than others your age. Being ahead of or behind your friends in growth and sexual development will have made you question whether you were normal. Even if you developed right in sync with those around you, the changes you were experiencing in your body may have left you feeling awkward. That is why we often refer to the male/female interaction at this age as the kiss-and-run, or bumbling, stage. Your feelings probably fluctuated wildly at this age anyway because of the hormonal activity going on in your body. Three years before you showed any physical changes, your hormones began to be secreted, at first very irregularly. These hormones were responsible for your body's changing from that of a child to that of an adult. But the hormones also triggered erotic sexual feelings that may have been identified as restlessness or irritability or clumsiness.

If genital touching was a practice for you, you may have been aware of these new erotic sensations in your body. Self-stimulation (masturbation) may have become a regular practice for you at this time. That is common for about 90 to 95 percent of boys and 60 to 70 percent of girls. Even if that practice was warned against, it is unlikely that you stopped the behavior. While the masturbatory activity probably continued after the warning it was most likely connected with guilt. If this is your situation, do everything in your power to disconnect your sexual arousal and release from that guilt! Married sex is not wrong, so it does not trigger the adrenal excitement that "wrong" sex arouses. That is why it is vital that you recognize that your sexual feelings and desires, even as a preadolescent, were given to you by God and were not wrong. If your masturbatory habit began in response to sexually explicit material, you may have become hooked on or addicted to pornographic materials. Overcoming this habit will require help. You may begin by reading the chapter on sexual addictions in our book *Restoring the Pleasure.* Your community or church may offer Sexual Addicts Anonymous (SAA—see chapter 12 for the phone number of the national headquarters), or you may seek private counseling. Whatever the resource, seek help until you find what you need to get and keep your addiction under control.

We hope that during your curious years, preschool through preadolescence, you learned the following attitudes:

- Sex is good and of God.
- Sexual curiosity is natural.

- Sexual responsiveness is inborn.
- Sexual responsibility belongs to each person.
- Mutual respect and biblical standards are the guide for all sexual relationships.

If you entered *adolescence* with these attitudes *positively* ingrained in you, you will have been comfortable in relation to the opposite sex and with your own sexuality. You will have been prepared to make the tough decisions that adolescence requires.

For adolescents, sexuality presents the most tension of all developmental stages. Physically the adolescent's body is ready to function sexually; in fact, in Bible times this was the age when most couples consummated their marriages! However, emotionally and economically the adolescent today is at least ten years away from being ready to consummate a marriage. This is what we refer to as the "gap dilemma." Christian adolescents need to make decisions to limit their sexual behavior while keeping their sexual feelings alive for marriage.

Separating behavior from feelings will have been vital for you. How did you handle those two dimensions of *your* sexuality? This may have been a lonely time for you, a time of being very aware of your desire for dating but having very little or no opportunity to date. For you, decisions to limit your sexual involvement were not even an issue. There were no opportunities for involvement. Or you may have become sexually active during adolescence. If you simply let that happen without consciously deciding to be sexually active, you may not have the sense that you are able to control the extent of your sexual involvement by making active decisions. If you deliberately chose to be sexually active, you may have regrets about it now. If you carry guilt about past sexual activity, it is important for you to work through a process of forgiveness with your spouse and with God. Lewis Smedes's book *Forgive and Forget* may be beneficial to you in releasing that past experience. Having intercourse during adolescence will likely have taught you to rely on physical connection for intimacy. As an adult, you will be wise to be very deliberate in building other forms of intimacy into your relationship. Learn to share your feelings and to be able to accurately understand and care about your spouse's feelings. Learn to work, talk, play, and pray together.

Who you are today as a sexual person depends on how successful you were at learning about your sexuality at each of these stages. It also depends on the modeling and interaction that took place between you and your parents. From your same-sex parent you learned what it was to be male or female. If your same-sex parent seemed secure and content with his or her sexuality, so will you be. From your opposite-sex parent, you learned how to relate to the opposite sex. If you were affirmed and respected by your opposite-sex parent, you will expect affirmation and respect from your spouse.

You will need to consciously work to meet any developmental, modeling, or interaction needs that were not met. This will enable you to be all you can be as a sexual person and as a husband or wife.

In getting to know yourself, you will learn whether you bring to your sexual relationship in marriage the capacity for intimacy. You will also learn if you have a naturalness in giving and receiving affection, a comfortableness with your body, an awareness of your sexuality, a high view of the sexual relationship in marriage as a mutual commitment, and a confidence that you can make sexual pleasure happen. We wish all of that for you.

3
......

Getting to Know
Each Other

avid and Emily came to us after thirty years of marriage having never had a single mutually satisfying sexual experience. Their sexual relationship had started as teenagers. David felt guilty for being "oversexed" and pushing Emily sexually. Emily had harbored years of hurt and resentment for having carried the burden of her pregnancy before their marriage. David had never shared the extent of his childhood beatings that left him anxious, insecure, and looking for affirmation through sexual union. Emily had never shared her painful secret of having been molested and raped as a preadolescent by a respected spiritual leader in their community. Neither of them understood how those pasts led them to their early sexual difficulties with one another.

Childhood physical abuse of young boys often produces an involuntary erection; thus, without even realizing it, as adults they seek affirmation through desiring that same sexual response in their love relationships. They may not know how to be intimate, open, and vulnerable because they were never allowed to be that way in their childhood home. Home was not safe. This was true for David. In the same way, sexual abuse of a young girl will stir up a high level of conflicted sexuality that may invite sexual activity in a dating relationship without the girl's awareness that she is sending those messages. Emily had been unaware of inviting David's sexual pursuits.

Neither David nor Emily understood that both of them, because of the abuse they had suffered as children, had contributed to their premarital sexual activity that led to pregnancy before marriage. Getting to know each other and how their pasts contributed to their sexual tension was the start to healing those past hurts and beginning a great sex life.

This is your opportunity to get to know each other more intimately so that you can *start* your marriage with a great sex life. Completely committing yourselves to a lifetime of abandoning yourselves to each other sexually requires more than just having intercourse. It is the difference between practicing a religion and giving yourself to God. Couples we see for sexual therapy may have been married for ten, twenty, or forty years and have been engaging in an ongoing sexual relationship, but have never given themselves totally to each other sexually because they do not really know each other. They have never shared the secrets of their pasts, they do not understand the differences in their personalities, and they have never learned to listen to each other.

Sharing Yourself

As you worked through the last chapter, you spent time pondering and exploring your inner worlds. Now is the time to share that self-discovery with each other. In his book *The Transparent Self,* Sidney Jourard wrote about self-disclosure as the "portal to man's soul." To reveal yourself takes both courage and knowledge of yourself, says Jourard.[1] You can only know each other as you know yourselves and make that self-awareness known to each other.

If you wrote out your responses to your self-descriptions, as suggested, take time now to share those reflections of your inner worlds with each other. If you did not write your reflections, flip back and talk through your responses to the "Who Are You?" topics and questions beginning on page 29. As you share, do the following:

1. Practice active listening skills or "mirroring" (described in the following pages).

2. Agree that understanding each other's past does not obligate either of you to fix that past.

3. Commit yourselves to never use any of the information you gain to hurt each other, but only to love and help each other.

Active listening skills are the tools to fulfilling a yearning for your partner to truly and completely understand and accept you. Recognize that understanding and accepting each other does not necessarily imply that you agree with each other. You may have difficulty putting your own thoughts, feelings, and opinions aside while you listen to and then repeat back, in your own words, what you understand your partner to have said. Sometimes it's hard to keep your opinions silent because you worry that the other person will assume you agree with him or her when, in fact, you disagree. Be assured that you will both become stronger individuals as you learn to momentarily withhold your own personal views while you focus on the other's.

Some communication experts refer to this process as reflective listening, active listening, or mirroring. In his book *Getting the Love You Want,* Harville Hendrix refers to "mirroring" as "a communication technique that serves two important functions: 1) it helps you minimize the semantic differences between you and your partner, and 2) it trains you to become more receptive to your partner's spoken messages."[2]

The process of mirroring begins when one of you has something to say. In this case, you will be sharing how you see yourself—your discoveries about yourself from the last chapter.

It is important to use "I statements" ("I am," "I see myself as," "I feel," "I like," etc.). The other person's responsibility is

Communication Model

SENDER:

Listen to your inner self.
Determine what it is you think, feel, or need.
Choose carefully the words, gestures, and emotions that will accurately reflect the message you wish to send.

RECEIVER:

Put aside your thoughts and feelings.
Listen to and observe the words, body language, and feelings of the other person.
Rephrase in your own words what you think the sender is trying to say.

Affirm that you indeed said what you meant and that your message was received accurately.

OR

Clarify, rephrase, or add to your message.

to pay full attention and listen to your feelings and words. This requires that, for the moment, you, the listener, must put aside your own thoughts, feelings, and reactions so you can accurately perceive and understand your partner. You then pretend that you are the mirror, helping your partner see what you understand him or her to have shared. This rephrasing without interpreting or judging communicates to each other that you understand and care about each other's perspective.

Effective communication takes constant discipline. As important as the two of us believe it is to practice active listening, we still struggle to make that a consistent reality in our lives. It is so much more natural to want to be heard and to preach, to offer advice, to come up with solutions, or to argue than it is to be motivated to understand. That is human nature. Yet the vibrancy, closeness, and even ecstasy that result when you let each other know you understand are dramatic and well worth the effort. Try it for yourselves, and you will quickly see what we mean. Enjoy the challenge!

After you have taken turns sharing your individual responses to the questions in the last chapter, set aside another block of time in the next week or so to complete the process of getting to know each other. Sometime before your next designated time to work together on this process, individually complete the following form. There are no right or wrong answers. All of the communication exercises in this book are to be seen as tools to open discussion, not as tests to label you right or wrong.

Sharing Myself

1. Usually I am the kind of person who _____

2. Right now I am feeling _____

3. When things aren't going well I _____

4. I want to become the kind of person who _____

5. I like such things as _____

6. My best attribute is _____

7. My greatest weakness is _____

8. I am happiest when _____

9. When I feel anxious I _____

10. In conflict situations, I usually _____

11. The most distressing experience I have ever had is _____

12. I usually react to negative criticism by _____

13. I fear _____

14. I prefer to be with people who _____

15. I prefer to be alone when _____

16. I believe in _____

17. The best thing about me sexually is _____

18. Five years ago my feelings about sex were _____

19. I am hoping that _____

20. Ten years from now I _____

When you are ready to communicate your responses, go somewhere private so you can be alone with each other. Take turns sharing. As you proceed, follow the communication model on page 46, which reviews all the active listening skills.

Sharing Your Past

The two of you bring to your sexual relationship unique past experiences. Your families will have modeled and communicated different views of sexuality. Understanding those differences and your uniqueness will be essential to knowing each other sexually. You may have sexual secrets that seem very risky to share. You may still suffer the consequences of past hurts. It is completely understandable that you might feel hesitant to talk about your sexual past. You may worry about the effect your revelations will have on your partner. That is a realistic concern.

In fact, you may want to discuss your decision to share certain information with a counselor before you take that step.

Individually complete the form below and at a designated time share your responses with each other using the Communication Model on page 46.

Background History

Describe your family of origin.

List the positive qualities of your mother.

List the negative qualities of your mother.

Describe your relationship with your mother.

In what ways is your partner similar to and different than your mother?

List the positive qualities of your father.

List the negative qualities of your father.

Describe your relationship with your father.

In what ways is your partner similar to and different than your father?

Describe your parents' relationship now and when you were a child.

What do you think your parents' sexual relationship is or was like?

How were emotions expressed in your family of origin?

What type of affection was expressed?

How were you disciplined?

Describe your siblings and your relationship with each of them.

What similarities and differences do you see between your siblings and your partner?

Describe any sex education you received.

What is your first remembrance of your genitals?

Describe any sexual experimentation:

> Exploratory play?
>
> Discovery of pornography?
>
> Sexual jokes?
>
> Masturbation (self-stimulation):
>
>> When did you start?
>>
>> What was your practice?
>>
>> What were you taught about it?
>>
>> How did you feel about it?
>
> Did you engage in adolescent sexual activity?
>
> Homosexual play and/or fantasies?

Describe any traumatic or abusive sexual event.
How was nudity handled? Was privacy respected? Were you ever exposed to a sexual scene or an older person's body for his or her sexual gratification? Were you ever touched on your breasts or genitals or kissed in a way that made you feel uncomfortable?

Describe your dating and marital history, especially noting any particularly significant events that might affect your sexual relationship in marriage. Do not share unnecessary details that would cause jealousy and comparisons.

Describe the person who has most significantly affected your view of yourself as a man or a woman.

Describe your favorite memory of your family.

As you have shared yourselves and felt heard by each other, you have experienced *empathy*. Christ was a perfect model of empathy; He denied Himself to become like us so He could truly understand us. In Philippians 2, Paul challenged his Christian friends not to be self-centered and to remember what Christ did for them. He encouraged them to be of the same mind, maintaining the same love and doing nothing out of selfishness. He said they should

> Have this attitude in yourselves which was also in Christ Jesus, who, although He existed in the form of God, did not regard equality with God a thing to be grasped, but emptied Himself, taking the form of a bond-servant, and being made in the likeness of men. And being found in appearance as a man, He humbled Himself by becoming obedient to the point of death, even death on a cross. (Phil. 2:5–8)

Even if you love each other deeply, getting to know each other completely, particularly sexually, is hard work and requires self-sacrifice.

Bringing Your Worlds Together

When Emily and David, the couple mentioned at the beginning of this chapter, came to us for sexual therapy, they knew they had differences but they had no idea of how to positively use their differences to enhance their relationship, sexually and otherwise. Yet each of their uniquenesses contributed significantly to the success of their sexual retraining process. David was a studious, serious rule-follower. Because of these qualities, the couple completed each assignment exactly as prescribed and moved through the learning process with the greatest of ease. Emily, on the other hand, had a lot of spark and spontaneity that added tremendous energy and distracted from demands that might have crept into the process and interfered with its success. While he would seriously check off every instruction in the list, she would teasingly say, "I'll take care of him." And she would!

How can you and your spouse utilize your differences to enhance your relationship? David Keirsey and Marilyn Bates's book *Please Understand Me* will be helpful in this process.[3] If you each completed the Myers-Briggs Type Indicator, as suggested in the last chapter, share your results with each other now. Then read aloud each of your types described in the appendix of

Please Understand Me. Next, read together the book's chapter titled "Mating and Temperament." Talk about the benefits as well as the needed adaptations that each of your personalities brings to your relationship.

Getting to know each other is a continual process. We are still surprised at little peculiarities or past events that we have not known about each other. But once you have established a basic understanding and acceptance of your uniquenesses, your backgrounds, and your personalities, the new discoveries that follow will become pleasant additions.

4

······

Clarifying Expectations

We could hardly wait for our wedding night. He was so passionate! He reserved the wedding suite at this beautiful hotel. Our wedding was wonderful. I enjoyed every minute of it, but I kept thinking about getting to our hotel and making love."

As Lori shared her memories about the start of her and Brian's married sexual life her eyes teared up.

"We got to the hotel and he was more excited about showing me around the hotel than going to our room. When we did get to our room, he turned on the television. I didn't know what to do, so I decided to take a leisurely bath and get into the beautiful white silk negligee my maid of honor had given me at my lingerie shower. I came out feeling hesitant, a little self-conscious, but with a sense of eagerness and confidence in how I looked." Lori had been a model in New York and Paris and was one of the most beautiful women we had ever seen. "When

I snuggled in beside him, he got fidgety. Nothing happened that night. I was so disappointed. We only had sex twice on our honeymoon, and we have never experienced the passion we had before marriage. He's happy with having sex once every week or two. I thought we would have sex several times a day on our honeymoon and every day or two thereafter."

Rachel's story was just the opposite. "We met overseas and fell madly in love. When we were alone together we would do everything but have intercourse. I felt guilty about that, but I felt good that we had set the clear boundary to not go all the way. Kissing was great. We always kept our clothes on, but we would roll around on the bed and eventually both come to orgasm. Then, on our wedding night, I freaked out. I thought we would start our lovemaking just like we had been doing during our dating days. I hadn't even changed out of my going-away outfit when he walked out of the bathroom in the nude with a full erection. It scared me half to death. Even though I had felt his erection through his clothes before, I had never *seen* an erect penis. I thought intercourse would never work—and it didn't. I was just too scared and too tight."

Many of the couples who come to us for sexual therapy say their sexual problem started on their honeymoon or shortly thereafter. Often the problem that has devastated their marriage for months or years could have been prevented. *The pain and disappointment could have been avoided if someone had talked with them openly about sex and taken the time to guide them through a process of discussing and negotiating their expectations for their sexual relationship in marriage.*

A fulfilling married sexual life is in part dependent on its start. Many couples have difficulty transferring their premarital passion into their marriages because they have false expectations about married sex (These are the myths we dealt with in chapter 1.), they lack accurate information, and they are unable to communicate openly about what each envisions as a healthy, fulfilling married sex life. That is what we hope to prevent by guiding you through the steps in this chapter. The rest is up to you. If you work diligently and seriously through the next pages, we believe you will learn to transfer your premarital sexual passion into a fulfilling marital relationship. Work hard—and have fun!

What Turns You On?

A colleague of ours once said, "If you want to turn on a woman, talk to her. If you want to turn on a man, stroke him." Even though that is a big generalization, there is some truth in our friend's observation of the difference between men and women sexually.

Not only are there differences between men and women, but each of us differs as to what works for us sexually and what doesn't. Paying attention to the ways you now relate to one another physically and otherwise can help you set realistic expectations for your ongoing sexual relationship after marriage. To help you do just that, complete the following statement. Using the active listening skills and communication model you followed in the chapter on knowing each other, each of you take turns finishing each statement.

You and Me

My first impression of you was _____.

What I like about you is _____.

My general image of you is _____.

What puzzles me about you is _____.

My most frequent daydreams about you are _____.

I love it when you _____.

I feel uncomfortable with you when _____.

When I am upset with you, I _____.

When you are upset with me, I _____.

I worry about you most when _____.

Our physical involvement makes me feel _____.

The best feeling in any physical, sexual contact is _____.

I feel sexual sensations when _____.

When I fantasize about sex, I picture _____.

What turns me on is _____.

The surest turnoff for me is _____.

What I think you need to know about me is _____.

When I imagine having sex with you, I feel _____.

When I think of our future, I _____.

What works for you sexually will continue to change, grow, and develop throughout your marriage. Thus, it will be important for you to continue talking about your sexual feelings, needs, and desires. You would be wise to plan into your marriage a yearly review of the previous communication exercise.

What Do You Envision Sexually?

Even though you may not have thought about it, you probably have a picture of your ideal sexual experience. What do you envision happening between the two of you and inside each of you during deeply satisfying lovemaking? When do you expect to have your first sexual time together on your honeymoon? Do you imagine that experience will lead to intercourse? How do you feel about that event? How often do you expect to have sexual times on your honeymoon? What about after the honeymoon? What percentage of those sexual times together will lead to intercourse? What parts of your current physical involvement would you like to continue after marriage? Which ones would you hope to change?

Your patterns of physical interaction before your wedding will likely continue after your marriage and can serve as indicators to how you will relate in a married sexual relationship. For example, if one of you is the boundary keeper (you are the one who stops the progression of your physical involvement) and the other partner frequently pushes for more, those roles are likely to naturally resume soon after marriage. The boundary keeper's reasons for saying no will change from moral standards to fatigue, work pressures, or the fact that his or her conditions for sex have not been met. On the other hand, if the two of you have talked about your boundaries, have helped and encouraged each other to enjoy your sexuality within those boundaries, and have respected each other's needs, you will continue that pattern of mutual respect and support even after marriage.

Sexual intercourse itself is not necessary to predict how you will function sexually after marriage. Those who advocate premarital sex say you should not think of getting married without making certain you are sexually compatible, just as you would not buy a car without test driving it. However, our observations suggest that premarital sexual intercourse is *not* the predictor of post-marital sexual adjustment. It is the patterns of relating with each other physically to whatever degree you are sexually involved before marriage that will affect your adjustment to sex after marriage.

Couples who have been sexually active before marriage sometimes carry that positive experience into their marriages. But we have had couples come to us for sexual therapy who had lived together for a number of years before marriage and had enjoyed a passionate sexual relationship, but once they got married and sex was no longer associated with guilt, their passion died. Couples who have mutually decided, with open communication and healthy passion, to wait until they are married usually move into their marriage and continue to grow in their delight of each other sexually. Yet, waiting for marriage to consummate your relationship does not guarantee a great sex life after marriage, either. We have worked with Christian couples whose faith was devastated because they believed God would bless their marriage with an incredible sex life if they waited until marriage. The Bible teaches that sex is for marriage, and we believe God's plans for us are for our good. But we are not promised a blissful life because we follow biblical guidelines. We are called to obedience, but we are not told that just because we are obedient life will be easy. Men and women in the Bible often *suffered* because of their obedience to God.

Studies have attempted to determine marital sexual satisfaction. For example, the Voter/Consumer Research firm, commissioned by the Family Research Council, conducted a nationwide telephone survey of eleven hundred randomly selected people in September 1993 and found that "sexual satisfaction is strongly and positively linked to marriage and traditional sexual ethics."[1] This is certainly a departure from the cultural input of our time. The survey also found that "Sexual satisfaction is often a by-product of, and a contributor to, marital satisfaction"[2] and that "Sexual responsiveness and satisfaction are significantly affected by the relational context in which lovemaking takes place."[3] The editor stated that "a number of research studies have found that sexual satisfaction is strongly linked to honest communication about sexual needs, desires, and feelings."[4]

We have observed that a high correlation between level of commitment and level of sexual involvement, an understanding of what goes on inside each person sexually, and effective patterns of interaction are critical for you to make a positive transition into a fulfilling sexual life together. Therefore, we recommend that you take some time to examine those factors carefully. Individually, write your responses to the questions on the following form, then share your responses with each other using the active listening skills you learned in chapter 3. If you dread or avoid writing, talk through it.

Your Sexual Patterns

Sexual Desire

How often do you feel the urge to be touched and to be close or for sexual arousal and release?

What stimulates those urges in you?

How do you handle those urges?

What changes have you noticed in your sexual desire since you started dating?

Initiation

How do you express that desire to each other?

How do you act upon that desire (e.g., ignore it, substitute physical exercise, call a friend, pray, masturbate, hold each other, or engage in other physical touching)?

If you act on the desire with each other, who initiates that action?

Are you happy with how that happens?

Is it mutual?

What about your response to your sexual desire would you to change?

What about your partner's response to his/her sexual desire would you like to change?

Pleasure

To what degree have the two of you been or are you currently physically involved with each other? Circle any behaviors on the list below.

Hand-holding

Hugging

Polite kissing

Total-mouth kissing

Intense, passionate kissing

Full-body rubbing with clothes on

Breast stimulation over clothes

Genital stimulation over clothes

Breast stimulation under clothes

Genital stimulation under clothes

Full-body pleasuring, no clothes

Oral-genital stimulation

Total sexual experience, except entry

Total sexual experience, including entry but without orgasm while inside

Total sexual experience, including entry and thrusting to ejaculation

Does your involvement agree or disagree with your beliefs?

If it agrees, is that mutual?

If it disagrees or is not mutual, how might you change or get control of your sexual activity without shutting down your desires for one another? List behavioral changes that you could make. (For example, plan your times alone so that you could be interrupted.)

Do you experience discomfort, guilt, or inhibitions when you are engaged in physical touching with each other?

If so, discuss how you might reduce or eliminate any negatives connected with your physical interaction.

What kind of touching is most pleasurable to you?

Are you aware of experiencing any arousal?

Are you aware of any restrictions you have on allowing yourself sexual pleasure other than the decisions you have made to limit your sexual involvement before marriage?

What events, feelings, or actions have contributed to your times of greatest pleasure without violation of your boundaries?

Letting Go

Are you a person who needs control in your life, or are you able to let go and take risks?

Have you ever experienced sexual release?

If so, through what forms of stimulation?

If not, has that been by decision or because of inhibition?

What expectations do you have for sexual release and satisfaction in marriage?

Affirmation

What do you feel after a time of being close physically?

What do you need from your partner at that time?

How might you express your affirmation of your partner?

What affirmation would you expect as part of a total sexual experience?

Your Sexual Expectations

Now that you have talked through your views of your current sexual pattern, take time to fantasize together about your ideal sexual experience in marriage. When and where would it happen? Who would initiate it? How would the initiation happen? What conditions would you want for yourself, for the setting, and for each other? How would you enjoy pleasuring each other's bodies? You might read the Song of Solomon together to get some ideas of how a married couple could fully enjoy one another. How would you feel if you let go? Describe how you would feel and what you would do afterward.

What expectations do you have of each other, generally and sexually? Take time to list ten expectations you have for your spouse. Then, across from each expectation, identify how you would be affected if your spouse did not fulfill these expectations. For example, if you are the wife or the wife-to-be and you were raised by a serving father, you are likely to expect your husband to be serving to you and your children. If your husband-to-be was raised by a serving mother and a pretty self-serving father, he is likely to behave as his father did. Both of you will have difficulty accepting each other's expectations.

How Do Men and Women Differ?

Although the wife wants to be sexually satisfied by her husband, this desire is awakened in her long after she has discovered that she loves him enough to die for him, while a man on the other hand desires to possess a woman physically long before he cares sufficiently to raise his little finger for her. That the love of a woman normally comes from the soul to the senses . . . forms one of the chief differences between the two, and often leads to the greatest misunderstanding.[5]

We love this quote from a 1957 guidebook for engaged and newly married couples. So many times when we deal with a husband who is frustrated with his wife's lower sexual desire, it is very difficult to help him understand and accept that the very best method to arouse her interest is to connect with her emotionally without any demand or expectation for her to be sexual. And even when he does experience positive results from this approach, he seems to have difficulty maintaining emotional intimacy without sexual expectations.

In our culture, emotional intimacy seems to be something women need much more than men. Women tend to feel the desire for sex when they feel connected with their husbands while men tend to feel connected as the result of a positive sexual experience. The most common stereotypes in our culture are that men "play" at love to get sex and women "play" at sex to get love. "Briefly stated, love is linked to self-esteem in women. For a man, romantic experiences with his wife are warm and enjoyable and memorable—but not necessary. For a woman, they are her lifeblood. Her confidence, her sexual response and her zest for living are often directly related to those tender moments when she feels deeply loved and appreciated by her man."[6]

It is true that many more men than women have difficulty identifying and expressing feelings. Dr. Graeme J. Taylor, associate professor of psychiatry at the University of Toronto Faculty of Medicine, wrote about this in *The Harvard Medical School Mental Health Letter* in 1990. He referred to the difficulty many men have with being able to bring their feelings into their conscious awareness as a disability called "alexithymia." People who suffer from alexithymia are aware of discomfort or unpleasant sensations but have difficulty identifying whether those are physical symptoms, boredom, anger, or sadness. Because of their lack of awareness, they may try to reduce their unidentified emotional tension through binge eating, sex, alcohol abuse, drug abuse, compulsive exercise, emotional outbursts, or even violence. Our observation is that men who are highly sensitive but unable to identify and express their emotions pull away from their wives who verbally express intense frustration toward their "unfeeling" husbands. It is much more beneficial to both the man and the woman if she can use her ability to identify and express feelings to help her husband by verbalizing *for* him rather than *at* him.

Whether the emotional differences between men and women are learned or innate is unknown. In our own family, our daughters were real talkers and question-askers by age four or five, but our son was not. The most vivid memory we have of his limited verbal expression occurred at age five. Cliff was driving Greg and his friend home from school. Cliff asked, "What did you do at school today, Greg?" Greg's response was, "Work." Then he turned to his friend and said, "One day I say 'work,' and the next day I say, 'play.'"

Janice Stapley and Jeannette Haviland of Rutgers, the State University of New Jersey, did a survey that revealed that adolescent boys and girls experience the same intensity of emotions but they differ significantly in the types of emotions they feel, what triggers their emotions, and how they deal with them. Girls look to relationships for expression while boys look to activities. If an adolescent girl is upset, she is likely to call her friends and talk about her feelings. In contrast, an adolescent boy is likely to either go to his room and think about how his disappointment might affect the rest of his life or act out his feelings physically.[7] Again we observed this difference in our own family. One daughter, Julene, more than the other daughter, Kristine, would spend hours talking about her disappointments. However, when Greg's new shoes, wallet, and watch were stolen out of his high-school locker, we didn't know about his loss until we noticed that he had used an ax to chop a wedge out of our tall palm tree.

We also see male/female differences themselves in our observations of male/female sexual patterns. Men use sexual activity to get close while women use talk to feel close enough to want sex.

How might you plan for these differences in your relationship? We find that it works best if connecting or relationship time is planned into your sexual times to allow the woman to be ready for sexual intimacy. Plan for the woman to lead during that time. It is easier and more important for both spouses if the woman does more of the sharing and the man more of the listening and reflecting. If the woman wants to know how the man feels about some issue, she might offer various options that he can choose from and to ask for his thoughts rather than his feelings.

For example, let's say Dave and Joanne got into a pretty intense conflict about a purchase Joanne made. The next day Joanne is still feeling quite tender and hurt. Dave is ready to have sex. How does Joanne get Dave to talk with her so that she can resolve her hurt and feel close enough to him to want sex with Dave? What Joanne might do is tell Dave she needs time to talk about their conflict before she can feel close to him. Then she might remind him that it would help her if he could listen to and reflect what he senses from her rather than reacting defensively or trying to prove his viewpoint. When Joanne talks to Dave, it is important that she use "I statements" to express how she feels and that she avoid criticizing Dave. If she needs to know how Dave feels about their past conflict, she might ask, "What thoughts have you had about what happened yesterday?" Notice the use of unemotional words like *thoughts* and *happened* rather than emotional words like *feelings* and *conflict*. If she gets a nonanswer, she might give him some options: "Was the issue resolved for you by the end of our discussion yesterday? Have you had any further thoughts? How would you like us to handle this type of difference in the future?"

There are obvious exceptions to this tendency for women to be able to identify and express feelings more easily than men. Sometimes a man may be the more expressive one and a woman may have the difficulty. What is most important is that you identify what is true for the two of you and then work together to find ways to maximize the benefits of your differences and minimize the hazards.

Other differences between men and women that affect sexual relationships are reported to us regularly. Which of the differences on the following list are true for you? You may have additional differences to add to the list.

Male/Female Differences

He likes the room cold.	She likes the room hot.
He is result oriented.	She is process oriented.
He wants to solve her problem.	She wants him to listen to her problem.
He wants sex.	She wants romance.
He wants to engage in activities.	She wants to talk.
He likes intense kissing.	She likes pliable kisses.
Sexually, he goes for more.	Sexually, less makes her hungry for more.

A great resource for dealing with male/female differences is John Gray's book *Men Are from Mars, Women Are from Venus.*[8]

Knowing what is a turnon for you and your partner, being clear about each of your visions of a positive sexual encounter, and understanding, accepting, and adapting to your male/female differences are positive ways you can validate each other's expectations for your married sex life. The intimacy that will develop between the two of you as you pursue this process of determining and maintaining clear expectations will be a key to a good sex life. The results will be well worth the effort!

5

••••••

Pursuing Biblical Passion

I am my beloved's,
And his desire is for me.
Come, my beloved, let us go out into the country,
Let us spend the night in the villages.
Let us rise early and go to the vineyards;
Let us see whether the vine has budded
And its blossoms have opened,
And whether the pomegranates have bloomed.
There I will give you my love.
The mandrakes have given forth fragrance;
And over our doors are all choice fruits,
Both new and old,
Which I have saved up for you, my beloved. . . .

Put me like a seal over your heart,
Like a seal on your arm.

For love is as strong as death,
Jealousy is as severe as Sheol;
Its flashes are flashes of fire,
The very flame of the LORD.
Many waters cannot quench love,
Nor will rivers overflow it;
If a man were to give all the riches of his house for love,
It would be utterly despised.

Song of Solomon 7:10–13 and 8:6–7

ursue passion in your marriage as Solomon's new wife so eloquently expressed it. Invite your husband to be adventurous in trying new locations for lovemaking, even the outdoors—the countryside; just be careful not to expose yourselves to others. Be creative in bringing together both the old and the new of your sexual experience. Plan, anticipate, and save ideas for your sexual times together, and recognize that the wife is the assertive one in this passage. Women, don't hold back on expressing your desire to enjoy your husband. Go for him with gusto! You will be honoring God as you do.

In Song of Solomon chapter 8, Solomon's wife continued by describing her need for security in his commitment to her because of the intensity of their love. She wanted the confidence of his commitment to her. She wanted his kingly seal to identify her as his. You might think of the wedding band as the "seal" you will someday (or may already) wear. The security that comes with that sense of belonging allows the spouses, especially the wife, to let go of all that fiery passion and love. And that is a love that cannot be bought with riches. It is love that overflows and is given freely out of one's desire, not by expectation or demand.

Begin pursuing biblical passion by reading the Song of Solomon together. If you find it difficult to interpret the symbolic language, read Joseph C. Dillow's book *Solomon on Sex*. Dillow guides his readers through each verse of Song of Solomon and applies Solomon's wisdom to the sexual relationship in marriage.[1] It is an excellent resource for sexual adjustment in marriage. We have often suggested that if a married couple could regularly enact the Song of Solomon, they would never need sexual therapy and would enjoy an ongoing, delightful sexual relationship in their marriage.

Passion

Sexual passion is not only demonstrated by the lovers in the Song of Solomon; it is also implied throughout Scripture. Why else would God's messages to us have been so consistently laced with instructions for handling our sexual passion? If He didn't design us with earthy passion, He wouldn't have needed to teach us how to manage it.

This earthy passion is revealed in the lives of the Old Testament men and women who are named in the "Hall of Faith" in Hebrews 11. Abraham, the father of our inheritance, visited his wife's handmaiden, Hagar, who then became pregnant (Gen. 16:4). Isaac lied about his relationship to Rebekah in order to save his own life and then was found fondling her in public (Gen. 26:7–8). Jacob (Israel) produced four of the twelve sons of Israel by sleeping with his wives' maids (Gen. 30:7–12). David, who by faith conquered kingdoms, was attracted to the beautiful body of Bathsheba, the wife of Uriah, and became sexually involved with her. He then committed murder to cover up his sin. Even Rahab the harlot, who helped the Israelites conquer Jericho, was honored for her faith: "By faith the prostitute Rahab, because she welcomed the spies, was not killed with those who were disobedient" (Heb. 11:31 NIV). In fact, Rahab is listed in the genealogy of Jesus Christ in Matthew 1:5.

It is clear that we are accepted by God as beings with a powerful sexual nature—a forceful drive. Sometimes that nature drives us to disobey God's standards, just as it did some of the biblical men and women of faith. God does not condone our disobedience, but neither does He condemn us. When our humanness causes us to fall short of His ideals, we violate His rules as well as ourselves and those close to us. We suffer the consequences of those actions. Nevertheless, God's grace is available for us, even for our sexual mistakes. We can be forgiven and continue to be used by God as were David, Rahab, and the other men and women of faith.

Sexual Freedom

While there are many biblical restrictions regarding extra-marital sexual involvement, love is the only rule within marriage; there are no do's and don'ts, no obvious limitations or instructions on how to enjoy sex within marriage. The Song of Solomon is our biblical example. As you study the beautiful love story and are free to act it out in your marriage, you will experience total sexual pleasure.

The writer to the Hebrews said, "Marriage should be honored by all, and the marriage bed kept pure" (Heb. 13:4 NIV). Translated into today's language, this passage might read, "In this troubled world, it is terribly important that we have a very high view of marriage. And by the way, sex within marriage is not dirty." What goes on in the sexual relationship as an outgrowth of the marital covenant is honorable, wholesome, and healthy. From Genesis 2:24 throughout all of Scripture, the sexual union is referred to as "becoming one flesh." Dr. Louis H. Evans Jr. has a wonderful comment that succinctly expresses the New Testament's teaching on sexuality:

> The one flesh in marriage is not just a physical phenomenon, but a uniting of the totality of two personalities. In marriage, we are one flesh spiritually by vow, economically by sharing, logistically by adjusting time and agreeing on the disbursement of all life's resources, experientially by trudging through the dark valleys and standing victoriously on the peaks of success, and sexually by the bonding of our bodies. In [intercourse], which is the expression created uniquely for marriage, the male and female fibers inter-twine in complementation, creating a living fabric that cannot be undone without serious damage to living fibers. When that happens, they are left scarred and therefore lacking in suppleness, circulation, sensitivity or strength. Scar tissue is not good tissue. Let [intercourse] be undefiled and untainted, undefiled and beautiful as God designed it.[2]

Because there are different uses and meanings of the word *flesh* in the New Testament, it is vitally important that we understand these differences. Evans described a positive use of the word. In other places in Scripture, for example in Galatians 5:19–24, the use of the word *flesh* is understood to depict man's sinful nature.

Desiring a healthy, enthusiastic, and fulfilling sexual life within marriage clearly does not mean following the lust of the flesh. Rather, this comes under the category of sharing our undefiled desires with the one to whom you have made a life-time covenant.

Our mission is to help you distinguish the difference between lust-driven expressions of sexuality and the God-given gift of sexuality. This can be achieved if sexuality is allowed to grow and find freedom within the context of your loving marriage so that your sexual activities build each other and glorify God.

Sexual Pleasure

Not only are passion and freedom to be a part of your married sex life, sexual pleasure within marriage is biblically encouraged and expected. You are to be available to respond to each other's sexual needs whenever the two of you desire it— not only at the time of the month when impregnation can occur. In this respect God created human beings to be different from the animal kingdom—animals only have sexual drives at the time of conception. To "be fruitful and multiply" is but one pur-pose of the sexual relationship between a husband and wife. The Bible also endorses the concept of sexual pleasure.

Solomon's wife again is an excellent model of a woman's desire for her husband's body.

> On my bed night after night I sought him
> Whom my soul loves. (Song of Sol. 3:1)
>
> My beloved is dazzling and ruddy. . . .
> His head is like gold. . . .
> His eyes are like doves. . . .
> His lips are lilies,
> Dripping with liquid myrrh. . . .
> His legs are pillars of alabaster

Set on pedestals of pure gold. . . .
And he is wholly desirable. (Song of Sol. 5:10–16)

Proverbs 5:18–19 talks about a husband's desire for his wife.

Let your fountain be blessed,
And rejoice in the wife of your youth.
As a loving hind and a graceful doe,
Let her breasts satisfy you at all times;
Be exhilarated always with her love.

Your bodies are each other's to enjoy in marriage. If you hold back for religious reasons you fool yourselves, because there is no biblical reason to do so. You are not being consistent with what the Bible has to say if you take an antisexual and antipleasure view of sex in marriage. The Scriptures teach that, because of Christ, Christian husbands and wives are freed of the sexual shame Adam and Eve felt toward each other and before God after they disobeyed Him. As believers you have the potential for greater joy, more intense release, and more complete freedom as you learn to enjoy each other ecstatically.

Integrated Sex

Lovemaking cannot be simply a physical experience for the Christian couple. In order to have a fulfilling relationship, you must share your total self—intellect, body, spirit, and will—with your partner.

The Old Testament's description of the human sexual experience, "they shall become one flesh" (Gen. 2:24), means more than physical union. This refers to that mystical union that Paul talked about in Ephesians 5:31–32. This union encompasses the emotional, physical, and spiritual dimensions. Becoming one means joining all of who you are to each other.

This integrated view of man and of the sexual relationship is most clearly portrayed in the Old Testament. The Hebrews always viewed the human person as an integrated whole, not as a person divided into good and bad parts. The Greeks, on the other hand, saw the physical body as something to put down and the human spirit as important to elevate. Their *dyadic,* or gnostic, view did not have high regard for the total person.

When we study all of Scripture, we recognize that the physical and sexual realms are integrated parts of us. The sexual part cannot be isolated. In generations past, there was little understanding that the integrated, whole person included the sexual dimension. As therapists, we realize how important it is to continue teaching the "whole-person dimension" of sex to help bring greater fulfillment and integration to couples' marriages.

Mutuality

Your passion will be expressed, sexual freedom will be pursued, sexual pleasure will be enjoyed, and a total sense of sexual union will occur only as the two of you highly regard the concept of mutuality for your sexual relationship.

The New Testament teaches that the barriers between men and women have been broken down because of Christ's death and resurrection. This teaching is a radical departure from the Old Testament culture. Men and women no longer are to live by different sexual standards; instead, the New Testament clearly teaches mutuality. This is not to suggest that men and women are sexually identical or that they play the same roles, but that because of Christ, men and women stand equally before God. This is symbolized in the sexual relationship. Gone are the days of male domination or control in the sexual realm.

Through Christ, we have the potential to reestablish the original design of creation—to be totally open and free with each other. This includes having an equal value, ability, and position before God: "There is neither Jew nor Greek, there is neither slave nor free man, there is neither male nor female; for you are all one in Christ Jesus" (Gal. 3:28).

Ephesians 2:13–22, an extremely important passage regarding this teaching, tells how Christ broke down the human barriers and made us one household of God.

It might be said that as we become new creatures in Christ, we open up the possibility for a new kind of relationship within marriage. This is the beginning of a restoration of the oneness that was lost in the Garden of Eden. In the same way Christ has restored the possibility of a relationship with God, He opens the door for us to enjoy new and deeper relationships with one another.

Because of the New Testament teaching that the barriers between men and women have been broken down, men and women have equal rights to sexual pleasure and release. Physically, emotionally, and spiritually a woman needs sexual pleasure and release as much as a man does. Pelvic pressure builds up in a woman just as scrotal pressure builds in a man. Spiritually, the biblical message clearly communicates the same rights and the same responsibilities for women as it does for men.

Both men and women have the right to expect sexual pleasure and fulfillment. You are to give yourselves to each other. Your bodies are each other's to enjoy for your pleasure, but not by demand. This is a mutual expectation. It is a command for each of you to apply *for yourselves* in relation to your spouse, not to use to demand sex of each other.

> The husband should fulfill his marital duty to his wife, and likewise the wife to her husband. The wife's body does not belong to her alone but also to her husband. In the same way, the husband's body does not belong to him alone but also to his wife. Do not deprive each other except by mutual consent and for a time, so that you may devote yourselves to prayer. Then come together again so that Satan will not tempt you because of your lack of self-control. (1 Cor. 7:3–5 NIV)

Each New Testament passage that addresses the husband-wife sexual relationship either begins or ends with a command for mutuality. Not only are husbands and wives equal in God's sight and not only do they have the same sexual rights, they also have mutual sexual responsibilities.

The concept of love between husband and wife is an expected part of the marriage relationship according to New Testament teaching. Love becomes the guiding principle for sexual behavior in marriage. Never should sex or any sexual behavior be engaged in that violates or diminishes pleasure for either of you. The husband-wife sexual relationship is to depict the kind of love Christ lavishes on the church.

> Husbands, love your wives, just as Christ loved the church
> and gave Himself up for her. . . . Husbands ought also to
> love their own wives as their own bodies. He who loves his
> wife loves himself. (Eph 5:25, 28)

The Scriptures present a highly prized view of sexuality. Sex
is designated for marriage because it is within this commitment
that the qualities of a highly held view of sexuality can be fulfilled. In that sense, sex is similar to a family jewel or heirloom.
It is a precious gift to be stored carefully and not allowed to
tarnish until the time it is given to a special person. However,
in modern society, sexuality is often treated more like a piece
of junk jewelry, something given to a child at age fourteen to be
worn to school and later thrown into the bottom of the bike bag.

The Bible values sex so highly that the sexual relationship
between a husband and wife is used as a symbol to describe
the relationship between God and His people. To give yourself
sexually to your spouse is the deepest commitment you can
make to another human being. It is a lifelong commitment to
honor, cherish, and be faithful to each other until death. When
you accept your sexuality as a precious gift from the Creator,
it clearly sets you apart from those who misuse it as junk.

In the book of Genesis, the Bible tells how Adam and Eve
were "naked and unashamed," experiencing a free, open relationship that had no barriers. Their relationship was not based
on power, intimidation, social myths, or cultural control.

Since Scripture refers to Christ as the "last," or new Adam
and teaches that believers are in Christ's image (1 Cor. 15:45–
50), sex without shame is a viable potential for the Christian.
Unfortunately, the church has let society dictate many negative
distortions about sexuality. As a Christian couple, you can rid
yourselves of these limitations and claim the total sexual freedom without shame that was there for Adam and Eve and is
available to us through Christ.

Questions and Answers

Couples who have taken our premarital classes have asked
questions about the Bible's teaching regarding sexual rights and

wrongs. You may want answers to those same questions, so we are sharing with you many of those questions and our answers.

What does the Bible say about masturbation?

The Bible says absolutely nothing about masturbation. The Biblical passages that have been used by some authorities to condemn masturbation have been taken out of context. So if you hear passages used for such teaching, study them for yourself.

For example, the passages in Leviticus 15:16 and Deuteronomy 23:9–11 refer to behavior that is acceptable "within the camp." Seminal emission, just like any other discharge from the body, was seen as unclean and had to be handled by going outside the camp and washing before reentering. This was true even if the man ejaculated involuntarily in his sleep. Even more time away from the camp was necessary for women who were menstruating. Other bodily functions were dealt with similarly, so it would seem that in this context, seminal emission is considered as a natural body function and not limited to self-stimulation.

The primary passage that has been used to condemn masturbation is Genesis 38:8–10. This is the story of Onan.

> Then Judah said to Onan, "Go in to your brother's wife, and perform your duty as a brother-in-law to her, and raise up offspring for your brother." And Onan knew that the offspring would not be his; so it came about that when he came to his brother's wife, he wasted his seed on the ground, in order not to give offspring to his brother. But what he did was displeasing in the sight of the LORD; so He took his life also.

This was not an act of self-stimulation, but rather intercourse and withdrawal so that Onan would not provide an offspring for his deceased brother. The Lord was displeased with him for refusing to do the duty of the brother-in-law.

The passages in the New Testament that have been used to condemn masturbation—1 Thessalonians 4:3–4, Romans 1:24, and 1 Corinthians 6:9—are references to homosexuality or immorality, not self-stimulation. Hence, we conclude that the Bible does not deal directly with the subject of self-stimulation.

How do you feel about masturbation in marriage to enhance self-sexual awareness and to teach my husband what areas are most sensitive to stimulation?

In 1 Corinthians 7, the Bible teaches that, within marriage, your body is not just your own but also each other's. This leads us to believe that self-discovery to benefit the sexual relationship in marriage is positive. Your body is your own, so you have the right to discover it, and your body is your husband's, so he has the right to benefit from that discovery. As a result, pleasure will be enhanced for both of you. Thus we would assume the behavior you describe would be acceptable as long as it is not experienced by your spouse as withholding, and your mind is focused on pictures of you with your husband.

What if my husband feels the need to masturbate after we are married? Should I feel guilty?

This is a complicated question to answer because, when applied to this question, the biblical teachings on sex within marriage seem to be contradictory. On the one hand, your bodies are each other's, not just your own, so we could say that you should meet your husband's sexual needs so he does not pursue masturbation. On the other hand, the husband is to love his wife as Christ loved the church and gave Himself for her, so we could say that he should never demand sex if that is not your desire. Instead he should give himself to you to love, and he should care for you until you respond to his nondemanding, nonexpectant, and unconditional love. The relationship usually works best if you both follow these biblical guidelines: Give your body as freely and lovingly as you can without pressure, demand, or guilt, and love each other without that expectation.

Sometimes self-stimulation by one spouse meets the criteria of a loving sexual act within the married relationship. This is most likely when one spouse has a significantly higher sexual drive than the other. In that situation, you as a couple might decide that masturbation is the most loving way to relieve pressure on and not completely squelch the sexual drive of the less interested one. However, if self-stimulation is used by your husband to replace intimacy with you, especially if you are replaced by pornography or fantasies of other women, then his self-stimulation violates the criterion that all sexual behavior within marriage must be loving and respectful of one another. If either of you should choose to masturbate on occasion after you are married and that is not a daily obsession that controls you and does not interfere with your relationship with each other or with God, we would consider that a natural response to a bodily appetite when the other spouse is not available. Whatever your husband's masturbatory patterns, you are not responsible for his sexual decisions. You are only responsible for yours. Thus, you need not feel guilty unless you are withholding yourself; then your guilt should lead you to struggle with your need to withhold rather than with his choice to masturbate.

What effect will my discomfort in touching my genitals have on my sexual experience in marriage? As a result of my church's teaching on sexual purity, I feel very uncomfortable with my genitals.

It will be difficult for you to share your genitals freely with your spouse until you are comfortable with them and have accepted them as a beautiful part of God's perfect design of your body. Affirm your genitals and your sexuality; they reflect God. Genesis 1:26–27 tells us we were created male and female in the image of God. As humans, our sexuality has unique characteristics that are not true of the animals: we think, communicate, act self-consciously, and respond and interact at a relationship level both with God and with each other. In fact, the Hebrew word for "to know" (Gen. 4:1 KJV) refers to sexual intercourse and is the same word used in reference to knowing God. It is also the word used for genitals.

There is nothing in the Bible to indicate that touching this vital part of your body that God designed for sexual pleasure is an impure action. Later, in chapter 6, we will give you specific directions for knowing your genitals before you get married. Thank God for your genitals, His design of them, and His intention for you to enjoy sexual pleasure in your marriage.

Is there any Scriptural advice on oral sex? It's going to be an issue for us. He feels it is dirty and I think it is a wonderful, intimate "non-demand" way to make love.

Oral stimulation, the stimulation of your partner's genitals with your mouth, is a form of sexual enjoyment that often causes conflict between spouses. This is a personal issue and can ultimately be resolved only between you and your husband. But some further information may help you discuss your beliefs and come to some agreement about oral sex. The three most common questions of concern are: Is oral sex morally wrong? Is it "dirty"? Is it an unnatural act? We'll address these questions individually.

Is it morally wrong? We refer to the Bible as our authority, and the Bible doesn't give specific instructions about love-making activities between a husband and wife. Thus, we look for other scriptural principles and go to the Song of Solomon as an example.

The biblical principle that says you are each to give your bodies to your spouse to enjoy would encourage your husband to examine and stretch his inhibitions. However, the concepts of mutual respect and love would encourage you to never pursue oral sex against your husband's desire. That balance continues to be the underlying guideline.

The Song of Solomon may be helpful to your husband's reconsideration of his feelings about oral sex. The lovers continually express their enthusiastic enjoyment of each other's bodies including tasting, eating, and drinking of them. He speaks of feeding "among the lilies" (4:5). She invites him to enjoy her: "Awake, north wind, / and come, south wind! Blow on my garden, / that its fragrance may spread abroad. / Let my lover come into his garden / and taste its choice fruits" (Song of Sol. 4:16 NIV). He says, "I have come into my garden. . . . I have gathered my myrrh with my spice. / I have eaten my honeycomb and my honey; / I have drunk my wine and my milk" (5:1 NIV).

Is it dirty? Your husband's discomfort seems to have more to do with cleanliness than with what is morally right. In both men and women, the anus is dirty. It is highly contaminated with disease-producing microorganisms. If the genital area is contaminated from the anal area, the genitals are "dirty." But if they are freshly washed and free of infection, the genitals of both men and women are clean. In fact, the mouth is more likely to contaminate the genitals than the other way around since the mouth is part of the gastrointestinal system that carries germs. But the only source of contamination of the genitals from the mouth is a cold sore or canker sore caused by the herpes virus.

Genital herpes is caused by a different strain of the herpes virus than the mouth carries; nevertheless, mouth herpes has been known to contaminate the genitals.

Is it unnatural? Even if your husband becomes convinced that oral-genital stimulation is clean and morally right, he may still feel it is unnatural. Some people believe that when the Bible refers to unnatural sexual acts, this is one of them. We have no way to prove those beliefs true or untrue, but if your husband feels violated by oral sex, you should not engage in it. It is not a violation for you to forego that pleasure; nor is omitting any form of sexual enjoyment a violation. Over time, your husband may become comfortable experimenting with oral stimulation. This change is most likely to occur if he feels cared for and loved by you without judgment or demand. Since the sexual act between a husband and wife should never include a violation, you are the one who will need to be patient.

Please comment on the appropriateness of anal intercourse from the perspective of physical design and function.

As we mentioned in the answer to the previous question, the anus is highly contaminated. Also, it does not have the capacity for accommodation that the vagina has. Thus, anal sex is not recommended by either secular or Christian authorities. It is highly dangerous. Entering the anus with the penis contaminates the penis with disease-producing microorganisms, thus causing danger to the man's reproductive and urinary structures. If the man enters the woman's anus and then her vagina, he then contaminates her reproductive tract and sometimes her urinary tract since it is so close to her vagina. When the man's penis enters the woman's anus, the stretching often causes the blood vessels in her rectum to burst, which makes both her and her husband vulnerable to infection.

Anal intercourse should be avoided for physical reasons. It is just not wise!

What part do sexual toys have in lovemaking?

Obviously, the Bible is silent on this issue. If the toys are physically harmful, they should be avoided. If the toys are substitutes for intimacy and pleasure between a husband and wife, they should be avoided. If either spouse feels replaced by a toy, it should be avoided. On the other hand, if an accouterment brings delight and pleasure to the lovemaking for both the husband and wife and does not inflict physical, emotional, or spiritual harm, we would see no reason to restrict it. The questions we encourage couples to honestly ask themselves and each other: Does any toy or sexual activity you wish to use or engage in bring the two of you closer together, or does it in anyway interfere with your relationship with God or with each other?

Is it normal for a man to get an erection from looking at a beautiful woman? This upsets me.

Some men do and some men do not. The erection for a man is an involuntary response controlled by his autonomic nervous system (see chapter 6). Men get erections every eighty to ninety minutes while they sleep, just as women lubricate vaginally every eighty to ninety minutes while they sleep. These responses also happen randomly during the daytime, but the man's erection is much more obvious than is the woman's lubrication. You may be lubricating in response to an attractive man and not even be aware of it. The genital response of arousal to positive stimuli in the environment is natural. It is the way God designed our bodies to function. What we do with that response is our responsibility. If a man pursues his response to a beautiful woman with his thoughts, feelings, or actions then he is going after something that does not belong to him. That causes trouble!

Is it biblically wrong to have intercourse during menstruation?

The passages from Deuteronomy and Leviticus that refer to the woman as being unclean while she is menstruating are laws regarding sanitation procedures of that time and of acceptable "in-camp" behavior. These rules regarding care of body excretions and the need for the woman who was menstruating or the man who had released seminal fluid to go outside the camp for a period of cleansing pertained to honoring the purity of God. It was not that the person was unclean or evil from a sinful sense; instead, these and other natural bodily excretions were not to occur inside the camp in the presence of the Lord Almighty. We find no evidence to support that intercourse is wrong during menstruation.

Is it either harmful or wrong to use pornography to arouse myself in my Christian marriage?

In 1 Corinthians 10:23, Paul wrote, "All things are lawful, but not all things edify." Earlier in 1 Corinthians, Paul gave almost the same teaching: "All things are lawful for me, but I will not be mastered by anything" (6:12b). Other translations talk about not being "enslaved" by anything. Pornography enslaves, especially when it is used for arousal. Secular research has discovered that when couples use pornography to increase their sexual excitement, their ability to be turned on by each other decreases over time and the explicitness needed to produce the arousal increases.[3] We would not recommend the use of pornography to enhance sexual arousal.

Based on the Scriptures' high view of sex within marriage, we encourage you to go after the passion the Bible so highly endorses and enjoy sexual freedom without enslavement. In Romans 14:14–23 Paul taught the principle that is also repeated in 1 Corinthians 10:23–31. The simplest way to sum up this principle is to say that many things in and of themselves are not evil or unclean, but they can become sin if they cause you discomfort (Rom. 14:14) or violate another person. If you believe something is wrong, for you it *is* wrong. If someone is offended by what you do, you should not do it (Rom. 14:20–21). Likewise, if you have the potential to become enslaved by anything, you should avoid it. You should not be possessed, mastered, or controlled by your sexual drive; instead, keep it in its proper subordinated place in your life. Your sexual drive is a natural, God-given part of you. But it is not a drive that must be fulfilled regardless of how it makes others feel, particularly within marriage.

It is vital for you to continue to study the biblical principles regarding sexuality and marriage. The number-one principle is to do what is loving. Enjoy each other's body for your pleasure but not at the expense of the other spouse. Share your beliefs and feelings about sex in marriage. Talk about your areas of conflict. Learn to back off if you are the more eager one and learn to stretch if you are the hesitant one. Remember, God rejoices as you enjoy each other sexually in your marriage!

6
•••••••

Discovering and Enjoying Your Bodies

T he wife in the *For Better or For Worse* comic strip is looking in the mirror with a frown. Then she says, "Bleah!" Her husband comes by and asks, "What's the matter?" The wife responds, "I'm ugly. That's all." He comforts her, "You're not ugly. You're just right!" She ignores him and goes on to describe all of her awful features. He insists, "And I love you just exactly the way you are!"

The wife walks away glowing, but then she hears him add, "Mind you, If *I* was perfect I might be a little more critical!"

Her glow fades.

A woman who attended one of our premarital classes asked, "I've never really liked my body. How do I bring this up to my fiancè before the honeymoon? I'd like to talk about it, but I don't know how."

In this chapter we'll look at some of the sexual issues related to your body—and we'll begin with that most important part of you: your view of your body.

Body Image

How you feel about your body will affect how openly you will be able to share yourself, how freely you will be able to soak in the pleasure of your spouse's touch, and how enthusiastically you will go after sexual pleasure for yourself.

Your self-concept affects how you relate to each other, particularly sexually. When Christ gave the commandment to love your neighbor as yourself, He was teaching that your feelings about yourself affect your ability to love someone else. You will have a hard time giving to or caring for someone else if you feel you are not a worthy person.

Your body image is your attitude about your body, especially your bodily appearance. Everyone would like to have that "perfect" figure or physique. Women are often concerned that their breasts are too big, too small, too flabby, too far apart, or too whatever. Men are concerned with the size of their penises, worrying that a smaller penis means they are less of a man and thus less likely to be able to satisfy a woman. The truth is that the size of breasts or penises are unrelated to sexual pleasure or satisfaction.

Some people are generally dissatisfied with their appearance; others are unhappy with their weight. Still others struggle with how they are proportioned. A premarital question we received asked about this issue rather bluntly: "How do you deal with fat when you are in a sexual relationship?"

If you are the one who is overweight and that bothers you, take action now. Develop healthy eating habits that will help you establish and maintain your ideal body weight throughout the rest of your life. Getting control of your weight will not only elevate your feelings about your body and enhance your sexual relationship, it will also improve your general sense of well-being. You may say, "But diets never work for me." We are not talking about dieting; we are talking about getting help that will change your eating patterns forever. You have to be willing to give up the foods and the habits that cause your excess weight. This change may require a combination of psychotherapy, nutritional consultation, and participation in a support group.

What if your partner's excess weight troubles you? That is much more difficult to deal with because it is your partner who will have to take responsibility to change. You cannot take responsibility for your partner's eating habits, but you can be of help if your partner is willing to lose the weight. You can avoid having foods in the house that your spouse cannot eat, and you can praise his or her efforts to exercise and eat correctly. When you are with your partner, you can avoid eating foods your partner must avoid in order to control his or her weight.

It is important to talk to each other about your bodies and how you feel about them. If you are already married, you can help break down barriers about your body by doing this in the nude in front of a full-length mirror. Take turns being the sharer and the listener; use the following guidelines:

Sharer: Describe your body as honestly as you can to your partner. Start with general feelings about your body as you see it. Then talk about each specific body part, starting with your hair and working down. Talk about how you feel about that part of your body, how it looks to you, what memories you have related to that part, how you wish it were different, and what you like about it.

Listener: Your only task is to listen, observe, and affirm. Listen to both the words and feelings of your partner. *Do not interrupt!* When your partner is finished, reflect back to him or her what you have sensed and heard. Note if there was any part of the body that your partner omitted or hurried past. If there is some part of his or her body that your partner feels is negative that is not negative for you, say so. Share any positive feelings you have about your partner's body.

Sharer: Clarify or expand on what your partner has heard from you. When you feel you have been understood accurately, reverse this procedure. You be the listener while your partner shares about his or her body.

If you are fairly accepting of your body and if your view of your body matches your ideal, you have a good body image. Body-image problems occur when there is a large gap between how you view your body and what you see as ideal. If the way you would like to look is different from the way you think you do look, you will have difficulty accepting yourself and will probably have difficulty being free with your body sexually. If that is the case, what can you do to bridge the gap? How can you bring your view of yourself closer to your ideal?

The first step toward body image enhancement is to examine your view of yourself. Is how you see yourself consistent with how others see you? When you talked about your body with your partner, did his or her feedback affirm your view of yourself? If not, what has contributed to your inability to accept and appreciate your body the way it is? Past sexual abuse, childhood physical abuse, a painful illness, and lack of warm touch and holding during infancy all contribute to a poor body image. Negative verbal messages about your body from peers, parents, or other respected adults may have contributed to a poor body image. You may need your partner's ongoing affirmation, both verbally and through touching, to mend those past hurts. You might spend some time in front of a mirror each day, praising God for having designed you the way He did.

The second step in bringing your own body view closer to that of your ideal is to determine ways you can change your body. There are many different ways this can be done. We've already discussed losing or gaining weight and exercising. Women may also use makeup and different hairstyles; men may choose to shave or not shave and vary their haircut. Both partners can vary their choice of clothing, straighten or correct faulty teeth, improve their posture; ultimately even plastic surgery is an option.

The third and final suggestion for bringing your ideal closer to your real view of yourself is to reevaluate your ideal. What are you measuring yourself against? Who are your models? Are you looking at the extremes held up by the media? How do these "ideal" images compare with the significant and valued people in your life? If your expectations are so far out of reach that you will always feel dissatisfied, we recommend the following process: Commit yourself to one other person who will hold you accountable to get rid of the current ideals and start selecting more realistic body models. If your new models are people with whom you can talk freely, ask them how they achieved their physical condition.

The struggle to feel good about your body is a process of becoming open with yourself and your partner. This includes honesty concerning your feelings about yourself, feeling comfortable being in the nude, caring for your body, and allowing yourself to receive validation through touch and verbal feedback from others in your world. A sense of comfort with and acceptance of your body will contribute to freedom and pleasure in your sexual experiences.

In all this, it is crucial to maintain a healthy perspective on where your value is as a person. God's message is loud and clear—man looks on the outside but God looks on the heart. Neither part can be disregarded: not the part that man looks at—the outside, and not the part God looks at—the heart.

Genital Discovery

"And God created man in His own image, in the image of God He created him; male and female He created them" (Gen. 1:27). Your bodies—including your sexual anatomy—are God's work. He created you with all of your internal and external body parts; all of your sexual organs were made by Him. "And God saw all that He had made, and behold, it was very good" (Gen. 1:31).

Even your sexual parts are good. They were not added as a result of sin. They were there from the moment of creation, and are to be enjoyed and discovered. The entire sexual anatomy is present in newborn babies. They are like miniature adults in newborn bodies.

It is natural for children to discover their genitals. During infancy and toddlerhood, a girl may find her clitoris and touch it because it feels good and it is soothing, much like sucking her thumb. In the same way, the boy finds his penis. These good feelings are God-given; they are natural and normal. Sexual feelings are God's gift.

If you accept this premise—that your sexual parts and feelings are of God—then it would follow that, as with any other gift from God, you should become familiar with them and develop them. A child will naturally become familiar with his or her sexual anatomy and feelings if allowed the freedom to do so. Sexual discovery may have occurred spontaneously for you.

Unfortunately, too often this is not the case. Like many others, you may have been brought up to believe that sexual exploration was bad or sinful.

You may not be familiar with the details of your genitals. Men have more difficulty avoiding their genitals because they are so external. But women often are totally unfamiliar with their genitals. You may be a woman who never felt free to sit down with a mirror and find out what your genitals look or feel like.

We encourage you to become familiar with and thank God for these intricate parts of your sexual anatomy. Thank Him for the good feelings associated with your genitals. Pray for healing from any pain or scars connected with them. You will be sharing this most private part of yourself with your spouse. The more comfortable with and knowledgeable you are about your sexuality, the greater confidence and freedom you will experience with your spouse.

Women: Discovering and Knowing Your Genitals

Begin with clean hands and body. Have a diagram of the female external genitalia (see Figure 6-1). Using a hand mirror, examine your external genitalia. What you see first are the thick outer lips (the labia majora) and the pubic mound; the soft part above the clitoris that is covered with pubic hair. If you have never given birth to a child, your outer lips probably close at the center, or midline, of your genitals. In women who have borne children, it is common to find that childbirth has interrupted the neat fit of the outer lips;they probably do not close at the midline.

Hold the hand mirror in one hand and use your other hand to spread the outer lips apart so you can examine the rest of the external genitalia. First you will notice the thinner inner lips (the labia minora). Next, look for the clitoris. The three parts of the clitoris shown on the diagram—the glans, the hood, and the shaft—may be difficult to identify specifically on yourself. The hood, which covers the shaft, flows down to form the inner lips. The shaft is a miniature penis-like cylinder located under the hood; the glans, or head, is the only part exposed. Even the glans may not be easy to locate. For some women the glans of the clitoris may tend to hide under the hood, and the hood may seem like the point where the inner lips join.

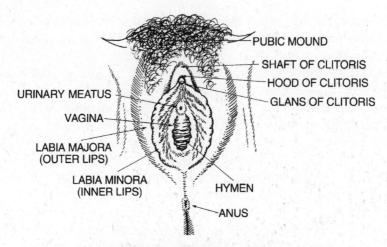

Labels: PUBIC MOUND, SHAFT OF CLITORIS, HOOD OF CLITORIS, GLANS OF CLITORIS, URINARY MEATUS, VAGINA, LABIA MAJORA (OUTER LIPS), LABIA MINORA (INNER LIPS), HYMEN, ANUS

EXTERNAL FEMALE GENITALS
(FRONT VIEW)

FIGURE 6-1

If you have difficulty identifying your clitoris, you may be able to find it by touching the place where you expect it to be. The tip of the clitoris is particularly sensitive to any touch. In fact, rubbing the tip may actually be painful to you. Many women report that the most pleasurable place to receive stimulation is around the clitoris, not directly on it. You may want to touch various points around and on the clitoris, not only for the purpose of stimulation, but to learn where the best feelings occur for you. This will be helpful to know so you can share this information with your spouse for the enhancement of your sexual pleasure.

Now identify the urinary meatus, the vaginal opening, and any other points of interest. The urinary meatus is not part of the sexual anatomy, but its proximity makes it important to locate. It is right above the vagina, or, for some women, it may actually be in the opening of the vagina. It may look like a little pimple. It is the opening to the urinary tract that leads to the urinary bladder. That entire system is sterile. The vagina is the largest opening you see. It is a clean passageway; that is, it is free of disease-producing microorganisms unless you have a vaginal infection. Because the vagina is a muscular passageway, it is an organ of accommodation. It can tighten up to prevent anything from entering it, and it can expand large enough to deliver an infant.

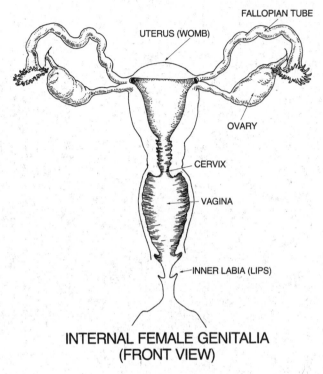

INTERNAL FEMALE GENITALIA
(FRONT VIEW)

FIGURE 6-2

The vagina is the woman's most important organ for sexual functioning. In Figure 6-2, you can see a front view of the vagina as a passageway from the cervix (opening) of the uterus to the outside of the body through the inner labia.

The outer one and a half to two inches and the G-spot area (Figure 6-3) of the vagina are sensitive to sexual stimulation. Some women are more aware of this sensitivity than are others. Regularly exercising the PC (pubococcygeus) muscle enhances that sensitivity.

To discover your areas of sensitivity, continue your genital exploration by inserting your finger into your vagina. Be sure your hands and nails are clean and have no rough edges. Gently press on the wall of the vagina. If you think of the opening of the vagina as a clock, start at the twelve o'clock position (nearest the front of the body) and slowly move around the wall of the vagina, pressing and stroking at every hour (see the figure below). Try varying degrees of pressure and types of touch. Be particularly aware of any points of pain or pleasure.

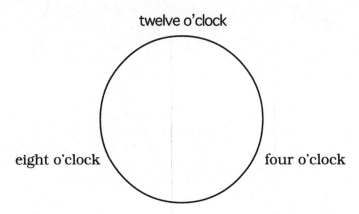

Opening of vagina with four, eight, and twelve o'clock positions identified.

After completing this exploration and with your finger still in your vagina, practice tightening and relaxing your PC muscle. Your ability to tighten and relax your PC muscle voluntarily can be enhanced. To learn to do that follow the exercise below. It is sometimes referred to as the Kegel exercise, named after the physician who taught pregnant women to exercise their PC muscle in this way to ease labor and delivery. A side benefit these women experienced was heightened sexual responsiveness.

PC Muscle (Kegel) Exercise: Begin by identifying the sensation of tightening and relaxing this muscle. While sitting on the toilet to urinate, spread your legs apart. Start urination. Then stop urination for three seconds. Repeat this several times before you are finished emptying your bladder. If you have difficulty stopping urination, you need to work on tightening the PC muscle. If you have difficulty restarting urination, you need to work on voluntarily relaxing the PC muscle. If you can do both easily, you only need to tighten and relax the PC muscle twenty-five times per day to keep it in good condition.

You might connect your PC muscle exercise with some regular daily activity, so that activity is a reminder to you. For example, you could do five contractions of the muscle every time the telephone rings. If either tightening or relaxing the PC muscle is difficult for you, follow the instructions below.

1. Gradually tighten the PC muscle tighter and tighter to the count of four. Then hold the muscle as tight as you can while you again count to four. Now gradually relax the muscle, letting go of the tension a little at a time as you count to four. Do ten to twenty repetitions of this exercise one to four times per day.

2. Start to tighten your vagina by thinking of bringing your labia (lips) closer together, like closing an elevator door. Imagine that your vagina is an elevator. You start to tighten at the ground floor. Bring the muscles up from floor to floor, tightening and holding at each floor. Keep your breathing even and relaxed. Do not hold your breath. Continue until you get to the fifth floor. Then go down, relaxing the tension of the muscle one floor at a time. When you get to the bottom, bear down as though you are opening the elevator door (the vagina) and letting something out. Do ten to twenty repetitions of this exercise one to four times per day.

3. Rapidly tighten and relax the PC muscle at the opening of the vagina in almost a flickering or fluttering movement. Do ten to twenty repetitions of this exercise one to four times per day.

Continuing the genital exploration, explore the sensation in the G-spot area (see Figure 6-3). With your finger in your vagina and the PC muscle tightened, move your finger in a little farther, just beyond the inner ridge of the PC muscle. Press, stroke, and tap toward the front of your body as though you are pressing the inside of your vagina toward your pubic bone. This is the G-spot area. Continue to massage that area with varying degrees of pressure. Note any sensations you experience. Some women feel pressure to urinate, which may be associated with a need for fluid release during orgasm. Many women do not notice any different sensation here than in any other part of the vagina unless they are already aroused. There is nothing right or wrong about what you feel or don't feel. It is just helpful to be aware of these sensations to aid communication and further discovery with your husband.

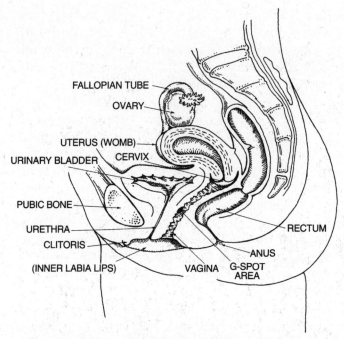

FALLOPIAN TUBE

OVARY

UTERUS (WOMB)

URINARY BLADDER CERVIX

PUBIC BONE

URETHRA

CLITORIS

(INNER LABIA LIPS) VAGINA G-SPOT AREA

RECTUM

ANUS

UNAROUSED INTERNAL FEMALE GENITALIA (SIDE VIEW)

FIGURE 6-3

You cannot go any further with "hands-on" discovery, but it is also important to know your internal sexual organs. Looking at the diagram of the front view of the internal female reproductive organs (Figure 6-2), you will see the ovaries, uterus, fallopian tubes, and vagina. The ovaries look like large almonds and are located on either side of the uterus, below and behind the fallopian tubes. They produce some of the sex hormones that affect the menstrual cycle and the sexual drive. They also produce the ova, or eggs, of reproduction. All the woman's eggs are present at birth. When a girl reaches puberty, the hormones trigger the maturation and release of these eggs, usually one per month until a woman is through menopause. The egg is usually released fourteen days before a woman's menstrual flow begins. It is carried through the fallopian tubes to the uterus, where it is implanted if it meets with a sperm. If it is not fertilized with a sperm, it is discharged from the body with the menstrual flow.

The uterus, or womb, is a pear-shaped organ located between the urinary bladder and the rectum, as you can see in Figure 6-2. In its unaroused position, the uterus is flexed toward the front of the body, pointing forward and slightly upward. If you have a tipped or retroflexed uterus, it is aligned in a straighter up-and-down position with the cervix hanging into the vagina. This can cause momentary, intense pain upon deep thrusting during intercourse. Exercising your PC muscle will help maintain the normal position of your uterus.

Men: Knowing Yourself

As the man, getting to know your genitals probably will not be a new or difficult task. While growing up, little boys automatically become familiar with their genitals—because the male genitals are so obvious. Even though you may be familiar with what it feels like to touch or stimulate your penis and scrotum, you may not be familiar with the various parts of your genitals and what they are called. In a private, well-lit room, use the diagram of male genitals (Figure 6-4) to identify all the specific parts of your genitals.

The scrotum is like a pouch that holds two small glands called the testes. The testes, or "balls", which you can feel moving around when you press on the scrotum, are the primary sex organs in the male. They produce the sperm that unite with the female egg to begin a new life. In addition to producing the sperm, the testes also produce a portion of the seminal fluid that carries the sperm from the testes through a series of ducts and out through the penis. The duct system passes through the doughnut-shaped prostate gland, which adds additional seminal fluid (see Figure 6-5 page 98). The seminal fluid carrying the sperm from the testes is called the ejaculate. The third function of the testes is totally unrelated to the duct system; it is the production of the male hormone testosterone, which is secreted directly into the bloodstream.

The ejaculatory system, as you can see in Figure 6-5, joins the urinary system and leads into the penis. The penis is the obvious essential organ for sexual intercourse. It is the means by which the ejaculate is introduced into the female vagina. The penis is composed of erectile tissue that has spaces called venous sinuses. These rush full of blood and fluid during

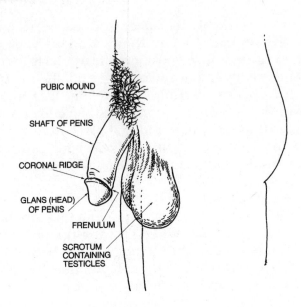

CIRCUMCISED EXTERNAL MALE GENITALS
(SIDE VIEW)

FIGURE 6-4

sexual arousal. This causes the penis to become enlarged, firm, and erect, which makes entry into the vagina possible.

The penis has various parts. There is the glans, the bulging tip with the coronal ridge. If a man has not been circumcised, the glans is covered with a loose skin called the foreskin. This can be pulled back from the glans for cleaning, and it automatically retracts during an erection. For the circumcised man the head (glans) is always exposed. There is no known difference in sexual satisfaction for the man or the woman if the man has or has not been circumcised. The shaft of the penis is the cylindrical structure that responds most pleasurably to being stroked. The skin around the shaft of the penis forms what looks like a seam down the back side of the penis. This is called the frenulum, and for some men is the part of the penis they find most responsive to caressing. This may or may not be true for you.

As you discover your genitals, think about the kind of touch and stimulation you have enjoyed. Imagine other kinds

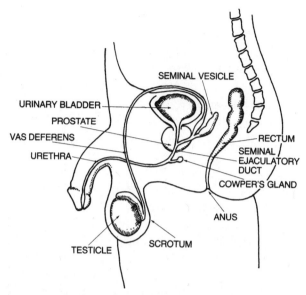

UNAROUSED INTERNAL MALE GENITALIA
(SIDE VIEW)

FIGURE 6-5

of touch and stimulation you might try. Think about how you might teach your spouse what you would enjoy without placing demands on her.

Sexual Responsiveness

Now that you have discovered how you have been made, we will acquaint you with how these various parts respond during a sexual experience. Not only is all sexual anatomy present at birth, involuntary sexual responses begin almost immediately. A baby boy has his first erection within minutes, and a baby girl lubricates vaginally within hours after birth. These early responses are not associated with the same sexual erotic sensations that are experienced once the hormones begin to be secreted during puberty.

The sex hormones, primarily estrogen and progesterone in women and testosterone in men, influence the development of the child's sexual organs, affect the adult's sexual functioning, and enhance sexual drive in adolescents and adults.

The sexual drive is not only the basis for sexual arousal, but also for the energy to get things done in life. That is why it is important to use up this energy for the tasks of life while you are postponing your sexual fulfillment and why it is important for married couples to save time and energy for their sexual relationship. If it is all used up with the stresses of life, you will have no desire for sexual arousal and release.

Arousal is an automatic, involuntary, pleasure-seeking response. Some men and women are more aware of the feelings of arousal than others; but all healthy adults experience arousal on a continual basis. A woman lubricates vaginally every eighty to ninety minutes while she sleeps, just as a man gets an erection every eighty to ninety minutes while he sleeps. Throughout the day, arousal may occur for various reasons: a full bladder, a brush of your genitals against some surface, an erotic thought, or any sexual activity.

Sexual arousal, which is controlled by the relaxed or passive branch of our involuntary or autonomic nervous system—the parasympathetic branch, may lead to the full sexual response of orgasm if positive sexual stimulation is pursued. Sexual response is controlled by the active branch of your autonomic, or involuntary, nervous system—the sympathetic branch. Thus your body shifts from being controlled by the relaxed side to being controlled by the active side of your involuntary nervous system as arousal peaks and triggers your orgasmic response.

Both men and women regularly experience sexual arousal without sexual release. The arousal gradually disappears when it is not pursued. It is also possible, though highly unlikely, for both men and women to experience orgasm without arousal. Some men ejaculate without an erection, a habit that must be changed before pursuing intercourse. Some women have an orgasm but never lubricate vaginally nor experience the sensations of arousal. While this is not the norm, it is important to understand that arousal and release are two separate responses.

Your sexual organs and their functioning during the sexual experience comprise an awesome and beautiful system. Physiologically, men and women have been created to respond in a similar way. The intricate details of this sexual response have been measured by Masters and Johnson and categorized into four phases (see Figure 6-6).

These responses may occur due to sexual intercourse; to manual, oral, or self-stimulation of the genitals; intense hugging; deep kissing; petting; fantasy; visual input; or any loveplay. Sexual intercourse is not necessary for full sexual release, nor does sexual intercourse guarantee full sexual release. This is vital information, especially for understanding the difference between sexual feelings and sexual behavior as it relates to your sexual decisions and responsibility.

As you read the following discussion of what happens in your bodies during each of the four phases of the sexual response pattern, find these details on either the man's graph (see Figure 6-7) or the woman's graph (see Figure 6-8). Circle any of the responses you are aware of or assume have happened to you. Put a check by any of the responses that you believe are difficult for you or have not happened. Share your graphs with each other.

FIGURE 6-6
SEXUAL RESPONSE PATTERNS

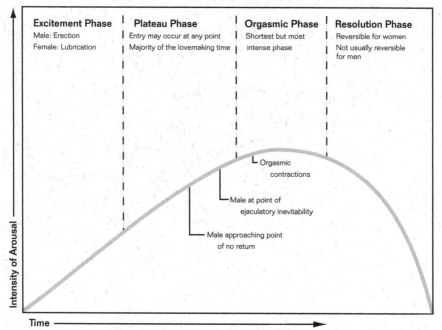

Excitement Phase	Plateau Phase	Orgasmic Phase	Resolution Phase
Male: Erection	Entry may occur at any point	Shortest but most	Reversible for women
Female: Lubrication	Majority of the lovemaking time	intense phase	Not usually reversible for men

Orgasmic contractions

Male at point of ejaculatory inevitability

Male approaching point of no return

Intensity of Arousal

Time

Adapted from Master and Johnson, *Human Sexual Response*
(Boston: Brown, Little, and Co., 1966)

Sexual Response Pattern
for Men

	Excitement Phase	Plateau Phase	Orgasmic Phase	Resolution Phase
External Genitals:	Penis becomes erect as it rushes full of blood Scrotum thickens and partially elevates	Penis engorges more and deepens in color Fluid containing sperm seeps from penis Scrotum thickens	Penis contracts expelling the seminal fluid	Penis becomes flaccid Scrotum thins and drops
Internal Genitalia:	No significant change	Testes enlarge Right testicle rises and rotates early: When approaching point of no return: Left testicle rises and rotates Prostate contracts Seminal vesicle contracts	Seminal duct system contracts	Testes descend and return to normal size
Total Body:	Nipples become erect in 60% of men	Skin flushes on chest, neck, and face Foot contracts downward (carpopedal spasm) Heart rate increases Blood pressure rises Pelvis thrusts Muscle tense	Rectal sphincter contracts Foot spasms continue Heart rate increases more Blood pressure rises more Breathing increases Facial muscles contract Gasping occurs	Relief of vasocongestion and engorgement Skin perspires Muscles relax
Characteristics:	Arousal	Entry may occur at any time Ejaculatory control must be learned for extended love play	Shortest, but most intense phase Internal experience	Tension loss Not usually reversible (rest period required before more arousal)

Level of Sexual Arousal

Adapted from Masters and Johnson
Human Sexual Response
Boston: Little, Brown & Co., 1966

FIGURE 6-7

Phases of the Sexual Response|

© Copyright 1993 Penner & Penner

Sexual Response Pattern
for Women

Excitement Phase	Plateau Phase	Orgasmic Phase	Resolution Phase
External Genitals: Clitoris lengthens; Outer lips spread flat; Inner lips enlarge	**External Genitals:** Clitoris retracts under hood; Inner lips turn bright red and enlarge (about 1 min. before orgasmic response)	**External Genitals:** No noticeable change	**External Genitals:** Clitoris returns to normal size; Inner and outer lips return to normal size and position
Internal Genitalia: Vagina lubricates (within 10-20 sec.); Uterus elevates	**Internal Genitalia:** Inner 2/3 of vagina expands; Outer 1/3 of vagina thickens and contracts forming orgasmic platform; Uterus elevates fully	**Internal Genitalia:** Outer 1/3 of vagina contracts 3 to 12 times; Uterus contracts	**Internal Genitalia:** Cervix opens slightly and drops into seminal pool; Uterus drops back toward front of pelvis; Vagina collapses and thins
Total Body: Nipples become erect; Breasts enlarge	**Total Body:** Skin flushes over abdomen, chest, etc.; Foot contracts downward (carpopedal spasm); Heart rate increases; Blood pressure rises; Pelvis thrusts; Muscle tense	**Total Body:** Rectal sphincter contracts; Foot spasms continue; Heart rate increases more; Blood pressure rises more; Breathing increases; Facial muscles contract; Gasping occurs	**Total Body:** Relief of vasocongestion and engorgement; Skin perspires; Muscles relax; Breasts and nipples return to prestimulated appearance
Characteristics: Arousal	**Characteristics:** Entry may occur at any time; Majority of love play	**Characteristics:** Shortest, but most intense phase; Internal experience	**Characteristics:** Tension loss; Reversible

Level of Sexual Arousal

Adapted from Masters and Johnson
Human Sexual Response
Boston: Little, Brown & Co., 1966

FIGURE 6-8

Phases of the Sexual Response

© Copyright 1993 Penner & Penner

The Excitement Phase—Arousal

The excitement phase, the first stage of the sexual response pattern, may occur involuntarily without any stimulation when you are relaxed or asleep. The excitement phase is either preceded by or triggers sexual desire, is the urge to be close physically or to be stimulated sexually. For both the man and the woman, the changes of the excitement phase are due to vasocongestion (blood and fluid rushing into the sexual organs).

Female Excitement. The clitoris is most important for the woman during the excitement phase. It becomes engorged with blood the same way the penis does. It doubles or triples in size as blood and fluid rush into its venus spaces.

The clitoris, the only organ in the human anatomy designed solely for receiving and transmitting sexual stimuli, confirms that God designed women to be intensely sexual beings, not just "vaginas" that are recipients of the man's sexual aggression. Physiologically, pleasure is the clitoris's only function. The woman, not the man, was created with the clitoris. Consider this fact very seriously as you begin your sexual life together. It should affect how you make love, how the woman feels about herself as a sexual being, and how the man relates to her sexually. Couples who are aware of the unique importance of the clitoris rarely fall into the "passive woman versus aggressive man" mentality that leaves the woman submissive, passive, and unfulfilled in the sexual act and the man unhappy with the woman's lack of involvement.

Intense pleasure and pain are closely related in our bodies. Those areas, such as the clitoris, that are loaded with nerve endings are most receptive to pleasure and, for the same reason, most receptive to pain. As the woman's arousal moves to intense pleasure, the clitoris becomes so sensitive she can readily experience clitoral pain, especially if the stimulation is directly on the head of the clitoris, too intense, or continues too long. That is why it is vital to understand that most women prefer stimulation *around* the clitoris rather than directly on the head. Most women also prefer the stimulation to vary in intensity, and they respond better if their arousal is allowed to build in waves with intermittent stimulation of the clitoris rather than continuous stimulation. A lighter, teasing touch satisfies most. Ultimately what works best is if the woman is the authority on her own body and guides her husband in clitoral touch. There is no way he can automatically know what is going to be most pleasurable.

During the excitement phase, other changes happen in the woman's body. The labia minora (inner lips) become engorged and extend outward while the labia majora (outer lips) spread flat as if the genital area is opening up to receive the penis. As the arousal builds, the woman's genitals take on a slight funnel shape in preparation for penile entry.

Internally, the uterus begins to pull up and away from the vagina; this pulls the cervix out of the way so the penis will not strike against it during thrusting. However, this preparation does not occur when the woman has a tipped uterus; the cervix does not get out of the way of the penis. That is why it can be struck, causing a sharp, stabbing pain during deep thrusting.

The vagina lubricates within twenty seconds of any form of sexual stimulation. The lubrication is secreted like beads of perspiration along the wall of the vagina to make the entry of the penis into the vagina a smooth and comfortable activity. Even though lubrication is the sign of *physical* readiness only the woman can determine when she is *emotionally* ready for entry. The involuntary response of lubrication cannot be triggered by will or determination. Anxiety or pressure to perform is likely to hinder lubrication, so during your first sexual encounters we recommend using a lubricant. Many different materials can be used to provide lubrication. K-Y Jelly is water-based, so it dries easily. If you are not using a rubber-barrier method of birth control such as a rubber condom or diaphragm, petroleum-based products like Allercreme (a nonallergic and nonlanolin body lotion) and Albolene (a facial cleanser) are very good. Natural oils are also popular. Newer products designed especially for this purpose that will not interfere with the effectiveness of condoms and diaphragms include Probe and Astroglide. When nothing else is available, saliva works well.

The breasts also change during the initial excitement phase; nipple erection is the most obvious response, and general engorgement causes a slight increase in breast size. The areola, the area around the nipple, usually darkens and becomes slightly engorged, especially as the woman's excitement intensifies. We have received letters from engaged women who were concerned about this change in their nipples as they became aroused or felt chilled. They wondered if this change in their nipples would be negative for their husbands. On the contrary, men are usually excited by the woman's nipple erection.

Male Excitement. The penis is the primary receiver and transmitter of sexual sensations in the man. The penile response of erection is parallel to clitoral engorgement and vaginal lubrication in the woman. It is that involuntary response that occurs throughout the day and night and can be brought about by sexual thoughts or by direct or indirect stimulation of the penis itself. Erection is necessary for intercourse, so men who have had difficulty with arousal or loss of erection worry about their ability to respond.

Erections can easily be interrupted by negative or nonsexual stimulation such as the telephone ringing, a loud noise, a negative thought, a special concern, a harsh word, or a critical comment. Erections can be lost and regained when relaxation and freedom allows that response. This is likely to happen during extended love play, yet erections can also be maintained for extended periods of time without ejaculation. The latter is most likely to occur when the stimulation is varied and the intensity of the experience flows in waves.

In addition to the penis becoming erect as blood and fluid rush into it, the scrotum thickens and elevates slightly. The man, as well as the woman, may experience a sexual flush in the upper third of the body. Nipple erection occurs in about 60 percent of men.

The Plateau Phase

The plateau phase is the phase that varies most in length; it can last a few minutes or continue for hours. It all depends on how quickly each individual responds and what the couple desires. The plateau phase includes all the bodily changes that happen from the time of arousal until orgasm.

The changes that occur during the plateau phase are due to the buildup of tension and increased congestion in the genitals.

When a long, extended period of love play occurs, this buildup of intensity will usually result in repeated waves of heightened arousal and then relaxation. They may continue as long as the partners give each other and themselves the freedom to ride these waves; then the intensity with one of the waves will build to the point of automatically triggering an orgasm.

Male Plateau. Externally, the penis becomes slightly more engorged and deeper in color during the plateau phase while the glans, or head, of the penis increases in diameter. The scrotum also thickens and elevates more. Fluid containing sperm may seep from the penis during the plateau phase before the point of ejaculation; that is why withdrawal of the penis from the vagina before ejaculation is not a reliable method of birth control.

Internally during this phase the testes enlarge 50 to 100 percent. The right testicle rises and rotates a quarter turn. Near the end of the plateau phase as the man nears the point of orgasm, three changes warn him that he is about to ejaculate. The left testicle rises and rotates a quarter turn, the prostate gland contracts, and the sphincter from the bladder shuts off so no seminal fluid will be forced into the bladder and no urine will be expelled during ejaculation. No man can identify these specific changes, thinking, for example, *There goes the left one,* but he *can* sense that he is about to ejaculate. The seminal fluid is traveling to the base of the penis.

Once these changes have occurred, the process is in motion. The man is approaching ejaculatory inevitability, the point of no return. He *will* ejaculate! If a man wishes to learn to delay his ejaculation, he must gain control *prior* to these physical changes.

Female Plateau. As the sexual experience progresses, more and more is happening internally for the woman, and less is occurring externally. This fact symbolizes women's more internal experience, in contrast to men's more external, obvious response.

The slight external changes include the increase in size and brightening in color of the labia minora a minute or two before orgasm. The Bartholin gland just inside the labia secretes one to three drops of a substance designed to enhance impregnation by changing the pH balance of the vagina. At the same time, the

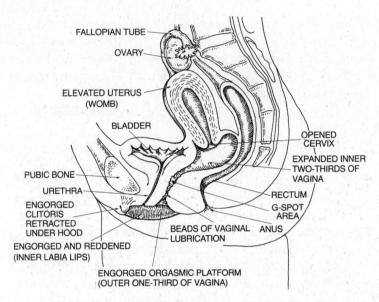

FALLOPIAN TUBE

OVARY

ELEVATED UTERUS
(WOMB)

BLADDER

OPENED
CERVIX

EXPANDED INNER
TWO-THIRDS OF
VAGINA

PUBIC BONE

URETHRA

ENGORGED
CLITORIS
RETRACTED
UNDER HOOD

RECTUM

G-SPOT
AREA

ENGORGED AND REDDENED
(INNER LABIA LIPS)

BEADS OF VAGINAL ANUS
LUBRICATION

ENGORGED ORGASMIC PLATFORM
(OUTER ONE-THIRD OF VAGINA)

**AROUSED INTERNAL FEMALE GENITALIA
(SIDE VIEW)**

FIGURE 6-9

clitoral glans retracts under the clitoral hood, allowing more direct stimulation.

Internally, many significant changes must occur for the woman before her intensity will be strong enough to trigger an orgasm (see Figure 6-9). The uterus, which began to elevate during the excitement phase, now elevates even more. The nonerotic upper two-thirds of the vagina expands or balloons to hold the seminar fluid for impregnation; this area is known as the seminal pool. The outer third of the vagina becomes intensely engorged to form the orgasmic platform. Some women are aware of the pleasurable vaginal grasping response as arousal during the plateau phase intensifies. These bodily changes verify that the woman's sexual response was designed for both reproduction and pleasure.

Male and Female Transition from Plateau to Orgasm.
The specific changes that happen for both men and women during the transition from plateau to orgasm usually go rela-

tively unnoticed. There is the involuntary extension of the foot called the carpopedal spasm. Both the heart rate and the blood pressure increase. Involuntary pelvic thrusting occurs as arousal approaches orgasm, and general muscular tension builds with spastic-like contractions.

More obvious changes also occur. The skin flushes in the chest, neck, and face—almost a blushing effect due to the widespread vasocongestion. Facial grimaces are common because of the involuntary contracting of the facial muscles. Gasping or moaning responses are due in part to hyperventilation (heavy breathing), which is virtually inevitable and necessary for both men and women in order to be able to orgasm. Women who have difficulty with orgasm usually stop these intense gasping, grimacing, and breathing responses because they feel self-conscious or unladylike. Yet these changes are necessary for both men and women to make the transition from the plateau phase to the orgasmic response, and men enjoy these responses in their wives.

The Orgasmic Phase

The orgasmic phase is the shortest and most intense of the four phases. It is a reflex response that lasts only a few seconds. You cannot choose to respond with an orgasm as you can choose to bend your elbow, but you can control or inhibit the response by stopping the natural, involuntary responses in your body. Or you can enhance the possibility of an orgasmic response by becoming active and pursuing genital stimulation—penile thrusting for the man and clitoral and/or vaginal stimulation for the woman.

As the intensity builds, the tension increases to the point where the orgasmic reflex is set off. The autonomic, or involuntary, nervous system has switched control from the relaxed branch (the parasympathetic) to the active, fight-or-flight branch (the sympathetic). Thus, the more active you are, the more your body is encouraged to respond orgasmically (which is usually what the woman needs); and the quieter and more passive you are, the more your response is slowed down (which is usually what the man needs). Since orgasm is a reflex, a person who actively receives enough stimulation will eventually be orgasmic.

Female Orgasm. All the significant orgasmic changes in the woman take place internally. That is why there has been so much confusion about women's orgasmic response.

Internally, the woman has two centers of orgasmic response, the uterus and the vagina. The uterus contracts similarly to way it contracts during the early stages of labor. (This is why doctors rule out orgasm when a woman is threatening to miscarry or go into early labor.) Sometimes women resist these contractions because they are experienced as slightly painful, but as women learn to focus on the intense pleasure of the contractions, they become highly enjoyable. Intense pleasure and pain are so close that the switch from one to the other is very possible. The second internal response center is the outer third of the vagina—the orgasmic platform. The contractions of the PC muscle that surrounds both the vagina and the rectal sphincter occur eight- tenths of a second apart, with three to five contractions in a mild orgasm and eight to twelve contractions in a more intense orgasm. These uterine and vaginal responses happen simultaneously.

Because the clitoris is retracted completely under the hood during orgasm, the woman may need very direct clitoral stimulation at that particular time. She can develop signals to communicate that need to her husband.

Male Orgasm. The man's orgasm is experienced in two stages. In the first stage, the internal genitalia respond a few seconds before ejaculation. The contractions of these internal structures—the seminal duct system, the prostate gland, the rectal sphincter, and the urinary bladder—occur at intervals of eight-tenths of a second just as they do in the woman. These contractions move the ejaculate to the base of the penis, preparing it for the ejaculation.

During stage two, the seminal fluid carrying the sperm, is expelled. This is the ejaculation. Having reached this point of ejaculatory inevitability, nothing can stop this response; it is, indeed, inevitable. The contractions at the base of the penis that cause the expulsion of the seminal fluid also occur at intervals of eight-tenths of a second. For the average male, a standard ejaculation contains 3.5 to 5 cubic centimeters of ejaculate (about 1 teaspoon) and 175 to 500 million spermatozoa.

Orgasmic Differences between Men and Women. Women's orgasmic responses seem to differ greatly from one experience to another and from one woman to another. Men seem to be more similar in their orgasmic responses. This may be due to the wide range of the contractions during orgasm for women (from three to twelve) and their capacity for having more than one orgasm.

Women have a physiologically unlimited potential for orgasms; they are limited only by their desire, their pursuit, and their stamina. In contrast, men, except for a very small percentage, need a refractory period of at least twenty minutes—and usually hours—before they can regain arousal, erection, and ejaculation. As a man ages, the refractory period increases. It also seems that the more frequently a man ejaculates, the longer it takes until he is able to be restimulated.

Even though women have unlimited potential for orgasms, many women struggle to even experience one orgasm. And not all women desire more than one response. For women who do wish to have more than one, there are two ways of doing that. Some women have multiple orgasms. These are orgasms that come one right after another with no refractory period. These are referred to by sexual therapists Alan and Donna Brauer as "extended sexual orgasms."[1] Other women have sequential orgasms. These women respond orgasmically, have a slight refractory period, then respond again with another orgasm.

The woman's orgasm can be interrupted at any point; the man's cannot. Once the man has reached the point of ejaculatory inevitability, nothing can be done to stop it; the reflex is in motion. Because of this irreversibility, women have often been taught they should not arouse a man because once a man is aroused he cannot control his behavior. This just is not true! Men are responsible for their own sexual behavior just as women are. Ejaculatory control—learning to gain control *before* the point of no return—is a separate issue that also *can* be learned.

The longer the time between sexual releases, the greater the difference between men and women's timing of sexual response. If the sexual experience is the first one in a long time, a woman will tend to be slower in her response and will experience less intensity in her release while a man will tend to be quicker in his arousal and release and experience more buildup and intensity. We believe this tendency—to go in the opposite direction—is one more indication that couples were designed to be together and to experience sexual release on a regular basis.

While women experience difficulty with and pressure to be orgasmic (the active phase of the sexual response cycle) men's pressure is with getting or keeping erections (the passive phase of the sexual response cycle) or with ejaculating too quickly. This is likely because men tend to be active during sex and women tend to be passive. If you wish to prevent these difficulties, both of you would do well to learn to enjoy both passively receiving pleasure and actively pursuing pleasure.

We are often asked orgasm-related questions during our work with premarital groups. We will answer some of the most common questions here:

When a woman has an orgasm is there fluid?

A small percentage of women release a fluid when they have an orgasm. The fluid comes from the urinary bladder and is released through the urinary meatus, but it is not urine. Researchers at Masters and Johnson's institute verified this response. They inserted a catheter into each woman's bladder, emptied it of urine, had her go immediately into a sexual time with her husband, and collected the fluid she released during orgasm. They found that it is not amber in color and does not contain the same components as urine. If you feel an urge to urinate when you are getting close to orgasm, have the bed protected and let go of the fluid. The release is accompanied by a very intense orgasm. If you wish to read more about this response, read *The G Spot.*[2]

Why do some couples have simultaneous orgasms?

Simultaneous orgasms are far from necessary for a fully satisfying sexual relationship, and striving for that goal will cause more trouble than it is worth, creating one of those demands that destroy pleasure. A husband and wife may incidentally orgasm at the same time, particularly if the wife has more than one orgasm, but it often is more enjoyable to orgasm separately and enjoy the intensity of each other's experience.

How does a woman know if she has had an orgasm?

Usually you will know by how you feel afterward. When you

have had release, you feel the relaxation after the buildup of the sexual tension in your body. If not, you will feel the frustration or alertness of not having had release. An orgasm is basically a pelvic sneeze. Consider how you feel when your nasal passages are congested and you need to sneeze but you can't. That is the same feeling that occurs in the pelvic area when you have gotten aroused but have not had an orgasm. Another analogy shared by a person in one of our classes is that an orgasm can feel like opening up a well-shaken can of soda. However, we might add that orgasms are not always that intense.

Can a man stimulate a woman is such a way that she will always have an orgasm?

No, it is not the man's responsibility to assure a woman of an orgasm. There are definitely techniques he can learn that will be more enjoyable for her than others. The woman has to learn about her body and teach her husband what she needs to become stimulated. She also has to learn to be active in going after the stimulation she desires. In turn, he has to learn to enjoy her body for his pleasure without focusing on whether he is producing a response. His focus on her response will produce demand, not an orgasm.

If you have never had an orgasm, how do you get one?

There are entire books written on this topic. The one we recommend is *Becoming Orgasmic* by Julia Heiman and Joseph LoPiccolo.[3] We also have outlined a whole process for that purpose in our book *Restoring the Pleasure*.[4] Basically, there are four simple steps: stop trying, focus on pleasure, reduce self-consciousness, and get active. The goal you can set for yourself is to enjoy longer times of arousal and higher peaks of arousal. Eventually the orgasmic reflex will be triggered.

What if the woman hasn't reached orgasm and the man gets to the point of no return?

The man can continue to stimulate the woman after he ejaculates. Or the two of you can prevent this from happening by enjoying a longer time of stimulating the woman both before and during intercourse and teaching the man to delay ejaculation. All of these are satisfactory options.

The Resolution Phase

During this final phase of the sexual response, the body returns to its unstimulated state. Both the man and the woman experience the sensation of tension loss due to the release of engorgement and the diminishing of vasocongestion.

Male Resolution. In the male, the most obvious sign of resolution is the lessening of his erection. For most men, the full, firm erection will diminish immediately, but it may take some time for the penis to return to its prestimulated, flaccid state. A question that was asked during a premarital class relates to this issue: "Is it possible to stay hard after ejaculation, continue making love, and ejaculate again?" A few men report the ability to do that, and Brauer and Brauer, in their book *ESO,* suggest possible ways to enhance that possibility.[5] We would discourage a focus on reaching this goal, especially early in your sexual life. Goals such as this usually take away from the pleasure and create demand.

During resolution some men experience heightened sensitivity, even pain, on the glans of the penis. If you should find that to be true for you, rather than draw away from your wife and leave her feeling rejected, inform her of this sensitivity and your need not to have any penile touching after ejaculation. You can hold and affirm each other without penile contact.

Men often feel relaxed and fall asleep quickly after an orgasm. This can be frustrating to the woman who may come down off her orgasm more slowly and desire a time of intimacy through conversation and touch. On the other hand, if the woman has experienced an intense orgasm or enough orgasmic release she, too, may fall asleep quickly.

Female Resolution. If the woman has been aroused but has not experienced release, she may feel the continued tension or engorgement for some time after the sexual experience. This can be frustrating for the woman, sometimes causing involuntary crying.

From a physiological perspective, we understand this crying to be the body's way of releasing the tension that did not get released orgasmically. Crying triggers the parasympathetic-nervous-system dominance, which helps the woman relax. When the couple can hold each other and share this crying release, the woman will eventually become more comfortable letting go with her husband and be able to allow an orgasmic release.

After an orgasm, the woman's clitoris returns to its pre-stimulated size within five to ten minutes. It takes about the same time for the labia minora and labia majora to return to their unstimulated size, position, and color. The uterus drops back into its original position relatively quickly after orgasm. The vaginal wall collapses within five to eight minutes while the congestion in the outer third of the vagina disappears in seconds.

When the woman has not had an orgasm, it will take longer for all of these changes to occur because the engorgement is released gradually. There have been no contractions to trigger the release. The greater the number of contractions, the more quickly the woman's body returns to its prestimulated state. During the resolution phase, you have the opportunity to affirm your intimacy regardless of the physical fulfillment that has been experienced. Some couples like to fall asleep together, others like to talk and cuddle, and still others like to get up and do something active together. Discover together what you enjoy. If your desires for handling the resolution time are different, negotiate those differences: One time go his way, another time her way, and sometimes compromise on both ways.

7

•••••••

Designing a
Successful Honeymoon

The fond memories of our happy honeymoon have lingered with us now for thirty-one years. As it was for us, your honeymoon will be a special time just for the two of you. After the hustle and bustle of all the planning, and after the delightful celebration of your wedding with friends and relatives, this will be your time to relish those fond memories, cherish each other, and anticipate your future together.

You are the two people who will create the atmosphere that will make your honeymoon a success. It might rain the entire week even though you choose the Kona Coast on the big island of Hawaii, where the rainfall is only six inches per year. One of you could be sick. Your luggage could get lost. One of you could forget your passports. You could discover you did not have a reservation at the motel you thought was confirmed for your first night. Most couples feel fatigued as their honeymoon begins; you may feel completely wiped out.

Disappointments need not interfere with this joyous time in your life. How you deal with the unexpected can add to, rather than distract from, your blissful getaway. Our oldest daughter, Julene, has the capacity to look at life's consequences so that the positives always seem to overpower the negatives. We have often said that her capacity for denial has served her well. During one of her college summers, she spent several months working for the Young Life Camp in France. Before the campers and staff arrived, she was asked to stay at the camp a few weeks and work with an older French-speaking maintenance man to get the facilities ready. She was clearly the Cinderella before the ball. Cleaning bathrooms, removing spider webs, and painting outdoor lawn furniture were some of her tasks. There was no one with whom she could speak English, and her French was limited. But she was in one of the most beautiful settings in the world—the French side of the Swiss Alps! So when she got up in the morning, she would look out over the Alps and enjoy the gorgeous scenery. Then, before she went to dinner, she would turn down the sheets of her camp cot and place a wildflower on her pillow. When she would come to bed at night, she would pretend she was at an exclusive hotel where the staff had prepared her bed for her.

You, too, may encounter some "spider webs" or messy "toilets" in your honeymoon, but you can look out and find the beautiful scenes in your life and create an exclusive hotel experience. We are convinced that *YOU* can make your honeymoon an experience that you remember fondly, even if there are disappointments and adjustments that must be made.

After twenty years of listening to stories of honeymoons that began with shattered dreams, painful disappointments, sexual pressure and conflict, and fearful avoidance, we have often asked ourselves, "Were we just lucky? Is happiness something that just happens to you, or do you make it happen?" Too often, we suspect, disappointments are the result of inadequate planning and communication because of the magic-wand myth: a widely held inner belief that happiness is the result of what happens to you rather than what you make happen. This myth implies if sex does not work out the way you wanted it to, or if your spouse does not respond to you the way you had imagined, or if the motel is not what you had visualized it to be, then you were not lucky. Those who end up unhappy tend to be those who believe the magic-wand myth. If they could just find someone to wave the magic wand and make life fulfill their fantasies, they would be happy.

What makes a honeymoon successful? Your fantasy might be never leaving your room because you are so exhausted from the sexual activity you are both enjoying. You may dream of being together nonstop. But if that is not your spouse's expectation, you may be sorely disappointed. You may be a couple who enjoys traveling together to new and exciting places. On the contrary, you may both look forward to a time of peace and quiet after all the busyness of the wedding. Only *YOU* can design the honeymoon that is right for the two of you! So use the information in this chapter only as it contributes to what will bring the greatest joy, fulfillment, and contentment to the two of you.

Honeymoon Choices

The honeymoon is a time of transition from singleness into marriage. It is a time to enjoy each other without outside demands. Usually this works best when you make choices that allow for privacy, unhurriedness, and freedom from scheduled expectations or interruptions.

The First Twenty-four Hours

Many couples err when they try to cram too much into their first twenty-four hours together. The reception may end later than they expected, then they may have a long distance to travel to their first-night hotel. They may have invested in an expensive honeymoon suite but get to it after midnight and have to rush out in the morning to catch a flight to their ultimate honeymoon destination. They may hardly remember that first night because they were exhausted when they arrived, their anticipatory anxiety was high, and they were pressured to pack up and leave in the morning. When this happens, the couple certainly does not get to enjoy what they paid for.

REMEMBER: THE HONEYMOON STARTS
WHEN YOU DRIVE AWAY FROM THE RECEPTION!

Careful planning of your time from the end of the reception and on can make a major difference for your entire honeymoon. It is easy to forget that the honeymoon starts when you drive away from the reception. So many couples think ahead to their honeymoon destination without planning the time between the reception and that final location.

Whether you spend your first night at a modest local motel or a three-room penthouse suite, you should anticipate your special needs and desired circumstances. This will often be more important for the woman since she will have borne the greater burden during the wedding planning and events. And women tend to be more affected than men by the circumstances of what is supposed to be a romantic time. Thus, the woman's needs should be given top priority. Nevertheless, both of you need to be aware of what will make the first night special for you.

There are several issues to consider in planning the first twenty-four hours of your honeymoon. The first is transportation. Do you want to drive yourselves or have someone else drive when you leave the reception? If someone else will drive, who do you want that to be? The second consideration is food. Often the bridal couple does very little eating at the reception. You might arrange with the person in charge of food for your reception to have a food basket packed for you to take along as you leave. It can be a fun connecting time to have a picnic in your room when you arrive.

The third consideration is timing. Allow more time than you think you need from the end of the reception until you leave for your honeymoon destination the next day.

The fourth is clothing and personal items. Consider what you want to wear when you leave the reception, what you will need to get ready for spending the night, and what you will need for the next morning. Have those items packed separately from the rest of your honeymoon luggage. That way you will not have to spend your time packing and repacking. If you don't want to take the first-night items with you on the rest of the honeymoon, arrange for a friend or family member to pick them up from the hotel desk after you leave.

Other plans might include any of your personal preferences. For example, if one of you dislikes certain color schemes, you might ask about the room decor at your honeymoon hotel.

Others have fears of heights or feeling closed in. Temperature may need to be anticipated; you might arrange to have
the heater or the air conditioner turned on in your room before
you arrive. Be aware of who each of you are and what would
add to the pleasantness of your first night together as a married couple.

Connecting Time

The purpose of the honeymoon is to provide connection between the two of you. The honeymoon conditions should help for
you do that. In what situations have you felt most connected?
What kind of setting has pulled you away from each other?

You may just love to spend time together. We sense that from
our son, Greg, and his fiancée, Carrie, who are now in the process of making honeymoon plans. Outside activities will not be
essential to their enjoyment. On the other hand, you may do
better with a balance of together time, alone time, and activity
time. Eating out together or taking walks together may be
good for you. Having a project may be a way the two of you can
connect. You may want to take along your gift list and write
thank-you notes together. You may enjoy reading material that
you either read out loud together or read separately and discuss.

If either of you needs a break from constant togetherness,
take responsibility for that. Let each other know when you've
reached your limit at connecting and you need time alone before
you will be ready for more intimacy. You may wish to read a
book, jog, walk, or climb a tree. It really doesn't matter as long
as you make it clear that you are not rejecting your spouse.

No Distractions

Issues or distractions that get in the way of your connection
may already be obvious. For others, you may not be sure of
what is likely to pull you apart.

Television is the usual culprit; it causes more trouble in
marriages than is imaginable. Most often the husband watches
and the wife feels neglected. Talk about the TV issue before the
honeymoon. We recommend that the television not even be
turned on unless the two of you decide together that you both
want to watch. Enjoy watching as a couple, then turn it off. No

show, sports event, or news program is worth tension and distance in your relationship. The TV can become a mistress, and most wives do not like sharing their husbands.

Also avoid interruptions from insensitive friends or relatives. You should not be expected to visit with or entertain others on your honeymoon. This is *your* time! Guard it carefully. If you should happen to run into someone you know, decide together how you might handle that. Usually a friendly chat or a stop for coffee is all that is expected. It would be wise to let it be known that you are on your honeymoon. It would probably benefit your privacy to be vague about where you are staying. If someone should drop by to visit you, you have every right to limit his or her stay. You can warmly thank the friend and then let him or her know that this is your time. If directness is difficult for you, tell the friend you have someplace to go and must leave right then. You don't have to say that you are just going for a walk by yourselves. Excuse yourselves and let the friend know you will look forward to seeing him or her sometime after your honeymoon.

Obviously, you as a couple may enjoy time with others. For example, some couples like to return to a family and guest brunch, lunch, or afternoon tea the next day before they leave. If that does not rush your first night, it can be a fun time to connect with those you love, open gifts, and then leave for your more extended honeymoon time. We were thrilled that our daughter and son-in-law, Julene and John, wanted to join our family to go out to dinner to celebrate our thirtieth wedding anniversary the evening after their wedding. Since their flight was not leaving until nine o'clock that evening, we had a delightful time of reviewing the wedding, the guests' reactions, our joy and excitement, and joining together as our newly expanded family. As an extra treat, Julene's close friend Jennifer had photos from the wedding developed and delivered to the restaurant before we arrived for dinner. This was a wonderful way for us to review this special event that was still so fresh in our lives.

Rest and Relaxation

It's vital to plan time during your honeymoon for adequate quiet relaxation and rest. This allows for restoration and a more enjoyable time together. It also helps you start your life together in your new home feeling rested.

Activities

Optional activities are a benefit to any honeymoon. These work best if they are flexible rather than scheduled so you can pick and choose what you would like to do and when. Avoid putting money toward an activity so that you feel committed to it. For example, if you buy a golf package, scuba-diving instruction, or a sunset cruise, you will feel obligated to do that activity even though it turns out not to be the best focus for you at that time.

However, if you are an activity-oriented couple, you may prefer to plan your favorite activities into your honeymoon. Hiking, mountain climbing, biking, camping can be physically draining for some people and not leave much energy to enjoy the new sexual relationship, but others find they need strenuous physical activity to keep their sexual vitality alive.

It is most important that you not plan an activity you love but your partner does not. An afternoon in the hot sun watching your favorite team lose another game may not be your spouse's idea of a great honeymoon. Even if this is your first chance to see a game in person, *forget it!* On the other hand, if you both are rabid fans and you met at a game, this might be an exciting way to spend a day. Work it out, but don't talk him or her into it. You will regret it! The honeymoon should be designed for both people's pleasure and enjoyment.

A man may really get into a sporting event, but totally lose his wife. Or the woman may plan a shopping spree and find herself with an irritable husband. You will have plenty of time during your married lives to engage in the activities of your choice; this is not the time for pursuing individuation.

Tour groups can be a distraction. If your time is controlled by a scheduled tour group for ten days, you will not be free to respond to your own timing needs and desires. You may decide to visit a museum or a scenic or historic site, and that will not take away from your focus on each other. But avoid committing yourselves to anything that is prescheduled. Your honeymoon is one of the few times you may have in life to do what you want to do when you want to do it.

No Surprises

The honeymoon is most likely to be enjoyed by both of you if there are no surprises. If you absolutely do not like to be taken by surprise, make certain your spouse-to-be truly understands how adamant you are about that before you plan the honeymoon. If he or she believes a particular surprise would be an exception and goes ahead against your warning, that can put you in a dilemma. It will be impossible to act like you are delighted when you may feel furious; in response, your partner may be crushed by your reaction.

On the other hand, if you love to be surprised, let your spouse-to-be know that. You may want to bring some little surprises for each other to enhance your romantic responsiveness.

If you don't feel strongly either way about being surprised, be cautious. Avoid major surprises. The risk is too great that you might not get the positive response you expect; your idea may not bring the joy you had hoped it would.

Likewise, avoid any major investment of time or money in something neither of you has ever tried. It would not be wise to plan a fishing trip on a lake in Northern Minnesota in August if you have never been to Minnesota in August and have never tried fishing. Nor would it be a good idea to plan your dream sailing trip if you had never sailed. You might get seasick and spend your entire honeymoon feeling nauseous. Similarly, if you are from the prairie and have always wanted a vacation in the mountains, this is not the time to find out if you're prone to altitude sickness. If you have not been out in the sun, be cautious about a tropical island setttings; sunburned bodies do not make for a delightful honeymoon.

Establishing Patterns

This is the beginning of your married life, and you will be establishing lifelong patterns of interaction and role responsibilities: Who checks in with the airlines? Who calls the cab? Who checks you in at the hotel? Who handles tipping? Who takes responsibility to correct situations that did not happen as you had planned them? Who showers first? Who initiates closeness? Who initiates bedtime? Do you keep the window open or closed? How dark do you have the room for sleeping? Which side of the bed do you sleep on? Who sets the alarm?

How close to each other do you sleep? Do you need bathroom privacy? How do you squeeze out and put the cap on the toothpaste? What do you do with used towels or dirty clothes? The list of issues to be addressed could go on forever. For some couples, these decisions seem to happen uneventfully. Others encounter many differences and have a greater need for deliberately developing patterns of responsibility to enhance their relationship and their individual well-being.

Not all patterns will be established on the honeymoon; you will have a lifetime of learning to live together with ease. You can design your honeymoon to be virtually free of any need to determine lifetime patterns, or you may have to address these issues. For example, staying at a cabin and doing your own cooking would be more similar to most couples' ongoing life while being on a cruise or in a hotel where all services are taken care of would be free of most normal life decisions or pattern-setting for most couples. Choose how you would like to use this honeymoon time to benefit you most.

Location

Setting. Privacy is a central criterion in planning your honeymoon. To feel free to express yourselves sexually, you will want to make certain you are not heard by and do not hear your neighbors. That is why bed and breakfast inns are not a wise choice—they are usually old, restored homes. The walls are not well insulated for sound, there is space under the door, and the wooden floors and beds usually creak with any movement.

Not only do you want sound protection, you also want privacy from socializing expectations with other people. This is another negative for bed and breakfasts as honeymoon sites. Communal mealtimes will take away from your ability to exclusively focus on your relationship and will obligate you to eat at certain pre-set times.

Cleanliness and decor can be important issues to some individuals. Some people have strong preferences for the stark newness of a modern setting as opposed to a country setting with antiques, handwoven rugs, a rock fireplace, and worn furniture. Some people's moods are affected by the lightness or darkness of their room. Earth tones may make your spirits dip; bright colors may activate your hyperness.

The cleanliness of a place would not even be noticed by some people and would ruin the honeymoon for others. If you are wondering what importance these external elements have to two people who love each other deeply and enjoy each other's presence, then you can skip these considerations. Just be certain your spouse feels the same way!

Weather. The weather can affect the setting, the activities, and you. If you don't like rain, do not honeymoon in Seattle in November. If humidity makes you sluggish and leaves you feeling that you do not want to be touched, don't honeymoon in Georgia in July. If you hate cold as much as Joyce does, do not go on a snowskiing vacation. If dry heat bothers you, do not go to the desert city of Palm Springs, California, in August when it is 125 degrees. Wind invigorates some and irritates others; avoid Chicago if you are the latter. No one likes mosquitoes, but if you are bothered more than a little (i.e., if you get huge welts from bites) you will want to make certain you do not choose a location that is swarming with mosquitoes or other insects.

To get information regarding the weather of the honeymoon locations you are considering, call the Chamber of Commerce for that city or contact a major hotel in the area. Ask them to describe the weather at various times of the year, including the time you hope to be there. So that they do not bias their weather report for your selected dates, do not tell them which time of the year you are interested in being there; ask for a seasonal overview.

Geography. There is nothing that makes a beach honeymoon better than a mountain honeymoon or a lake honeymoon. You might prefer to honeymoon in the desert or on a lake, at a coast or beach, in the mountains, on the plains, in a city, or on an island. The type of scenery and location is a personal choice.

Travel. How you prefer to travel may affect the location you choose. If you are afraid of flying, that will limit your choices to travel by ground or sea. Some people's ears are severely affected by the change in air pressure when they fly. If that is true for you, you may need to get medication to reduce or eliminate that complication, which often makes people irritable after a flight.

You may have a personal preference or idiosyncrasy that will affect your choice of travel. Some couples love a leisurely driving trip. That would not have worked for us. While vacationing in northern Minnesota for our August honeymoon, Cliff wanted to take Joyce to see the Northshore Drive of Lake Superior, which reminded him of the beautiful evergreens of his British Columbia home. After driving fifteen miles, Cliff noticed that Joyce was asleep. He stopped so we could look at a beautiful scene (and to wake up Joyce), then we drove on. Before long, Joyce was asleep again. After a third stop, Cliff decided to turn back and go to our cabin. We discovered on that trip that Joyce falls asleep almost as soon as a car starts moving. A ten-day driving trip would have been very restful for Joyce and very lonely for Cliff.

Train travel can be fun, free of responsibility, and very relaxing. The bed and privacy situation would not be a great setting in which to spend most of your nights, however. And you might feel too much a part of a "community" because many train travelers enjoy getting acquainted with fellow passengers. But it's also possible to remain anonymous.

Travel by water is high risk unless you are experienced sea travelers. Sea sickness definitely deadens a sexual relationship. Cruises can be fun, but also may feel too confining within a communal-type situation. Usually you are assigned to a particular table for meals, where you see the same people each time. Thus, cruises carry many of the negatives of a bed and breakfast inn.

How you travel is a matter of personal preference, or your destination may dictate your choice of travel.

Responsibilities

Traditionally, the man plans and pays for the honeymoon, but that is not a rule. We believe you will be happiest with your honeymoon if you plan it together. The financial responsibility can be shared or assumed by anyone. It is important that the money spent on the honeymoon is realistic. A glamorous honeymoon that eats up all your financial resources will leave you in a rough situation when you return home, and there's unlikely to be much sympathy from your parents. If you will be sharing income and expenses after the honeymoon, you should decide together how much you can spend without affecting your living arrangements afterward.

What if the man is just not a planner and arranger? Work together. Divide the responsibilities. Together decide which ones each of you does better. Whoever does telephone negotiations better should call to make various reservations. The other one of you may have better organizational skills. This is a great time to learn more about what each of you does well. It is better for the one who is a natural at some task to assume that responsibility. Just make sure the responsibilities basically even out.

Troubleshooting

Ideally, your thorough preparation will prevent any need for troubleshooting. But be prepared, just in case you have difficulties. Take the telephone numbers of your medical doctor, your premarital counselor, and any other resources you might need. If you should experience any of the sexual difficulties we address in chapter 12, you may want to give us a quick call (818-449-2525). Sometimes five minutes of correct guidance can make all the difference in the world. If you need to pursue more involved counseling, we can refer you to some professional in your area, or we can arrange for ongoing paid appointments by telephone.

For sure, take *Getting Your Sex Life Off to a Great Start!*

8

•••••••

Preparing for Your First Time

By reading and sharing the exercises in this book, you have already begun the process of opening your sexual inner worlds to each other, and you have probably prepared yourselves for your sexual relationship in marriage more thoroughly than most couples have. Whether or not this is your first sexual intercourse experience, there are specific steps you can take to make that first time after your wedding an event that is associated with lasting positive memories. In this chapter we'll discuss those important preparations.

Prepare Your Minds

Your most influential and positive sex organ is your mind; it controls your body, how you think about sex, how you feel about sex, and how your body responds to sex.

In reading and completing the exercises in chapter 2, you

spent considerable time getting to know your sexual self. You discovered your view of yourself and how that view developed throughout your growing-up years. In chapter 3 you shared with each other what you had learned about yourselves. Chapter 4 helped you accurately look at and share your sexual expectations for your married life. The next two chapters provided biblical and bodily background information. You have even designed the honeymoon to give you a positive start to your marriage. Now it is time to define the attitudes you have formulated out of all of the preparation you have done thus far. What is your mind-set toward sex in marriage? In the following pages we'll discuss the attitudes mentioned in chapter 2 as the five basic attitudes we hoped you had already acquired before adolescence (see page 40). If these attitudes are not representative of your mind-set about sex and marriage, we hope you will attempt to integrate these into your way of thinking.

Sex Is Good and of God

Sex was God's idea. God created us male and female in His image. And when God completed His work of creation, He looked at His work and was pleased. It was good! So our sexuality, our differences and uniquenesses as men and women, are part of God's perfect, sinless design for us. Then God instructed men and women how they were to live with one another. He told the man to leave his mother and father and become one with his wife. This was the instruction to consummate their physical relationship—to become one physically, emotionally, and spiritually. This sexual union was part of God's perfect design for mankind, not the result of sin.

If you have difficulty accepting that the sexual relationship in marriage should be pursued with passion and without inhibition, you may need to read and discuss chapter 5 again and again. If that does not help you connect your sexuality with your spirituality, you may need to get permission to enjoy God's blessing of your sexual relationship from someone you would consider your spiritual mentor. You may also find it helpful to study for yourself the Bible's teaching about sexuality. That is what we did for our devotional times together during the first year of our marriage. That study became the basis for what we believe and teach today.

Sexual Curiosity Is Natural

As human beings grow from infancy to adulthood, it becomes evident that God's design of our sexuality includes a natural pursuit of sexual discovery. That begins with genital touching in infancy and toddlerhood, continues with question-asking and exploratory play during the preschool and school-age years, and remains a vital part of sexual development through-out preadolescence, adolescence, and into adulthood.

Your interest in knowing each other sexually is completely natural. There is no need to feel guilt or shame or embarrass-ment while exploring one another as a married couple. Scripture confirms this: "And the man and his wife were both naked and were not ashamed" (Gen. 2:25). That freedom to become com-fortable and familiar with each other will grow gradually for some. Others will be unashamed of their curiosity about each other right from the start. Be sensitive to your individual needs in that regard and be sensitive to each other's needs for privacy, as well as for familiarity. As Paul Popenoe wrote in *Preparing for Marriage:*

> The change from the restrictions of the engagement period to the freedom of marriage is, in many cases, made too rap-idly. There is a gap which must be bridged over carefully, by a steady process of mutual education and adjustment during the engagement, and by continuing this uninter-ruptedly after the wedding. The inherent tendency of all male animals to delight in exhibiting themselves must be repressed, particularly on the wedding night and during the early part of the honeymoon, if a modest and sensitive bride is not to be distressed. [1]

Popenoe's book was originally written in 1938 and was the marriage manual we used in preparation for our marriage. In preparing to write this book, we went back to look at both cur-rent and original manuals, and this book continues to amaze us with its relevancy.

Many of the unconsummated marriages we see in sexual therapy started with the bride tensing up on her wedding night when her husband surprised her with his nude body and a full erection.

It would be best to assume your curiosity about each other on the wedding night will begin with the degree of openness you have experienced with each other before marriage. Gradually continue learning to know more about each other as you grow in trust and familiarity after marriage. Eventually, it will be helpful to your sexual relationship to become specifically familiar with each other's genitals.

When you are both ready for that degree of openness, use the self-discovery genital diagrams from chapter 6 to share your genitals with each other. This is a time of "show and tell." Show your spouse the various parts of your genitals as identified on the diagrams. Then teach each other about the genital touching that is most pleasurable to you. Continue to learn about your bodies as you mature in your sexual life as a married couple.

Sexual Responsiveness Is Inborn

Your bodies confirm the perfect design of God's creative power. Your responsiveness demonstrates the beauty of how your bodies have been set in motion sexually.

Sexual responsiveness is an involuntary response. It is not an action you can *will* or make happen by a mental decision. But it is a response you can *allow* to happen by a positive, sexually aggressive attitude.

You can encourage this response in your marriage by honoring the fact that both of you were born as sexually responsive people and that sexual responsiveness is to be fulfilled in marriage. Both of you have the privilege of enjoying one another's body to go after that fulfillment. That will work only if sexual enjoyment is pursued for both of you. It must be kept mutual.

The potential for sexual responsiveness is equal for men and women. Physiologically, men are no more or no less sexual than women. Men and women have been designed with equal capacity for sexual pleasure and release. Because of how our bodies work and because of the teaching of 1 Corinthians 7:1–3, we believe men and women have equal sexual rights.

In our society a prevailing attitude about men and women contradicts this concept of equality and causes a lot of destruction in marriage. It assumes that men are more sexual than women and men have a need and a right for sexual release whether or not the woman does; thus, according to this attitude, the role of the wife is to sexually please her husband. Sexual pleasure in this view is not something the woman seeks out, but rather is something she provides for her husband. It is her job to increase his feelings of masculinity and control and to let him use her body for his pleasure, but not to expect that for herself. This sense of *duty* for a woman to have sex to keep her husband satisfied and at home doesn't work. The wife who is involved sexually *only* to please her husband without going after sexual enjoyment for herself eventually ends up with a husband who is not pleased. As sex becomes a task rather than a pleasure, she becomes less and less responsive, and sexual encounters become an event she dreads. The husband senses her absence of vitality and becomes anxious about her lack of involvement but often doesn't understand what went wrong. Tension and distance build.

This is not an inevitable scenario, however. Pursue your natural responsiveness with vigor but never at the expense of one another.

Sexual Responsibility Belongs to Each Person

Sexual responsiveness has to do with sexual feelings and desires. In contrast, sexual responsibility has to do with the choices you make about those feelings. It is natural to have sexual feelings toward people of the opposite sex at various times throughout life. It is your responsibility not to pursue those feelings or actions with anyone other than your spouse. Sex is not something that happens to you. You can choose to not act on your sexual feelings toward anyone other that your spouse, and you can choose to be sexual with your spouse even when you are not particularly aware of those desires. You can also choose not to pursue sex with your spouse when he or she would perceive that as a demand or violation.

Sexual responsibility is not only important to practice in pursuing your sexual feelings with the correct partner and in being respectful of that partner; it is also vital to practice in your actual sexual experiences.

A popular mentality about men contradicts this attitude of individual responsibility within a sexual relationship. This mentality assumes that men are more qualified sexual partners than are women. Thus, the man is expected to come to marriage with the ability to tactfully and skillfully lead his innocent bride through the most delightful sexual time of her life. According to this mentality, it is his responsibility to turn her on. If he really loves her, according to this theory, he will automatically sense what she likes and doesn't like. Having this innate ability, he will sensitively woo her to a state of ecstatic arousal and release. Meanwhile, she is the passive receptor of his natural male skills. As one woman expressed it. "He's got to do something to turn me on."

When either the husband or the wife puts this demand on the man, it gets in the way of open communication and mutual enjoyment. Neither of them ends up happy! Even Dr. Popenoe recognized this reality when he wrote in *Preparing for Marriage,* "It is indispensable to the husband's happiness that his wife be a real partner, not a silent and passive instrument."[2] There is no way a man can come to marriage as a skilled lover unless he has had effective previous sexual experience. To demand that the husband is responsible for the wife's pleasure will only cause anxiety and frustration. You both need to learn to listen to the desires of your bodies, take responsibility to communicate those desires to each other, and go after them—letting each other know what you would enjoy but never demanding or violating the other.

Assuming responsibility for your sexuality outside of marriage will help prevent unintended sexual encounters from happening. Assuming responsibility for your sexuality within marriage will reduce demand, allow greater freedom, and help protect your marriage from sex with someone other than your spouse.

Mutual Respect and Biblical Standards Are the Guides for All Sexual Relationships

The biblical expectation is one of mutual respect and enjoyment of sex in marriage. The New Testament consistently teaches mutuality within the sexual relationship. The barriers between men and women have been broken down because of Christ (Gal. 3:28) and the husband and wife are free to enjoy each other's bodies with mutual abandonment (1 Cor. 7:1–3).

If you begin your sexual relationship in marriage by believing and practicing these five principles of biblical teaching on
sexuality your chances for enjoying many years of a free, pleasurable sexual relationship together are very promising.

Prepare Your Bodies

You are going to share your bodies most intimately. To feel
most relaxed and open with each other, it is important that your
bodies are ready for this experience. If it will be the first time
for either or both of you to have sexual intercourse, if it will be
the first time for you to have sexual intercourse with each
other, or if it will be the first time in a long time, the following
preparations will make this a special event.

The Woman's Preparations

Get a recommendation for a gynecologist, medical practitioner, or nurse practitioner who is known to be thorough yet
sensitive in examining and guiding women in preparing for
marriage. Ask the examining clinician to inform you very specifically of the condition of your genitals and your readiness for
sexual intercourse. You may ask about the condition of both
your hymen and your vaginal muscle. If either seems tight, you
may need to ask for graduated vaginal dilators. Never agree to
surgery for relieving tightness unless that treatment is vali-
dated by at least two other clinicians.

Be prepared to discuss contraceptive measures. Write out
your thoughts and questions after reading chapter 9. If you plan
to use a hormonal contraceptive, get started on the hormone
of your choice at least two months before your wedding so your
body has time to adjust. If you have complications or serious
side effects, that will give you time to stop and start a hormone
that interacts differently with your body. When you have the
required blood tests for getting your marriage license, ask to
be tested for AIDS, herpes simplex II, genital warts, and any
other tests for sexually transmitted diseases your clinician
would recommend. It would also be good to make sure you
don't have a yeast infection. If the physician is willing, we would
recommend getting a prescription for an antibiotic (such as

Azo-Gantanol) to treat "honeymoon cystitis," should you get it. Honeymoon cystitis is an infection of the bladder that is common because of the sudden frequent sexual activity. Germs can easily travel into the urinary tract and cause a bladder infection that can be very painful. That pain is usually relieved relatively quickly after appropriate antibiotics are taken.

In the months before your wedding night, get into the habit of tightening and relaxing your PC muscle as described in chapter 6, "Discovering and Enjoying Your Bodies." Stretch the opening of your vagina every time you bathe or shower. Relaxing in warm water will help you relax your vaginal muscle so you can insert the dilator or your clean fingers. Begin with inserting one finger or a dilator the size of a tampon applicator. If you have difficulty inserting something that size, you can try a cotton-tipped applicator with a lubricant on it. Gradually increase the size of the object you insert to stretch the opening of your vagina until you are able to insert three fingers and stretch them apart or insert the largest dilator. The circumference of an average erect penis is about four and a half to five and a half inches. When you insert the dilator, leave it in the vagina for about twenty minutes per day. The more faithful you are in preparing your vagina for entry, the more comfortable that initial experience will be. Since your vaginal muscle has either never been used for sexual intercourse before or it has been a long time since it has been used, you must think of preparing it for this special event as an athlete would prepare for an athletic event.

Groom your body especially carefully as the time for the wedding gets close. Different cultures and ethnic groups have standards of what is expected bodily preparation. In many Western cultures, the woman is expected to have smooth legs and underarms that have been freshly shaved, epilated, or waxed. If you have concern about other body hair, like above the lip, on the abdomen, or along the bikini line, those may be permanently removed by electrolysis. That must be done long before the wedding date since it is an expensive, tedious process that requires healing afterward. The other hair-removal methods can work just fine if you cannot invest money or time in electrolysis. The primary goal is for both you and your husband to feel good about your body.

The Man's Preparation

Just as the woman should make certain her body is healthy, free from infection, and ready for sexual intercourse, so should the man. It is wise to have a complete physical examination by a medical doctor. If you have any concerns related to your genitals, these can be dealt with at the time of your examination. The privacy of the physician's office is the place to address any questions. If your concerns or questions are minimized by the physician, that is a sign of the physician's inadequacy, not that you asked an inappropriate question. Find another doctor. When you get your blood tested for your marriage license requirements, get tested for AIDS, genital warts, herpes simplex II, and any other sexually transmitted diseases that might be of concern. Testing for sexually transmitted diseases is a gift of trust you give each other. That is true whether or not you have been sexually active previously.

Whatever your practice of masturbation or your past sexual experience has been, you would do yourself and your new wife a big favor if you practiced, through self-stimulation, learning to extend ejaculation.

You can learn ejaculatory control by focusing on and savoring the pleasurable sensations, becoming aware of the warning signs that you are nearing ejaculation, stopping and starting stimulation, and/or squeezing the coronal ridge of the penis. Stimulation must be stopped or the squeeze applied long before you notice you are approaching the point of no return when you are about to ejaculate. Another important ingredient to learning to delay ejaculation is to rest or allow the intensity of the arousal to dissipate while you stop stimulation or apply the squeeze. Then resume stimulation. For more information refer to chapter 16 in our book *Restoring the Pleasure* or Helen Singer Kaplan's book *P.E.: Learning to Overcome Premature Ejaculation.*

Stimulating yourself to ejaculation within twenty-four hours before your wedding night will also be of great benefit to both you and your bride because you will likely be more excited and fatigued than usual and more apt to ejaculate quickly. This can be disappointing to both of you. A recent ejaculation will increase the time of pleasure and enjoyment for this first, memorable, married sexual experience.

Preparations to Do Together

Take time to talk about and decide which contraceptive method the two of you would like to use. The next chapter provides information to help you with this decision. Decide which method has the most likelihood of success and is the most desirable for both of you. Once you have made your decision, obtain all of the necessary supplies you will need to effectively practice this method. Then familiarize yourselves with the process you have chosen.

If you will be using condoms, the man should practice applying the spermicide and the condom. If the diaphragm, cervical cap, sponge, or vaginal condom is your choice, the woman should practice inserting the device until it can be done with ease. If you are following a "natural" family-planning program, you both should be aware of where the woman will be in her cycle at the time of your wedding and honeymoon. Since the excitement surrounding the wedding can disrupt a woman's usual cycle, it might be wise to use an additional contraceptive for your wedding night and honeymoon. Or you might purchase and use an ovulation test kit. That would be an additional expense, but a worthwhile one.

Whatever your method of contraception, it is important that you are comfortable with it and can safely and efficiently use it so you avoid frustration—and pregnancy.

Once you have settled on your method of contraception, choose and purchase a lubricant. Since a woman lubricates vaginally early in a sexual experience, a time of long extended love play will require a lubricant. Whether or not you think you will need a lubricant, we recommend that all newly married couples automatically use one and that all couples have a lubricant available. Using a lubricant is not a sign of failure. Rather, to use a lubricant reduces demand and enhances pleasure because you do not have to pay attention to whether or when lubrication is occurring.

If you have chosen to use a rubber (latex) barrier contraceptive method, you should not use a lubricant that is oil- or petroleum-based. Oil and petroleum decrease the effectiveness of rubber (latex). Thus, you should not use Vaseline or other petroleum jellies, natural oils, mineral oil, butter, grease-based sexual lubricants, or some vaginal creams. These are unsafe to use with condoms, diaphragms, or cervical caps. You can use aloe, water, saliva, glycerin, and contraceptive foams, creams, and gels; commercial sexual lubricants include Probe, Astroglide, PrePair, Lubrin, Transi-Lube, Aqua-Lube, Condom-Mate, Duragel, and others; and water-based lubricants such as K-Y Jelly or Lubrafax. The water-based lubricants dry more quickly than others in the list, so they are not quite as desirable.

The more carefully you have prepared your bodies for one another and the better prepared you are, the more positive your first sexual experience together will be. So take time to prepare carefully, and deliberately try to anticipate your every need and desire.

Prepare Your Spirits and Souls

You will not just be joining your bodies; you will be joining all of who you are. Throughout the busy times of planning for and enjoying the events connected with your wedding, you will need to carve out time for yourselves, individually and together. This time is vital to your own personal inner self, your relationship with God, and your relationship with each other. Make certain you take time to keep your spirits and souls nurtured. If you come to the wedding and honeymoon totally depleted, you will have nothing to give and may even have difficulty receiving.

A great engagement or shower gift to request would be a calendar that has a meditation or Bible verse for each day between now and the wedding. Or a book of short daily inspirations or devotions would be great. Even if you take just fifteen minutes each day to read, reflect, and pray you will give yourself a great gift to prepare your inner spirits for each other. To keep your spirits connected, you might share a similar daily or weekly time together. Also, frequent walks and talks can help relieve stress and keep you connected.

Make a detailed time plan for the week of the wedding. Be realistic about allotting enough time for the required tasks; even when you think you've designated enough time, allow more. Plan to do very few tasks yourself. Be bold; ask friends and family members to help. Make task lists. Block out time each day for a nap. It will be important to spend time with family and friends who are visiting from out of town, so try to arrange relaxed settings where these guests can gather and enjoy time with you, but keep these times limited.

The day of the wedding is most critical. Plan your day so that you can sleep in as long as your body will allow you (unless you have a morning wedding). The rest of the day should include as much rest and pampering as time allows. You may want to get ready for the ceremony with the help of your wedding attendants or just your family or by yourself. If you are a person who is energized by being with people, you probably will want others around. If you get fatigued and need to restore your energy by being alone for a while, plan some rejuvenation time into the day's schedule.

Questions and Answers

Preparing for your first married sex is a topic that has elicited numerous questions from the premarital couples we have taught. We will attempt to answer the most commonly asked questions on this topic.

Are you at risk for contracting an STD if you have never had sexual intercourse?

If neither you nor your spouse have had genital-to-genital, oral-to-genital, or genital-to-anal contact, you are not at risk of contracting most STDs. Sometimes an individual who has not been sexually active can carry the virus that causes genital warts. It may remain dormant for years and become activated during sexual intercourse. Authorities are not certain how the person's body acquired the virus in the first place. It might have been through sharing used swimming suits or public swimming pools. The oral herpes simplex I virus may have been transferred to the genitals through oral-genital stimulation. We recommend that you both be tested for STDs whether or not you have engaged in behaviors that transmit them. It will take care of any doubts and build trust that the two of you are starting clean with each other.

If I was tested for AIDS six months after my last sexual contact, do I need to be tested again?

Yes, you do. The virus causing AIDS may not show up on a blood test until after six months, so you need to keep getting tested every six months until the wedding. Usually you will be considered safe after a year, but new information is continually being made available on the reliability of AIDS testing, so call an AIDS testing service for the current information.

Because we are considered "new" through Christ, can we let go of past experiences and look at our wedding night as a first experience?

Yes and no. In God's eyes—and spiritually inside your-selves—you can reclaim your virginity, and your wedding night will be your first sexual experience. Emotionally and physically, however, you must deal realistically with your past experiences and how they will impact your wedding night.

How do I deal with the memories of past sexual partners, positive and negative? How can I rid myself of the guilt connected with these past experiences? What can I (or we) do now to minimize the negative effects my past may have on our marriage?

This is a difficult, yet common, struggle for many couples entering marriage today. We believe Scripture's teaching that sex is for marriage was designed to prevent this very dilemma. The conditions of married sex are different than sex outside of a committed relationship. That sex is often associated with risk, guilt, winning, keeping, conquering, rebelling and/or deceiving. If your previous sex was connected with any of these condi-tions, you will need to "undo" that past so it won't negatively affect your sex life in your marriage. Memories of past sexual partners easily move into the marriage bed with you. They may show up in your marriage as comparisons, self-doubt, distrust, dissatisfaction, or fear.

First, you need to deal with your guilt. God's grace is ad-equate to forgive and erase any past sins. Confession is often as much for one's peace of mind as it is for one's relationship with God. You may want to take some time to pray with someone about your past. It may be helpful to write out all the incidents that haunt your memory and need to be cleansed. Then ask

God to erase them for you. Keep bringing them to Him until you are freed of their presence in your life.

Second, how you deal with your fiancé is important. It is important to tell him or her that your past still affects you and that you want to be free of it and get it out of the way of your current relationship. Do not share details of that past; otherwise the memories will also haunt your fiancé. Share how it affects you, what you have done about it, and how you would like to work together to minimize or eliminate its effects on your marriage.

Listen to, reflect, and care about your fiancé's feelings about your past. It will be easy for you to get defensive if his or her reaction is one of hurt, anger, or distrust. The more you understand that your fiancé's reactions are most natural, the sooner they will decrease.

Third, together make a plan for dealing with this past within your marriage. Start as if your married sexual relationship is the first experience for both of you. Learn about each other as unique sexual beings totally different from those past partners. Do not start sexually at the place you left off. Start as a new learner. Let your spouse teach you about himself or herself. When that past sneaks in, have a plan to signal each other and distract from those thoughts, feelings, or comparisons and focus more diligently on each other. Continually affirm your love and commitment to each other by your words and your actions. You will need to be more deliberate about this than someone without past sexual partners.

We have decided to wait for marriage to consummate our sexual relationship. That used to be a struggle for us, but it no longer is. Could we have shut off our feelings for each other?

It certainly sounds like that may be what happened. When we teach premarital classes, we always caution that if a premarital couple has decided not to be sexually active before marriage and that is not a struggle for them, they better get some help. God has designed us to desire sexual intimacy with the person we love and commit ourselves to. That is our responsiveness. We are given the responsibility to manage that drive so we do not violate ourselves, our partner, or our relationship with God. Therefore, sexual activity should be controlled by the decisions we make and the conditions we put ourselves into, not by turning off our desire for that intimacy.

Since the two of you seem to have already turned off your "pilot lights," it is time to relight those desires. Saying, "I do," will not turn the switch back on. Between now and your wedding, reengage in times of passionate kissing that go no further than that. If you sense an urge for more, affirm those good feelings by telling each other about them, but stick to just kissing. As desire builds, allow yourselves more bodily contact, but always after deciding upon very clear behavioral boundaries. Don't allow your actions to go further than what you have decided upon, but allow your desire for more to build. Don't ever stop those natural urges, but control the level of your sexual involvement by the settings you allow yourselves to be in and the physical behaviors you allow yourselves to engage in.

While we are going to wait until we get married before having sex, what sexual activities are permissible until that time?

We use the Bible as our standard, and it offers no direct answer as to what sexual activity other than intercourse is not permissible outside of marriage. Therefore, we apply to this specific question the Bible's consistent message that sex is for marriage. And marriage throughout Scripture is clearly identified as a monogamous, heterosexual relationship characterized by fidelity. Therefore, we look at how the activity a couple engages in *before* marriage is likely to affect their sexual life *after* marriage.

What we find most positively affects sex in marriage is keeping sexual feelings and desires alive before marriage while engaging only in sexual activities that do not violate either of you, your relationship with each other, or your relationship with God. Thus, you should not practice any sexual behavior that is associated with risk or guilt. You should not be doing sex to keep your husband-to-be; nor should sex be used to conquer your wife-to-be. Sex should not be connected with rebellion, drugs, or alcohol, or any other conditions that will tarnish sex after marriage. Remember that 1 Thessalonians 4 teaches that one who abstains from sexual immorality knows "how to possess his own vessel" and does not "transgress and defraud" another person sexually.

Choose together what your sexual boundaries will be, how you will keep to those decisions, and what action you will take if your boundaries are violated. Before marriage, keep sexual desires and feelings alive while making conscious, active choices about your behavior. This will best prepare you for a life of marital sexual fulfillment.

9
•••••••

Choosing and Using Family-Planning Options

P reparation for your wedding night—and for your life as husband and wife—must include consideration of whether you want to use contraceptives and if so, what method is best for both of you. Many couples assume the responsibility to plan the number of children they hope to have and when they hope to have them. Family planning is the process of setting up a program for your reproductive life. It is thinking, praying, and talking with each other about this decision. Whenever a couple decides not to allow the wife to get pregnant any time that would happen naturally, they have chosen to control conception.

It is estimated that if couples decided to let nature take its course for their reproductive life spans, most women would produce between ten and thirty babies! That would not only create an incredible personal and financial burden but also a world-overpopulation problem of monumental dimensions! The command God gave to be fruitful, multiply, and fill the earth has already been completed. The current concern is how we are going to responsibly care for the children already in the world. This has led couples to approach reproduction by choice, rather than by chance. When that choice fails, either because of the inability to reproduce òr because of an unwanted pregnancy, both the individuals involved and the family unit are strongly impacted.

Moral and Religious Issues

Over the years, the church has struggled with the issue of contraception. The concern has been that taking reproduction into our own hands is interfering with God's plan for our lives. In other words, we are in some way interrupting the work of the master Creator.

Some religious leaders recommend responsible choices but insist that no "unnatural" methods of controlling conception be used. In 1984, Pope John Paul II took a bold stand on birth control, proclaiming that the practice and attitude of contraception are "harmful to man's interior spiritual culture."[1] The earlier challenge from Pope Paul VI to the members of the Roman Catholic Church had been to be available for motherhood and fatherhood. The Roman Catholic Church has held that abstinence during the woman's fertile time is the only acceptable means of preventing conception. The belief is that sexual union and procreation are inseparable in the plan of God. These pronouncements are based on "natural law" rather than direct biblical teaching. Natural law promotes the concept of a moral order or reasonable principle of humanity that fits with creation as determine by the Roman Catholic Church.

Others would put no restrictions on contraception; instead, they see it as a personal choice. The belief is that God created us as intelligent human beings and gave us dominion over the earth. His primary message is how He wants to relate to us as His people—how we can come to Him, be forgiven by Him, and become members of His family. He gave us free choice and expects us to use that freedom wisely.

Each of you must come to grips with the religious and moral issues of contraception, then the two of you must work through those issues together. It is best if the family-planning decisions are settled before marriage. Ask yourselves, "How does our reproductive plan fit with our religious beliefs? Would we like to have children? How old would we like to be when we have children? How would we feel if we couldn't have children? How would we feel if we got pregnant without planning for it?"

Each of you comes to the marriage with attitudes regarding childbearing that will affect your feelings about using contraception. These attitudes need to be cleared with each other.

We know women who married older men and then discovered their older husbands were adamantly opposed to having children. Those couples are now divorced. The opposite can also happen: One spouse may be totally against using contraception and the other not ready to allow babies to arrive at random. Agreement concerning your attitudes and feelings about contraception is vital to family planning—and to your marriage.

The History of Family Planning

Contraception prevents the man's sperm from uniting with the egg cell from the woman. Note that contraception is used to prevent pregnancy, not to interrupt it once conception has taken place. That is an important moral and religious distinction. We are not talking about taking life; we are talking about preventing a new life from beginning.

There is no perfect method of contraception. What works well for one couple may not be suitable for another. All methods currently practiced have both advantages and disadvantages. The method you choose will be as effective as you are in using it.

The rhythm method, attempting to avoid intercourse during the woman's fertile time, and the withdrawal method used by Onan in the Old Testament have always been with us. Contraceptives have existed since the 1500s, when crude forms of condoms were first used. Rubber condoms and diaphragms came into use in the 1840s. These barrier methods designed to keep the sperm and the egg apart were the only methods of birth control until the 1930s. About that time, Dr. Ernst Grafenburg, the discoverer of the G-spot in the woman's vagina, developed the first Intrauterine Device (IUD) from silkworm gut. Ironically, oral contraceptives (the pill), which came onto the scene in the late 1950s, actually resulted from the search for a method to *increase* fertility.

Today a variety of reliable methods are available. Choosing a proper contraceptive method is a serious matter. It is not the woman's decision. It is a decision to be made by both spouses with thought and care.

Making the Choice

In choosing a contraceptive, four issues need to be considered:

- Safety
- Effectiveness
- Convenience
- Personal preference

In the following discussions of the various contraceptive methods, we will provide information on the safety, effectiveness, and convenience of each method. The fourth consideration, personal preference, will be yours to determine. That preference may be based on the other three, or it may be connected with choices that have nothing to do with the facts. It may be based on something you've heard or some past experience. Remember, if you are not going to faithfully use the method you choose it will not be effective, even if it is, by general definition, safe, effective, and convenient. Your personal preference may depend on how a method will interfere with your sexual relations. That is why this issue needs to be discussed by the two of you.

Abstinence

Refraining totally from sexual intercourse as a method of contraception is 100 percent effective. Even though it may seem convenient, it certainly isn't much fun; nor is it free of risk. The risk is divorce! We believe abstinence is the method of choice before marriage but is clearly against biblical teaching after marriage. First Corinthians 7:3–5 says we are not to withhold ourselves from one another except by agreement for a season of prayer, and then we're to come together again quickly lest we be tempted. Nowhere does the Bible state that we should abstain from sex to prevent pregnancy.

Withdrawal

Having intercourse (entry of the penis into the vagina) but removing the penis from the vagina before the man ejaculates (releases seminal fluid containing sperm) is frequently practiced as an attempt to prevent conception. It is NOT a method of contraception, however, and it has many disadvantages. First, it can be emotionally and physically upsetting. Two people have united themselves intensely; then (and at the height of openness and vulnerability) they pull apart.

Second, many men do not have complete control over when they ejaculate, so accidents are almost inevitable. A man has five to ten seconds' warning before he is about to ejaculate. Once he has felt those warning signs he cannot stop the ejaculation. He may not get out in those five to ten seconds, or he may not get far enough away from the vagina. Also, the higher the degree of arousal, the less self-control he has. So even if he started with the best intentions of withdrawing at the peak of arousal, he may not do so.

Third, and of utmost importance, seminal fluid containing sperm is released *before* ejaculation. Thus, withdrawal is not effective or convenient.

Douching

Using some means to flush the seminal fluid containing sperm out of the vagina has been attempted for ages, but this practice is neither effective nor safe. Those tenacious little sperm are fast and determined; they get into the uterus and go looking for the egg in the fallopian tube long before the woman can get to her douche bag and douching solution! In addition to being ineffective, douching is not recommended because it upsets the natural environment of the vagina and makes a woman more susceptible to infection.

One of the most dangerous douching methods is practiced by teenagers who douche with cola soft drinks. Yes, the colas are spermicidal, so they kill any sperm that haven't already found their way into the uterus. However, the bubbles of the pressurized carbonated soda may be forced into the uterus where they can be absorbed into the bloodstream as an embolus and cause sudden death!

Douching is NOT a method of contraception even though it is thought to be.

Barrier Methods

Barrier methods of contraception prevent the sperm from meeting the egg. Modern barrier contraceptives include condoms, the sponge, diaphragms, cervical caps, female condoms, and spermicides.

Condoms. A condom is commonly referred to as a rubber, prophylactic, safety, or sheath. It is actually a rubber (latex) or animal-membrane device shaped like the finger of a glove that is placed over the erect penis before entry into the vagina.

Besides their use as contraceptives, latex condoms provide a barrier to reduce the risk of contracting sexually transmitted diseases (STDs). As a result of the AIDS epidemic, condom use in the United States has increased significantly during recent years. However, there is increasing concern about how effective condoms are in protecting against AIDS. The spermicide nonoxynol-9 is recommended for use on and inside the condom to kill both the sperm and any disease-producing viruses. Animal-membrane condoms, often referred to as "skins," do *not* effectively reduce transmission of STDs. Since some people are highly allergic to the latex type of rubber, a nonlatex, nonallergenic rubber condom is expected to be available on the market soon.

Other reasons for condoms' popularity are their inexpensiveness, their advantage of being easy to purchase without a physician's prescription, and the fact that they require the man's involvement and prevent a woman's allergic reaction to the man's sperm. Except for the occasional allergic reaction to latex, there are no side effects from the use of condoms, so they are safe.

Condoms' effectiveness depends on how they are used. The statistics for effectiveness vary from a 3 percent failure rate with perfect use to a 12 percent failure rate with typical use. This means that 3 out of 100 couples using condoms perfectly for one year got pregnant. If these couples were having intercourse an average of two times per week, that would mean three pregnancies result from 10,400 condoms used.[2]

To use condoms successfully, you must be certain the condom is new and free of holes or tears. The condom should be applied before the penis has any contact with the woman's genitals. It is important that the condom be rolled over the erect penis all the way to the base, leaving one-half-inch slack at the tip of the penis to catch the semen. The woman's vagina needs to be lubricated before entry with a condom because a dry vagina may cause the condom to come off during thrusting. If vaginal lubricant is not adequate, saliva or water-based or other commercial lubricants can be used. Natural oils, mineral oil, and petroleum-based products such as lotions, Vaseline, Albolene, and some sexual lubricants should not be used with rubber condoms because petroleum breaks down the rubber.

After the man ejaculates, he must hold the rim of the condom against the base of his erect penis as he withdraws from the vagina so that no seminal fluid containing sperm will seep out.

Condoms will be inconvenient; love play must be interrupted to put them on, and the man must keep an erection until he withdraws from the vagina. That can cause considerable anxiety for some men and interfere with their sexual response. Condoms also interfere with some men's pleasure by reducing sensitivity. For others, it is just a nuisance. Repeated experience with putting on condoms as part of the love play can reduce the inconvenience and enhance their use.

The Sponge. The vaginal contraceptive sponge was approved for use in the United States by the Federal Drug Administration in 1983. It can be purchased by anyone without prescription and does not have to be fitted by a physician. It is a two-inch-wide, round, soft, pillow-shaped polyurethane sponge permeated with spermicide (one gram of nonoxynol-9). The sponge's advantage over the condom is that it is inserted before sexual activity and can be left in place for twenty-four hours with equal effectiveness for repeated intercourse. To prevent pregnancy it must be left in place at least six hours after intercourse.

Inserting the sponge is easy. First, wash your hands and wet the sponge with two tablespoons of clean water, squeeze it once, and then fold and place it deep in the vagina with your finger.

The concave side with the dimple fits over the cervix (the opening of the uterus) while the side with the loop faces the outside, the opening of the vagina. The pressure of the vaginal wall holds the sponge in place against the opening of the cervix. The loop facilitates easy removal.

When used by women who have never been pregnant, nine out of one hundred who used the sponge perfectly got pregnant during the first year of use while eighteen out of one hundred typical users had accidental pregnancies. The numbers are much higher for women who have been pregnant. Twenty-six out of one hundred got pregnant with perfect use, and thirty-six out of one hundred got pregnant with typical use.[3]

Although there is no evidence of significant health risks for women using the sponge, some users have reported allergic reactions to the spermicide and chronic vaginal irritation. Toxic shock syndrome has occurred in a few cases when the sponge was forgotten and left in for more than thirty hours. Even though a woman can purchase and use a sponge without professional assistance, it is recommended that she seek help to learn to find her cervix and properly place and remove the sponge. She should make sure the position of her uterus is such that the sponge can adequately protect her cervix.

The Diaphragm. This barrier method has been used effectively for well over one hundred years. The vaginal diaphragm is made of soft rubber and is shaped like a bowl, with a flexible spring at the outer edge. A spermicidal jelly or cream must be used with a diaphragm to ensure effectiveness since the diaphragm, itself, cannot prevent all sperm from reaching the cervix.

To insert the diaphragm, first wash your hands, then hold the diaphragm with the dome down, like a bowl. Be sure your diaphragm has no holes, cracks, or tears. Put a small amount of spermicidal jelly or cream in the bowl and around the edge of the diaphragm, then pinch the opposite sides of the rim together so the diaphragm folds in the middle. The flattened shape can then be inserted into the vagina. Stand with one foot on a chair or squat or lie down and pull your knees toward your body. Then open your vagina with your other hand and put the folded diaphragm in the vaginal canal, pushing the diaphragm along the back wall of your vagina as far as it will go. Then the front rim can be tucked up along the roof of your vagina behind your pubic bone. The back rim should be below and behind your cervix. Once inserted, the flexible rim resumes its original shape. Check to make sure the diaphragm is properly positioned to completely cover the cervix.

With typical use, the diaphragm is 82 percent effective in preventing pregnancy. That means eighteen out of one hundred women during the first year of using the diaphragm get pregnant. That estimated risk is reduced to six out of one hundred women when used perfectly every time during sex. For women over thirty years old who have intercourse fewer than four times per week, the risk is even less. Likewise, a woman's risk of getting pregnant using the diaphragm as her only means of contraception increases to more than 18 percent if she is twenty-five or younger and has intercourse four or more times weekly.[4]

One advantage of the diaphragm is that it has no side effects. Also, it is usually inserted before intercourse and thus does not interfere with scheduled love play. However, the diaphragm must be prescribed and fitted by a physician. The fit should be checked after pregnancy, pelvic surgery, or a weight change of ten pounds or more. The position of the diaphragm should be checked every time you have intercourse.

Some women cannot use a diaphragm because of poor vaginal muscle tone, a sagging uterus, or vaginal obstructions. A regular diaphragm will not stay in place for women with these conditions; instead, an arcing, or bow-bend, diaphragm may be needed.

All women must leave the diaphragm in place for at least six hours after intercourse, and they should not douche during this time. After removal, the diaphragm must be washed with soap and water, rinsed, dried carefully, checked for holes by holding it up against the light, powdered lightly with corn or potato flour, and placed in its special container. When using a rubber diaphragm it is important not to use petroleum-based lubricants because they interfere with its effectiveness.

Cervical Cap. The cap is similar to the diaphragm in function and effectiveness. It is made of soft rubber, is thimble-shaped, has a rim, and fits over the cervix. Just like the diaphragm, the cap needs to be fitted by a professional on a healthy cervix. It comes in four sizes.

The cap is inserted similarly to the vaginal diaphragm. With freshly washed hands, insert your finger into your vagina and find your cervix. Have the cap filled one-third full with spermicidal cream or jelly. Press the rim of the cap together and push it along the back wall of the vagina until it comes to rest against the back of the cervix. Allow the cap to open, then push it up to cover the cervix. Its placement over the cervix needs to be checked by pressing the dome of the cap and all around the rim of the cap to make sure your cervix is covered. The cap should be left in place for at least six hours and can be left in place for forty-eight hours. Once in place, the cap is less likely to dislodge than the diaphragm.

The cap has about the same effectiveness as the diaphragm for women who have never been pregnant, but it has a higher failure rate than the diaphragm for women who have been pregnant at least once.[5]

The only cervical cap currently available in the United States is the Prentif Cavity Rim, which was approved by the FDA in 1988. Your physician or clinic can order it from Cervical Cap Ltd., P.O. Box 387003-292, Los Gatos, California 95031.

Vaginal Spermicides. Spermicidal creams, jellies, film, foam, and tablets inserted into the vagina contain both a carrier and chemicals. The chemicals are nonoxynol-9 and octoxynol, which immobilize and kill the sperm. They must be inserted at a designated time before intercourse, depending on the type of spermicide used. Film suppositories and tablets must be inserted fifteen minutes before entry while foam, jellies, and creams are effective immediately. The effectiveness of most spermicides lasts an hour. Read the directions of the product you are planning to use to determine when effectiveness begins and how long it lasts.

Foam is the most effective method in this group, but all of these products increase their effectiveness when used in combination with another barrier method. They are increasing in popularity because they can reduce the transmission rates of sexually transmitted diseases.

Female Condom. The Reality Female Condom, approved by the FDA in 1993 for over-the-counter sale in the United States, is a plastic pouch, or sheath, that lines the inside of the vagina. A flexible ring on each end holds the condom in place. The inside ring is used for insertion and as an internal anchor. The outer ring remains outside the vagina after insertion and covers part of the perineum providing protection to the labia and the base of the penis during intercourse.

The female condom, which is prelubricated on the inside, is inserted much like the diaphragm and cervical cap. However, it should not be used with a latex male condom. With clean hands, remove the condom from its package, making sure the inner ring is at the closed end of the pouch. The package directions and illustrations will guide you. As you insert the inner rim of the pouch into the vaginal opening, push the inner ring way up into the vagina. The condom is best removed immediately after intercourse, before you stand up. It should be discarded and not reused.

Even though the statistics do not show the female condom (5 percent accidental pregnancy rate in the first year with perfect use; 21 percent failure rate in the first year with typical use) to be as effective as the male condom (3 percent accidental pregnancy rate in the first year with perfect use; 12 percent failure in the first year with typical use), it does have some advantages.[6] The polyurethane of the female condom is not negatively affected by oil and petroleum-based products as is the latex of the male condom, and the polyurethane may prove to be more effective against viruses than the latex. A spermicide is not used with the female condom, so it may be preferred by women who react to latex and/or spermicide.

Intrauterine Device

The intrauterine device (IUD) is inserted into the uterus by a physician to prevent pregnancy. The devices have been made of various shapes and materials, including silver, copper, and plastic. A string is attached to the device to allow the woman to check that the IUD is still in place and to allow the physician to remove it. In the 1970s, 10 percent of contraception use in the United States was by the IUD. Today that use is less than 2 percent, and the majority of users are in their thirties and forties.

Because of past complications with the IUD, women are warned not to use an IUD if they have a history of pelvic inflammatory disease (PID) or sexually transmitted disease or if they are sexually active with more than one partner or with a partner who has multiple sexual partners. IUD users should be very alert to any signs of infection (fever, pelvic pain or tenderness, and unusual cramping or bleeding) and seek medical help immediately if those symptoms occur. Other possible complications while using the IUD are abnormal bleeding, cramping and pain, partial or complete expulsion of the IUD, or problems with the string. Any of these merit medical attention.

What about effectiveness? The IUD is considered highly effective. However, the skill of the medical person who inserts the IUD and the woman's checking to make sure it is still in place are essential to its effectiveness. Expulsion is the biggest hazard in the IUD's effectiveness. but the statistics present a good picture. Only 0.1 percent (one out of one thousand) to two percent (two out of one hundred) of women who used an IUD got pregnant during their first year.[7]

Convenience is the IUD's biggest advantage. A physician can insert it at any time, even ten minutes after delivering a baby. It remains in place; thus, it does not require insertion and removal by the user. Nor does the woman have to remember to take a pill.

How does the IUD prevent pregnancy? The mechanism of action is not certain. For some time, the belief was that the IUD caused abortion by expelling the fertilized egg. This theory is currently in doubt because of a study that collected released eggs from women using the IUD and from women using no form of contraception. Half of the eggs from the women not using contraception had been fertilized and expelled, while none of the eggs from the IUD users showed signs of fertilization.[8]

IUDs may interrupt pregnancy by affecting the sperm, the egg, the fertilization process, implantation, or the endometrium (the lining of the uterus). It appears to prevent fertilization by immobilizing sperm and speeding the movement of the egg through the fallopian tube so the two do not connect.

If you are considering using an IUD for contraception, get thorough and recent information. Work with a medical professional who has inserted many IUDs and has had few complications. Be sure you are taught how to check the string, and follow those instructions consistently. Be alert to infections or other complications, and seek medical help immediately if they occur. Never attempt to remove the IUD yourself.

Hormonal Pregnancy Prevention (The Pill)

Various forms of "the pill" have been researched and debated before and since their approval by the FDA in 1960. Their convenience and effectiveness make them highly desirable. When the pill is taken consistently, it has an effectiveness of 99.7 to 100 percent. When taken at the same time every day as directed and when extra precautions are used when you have diarrhea or vomiting or are taking certain drugs that may interfere with the pill's effectiveness, only one out of one thousand women (0.1 percent) will get pregnant during the first year of use.[9] Most women get pregnant because they stop the pill to validate whether they are having side effects from it. But when they stop the pill, they fail to use other effective contraception. If you want to test the pill's effect on you by going off of it for a while, have other contraception planned and ready to use before you stop.

The pill is a combination of synthetic estrogen and progesterone hormones that, when given to a woman, shuts off the release of eggs so she no longer ovulates. It also inhibits other processes of impregnation. If the pill is started or resumed on day five of the cycle, day one being the first day of any menstrual spotting or bleeding, inhibition of ovulation is virtually assured.

The ratio and amount of the chemical activity of progesterone, estrogen, and androgen vary with the various types and brands of pills. Each woman's body has to be evaluated to determine which pill will be most effective with the fewest side effects. Unfortunately, some women try one pill, have side effects, and decide this method is not for them. Instead, they may need to change to a lower-level dosage or a pill that has a different proportion of estrogen, progesterone, or androgen.

The Oral Contraceptive User Guide by Richard P. Dickey can be ordered from Essential Medical Information Systems, Inc., P.O. Box 1607, Durant, Oklahoma 74702-1607. If you are going to use the pill, we recommend that you order this book to help you choose the correct pill for you and to guide you in using it most effectively. As Dr. Dickey says in another book, "I have placed a major emphasis on two indisputable points: 1) patients are different in their responses to OCs [oral contraceptives], and 2) OCs are also different in their steroid contents and therefore, in the reactions they elicit in patients.[10]

Even though many different pills are available in the United States, they all have two components—synthetic or natural estrogen and synthetic progesterone—and they all fit into one of three types:

The Combined Pill. This is the most common type of birth-control pill. It is taken daily for twenty-one days, starting with the fifth day of the cycle. Then it is discontinued or placebo pills are taken for seven days. The bleeding starts on the twenty-eighth day. The name refers to this type's having a fixed dosage and a particular type of estrogen and progesterone.

The Biphasic and Triphasic Pills. The estrogen and progesterone ratios in these pills change throughout the monthly cycles. Twenty-one pills are taken, but they have varying levels of estrogen and progesterone in each of two or three phases. The varying dosages are an attempt to reproduce more directly the normal female cycle. They need to be taken in the order prescribed to be effective.

The Mini Pill. This pill comes with progesterone only. It is taken daily without a break. Unlike the other oral contraceptives, it prevents the sperm from getting through, rather than stopping ovulation. It is not as effective as the other two types of pills.

Cautions. All pills contain powerful chemicals that are absorbed into the circulatory system and affect the total body. One report suggests that more than fifty possible metabolic side effects are associated with taking oral contraceptives. So even though most women tolerate the pill very well and even benefit from it, their body chemistry *is* being affected.

The estrogens and progesterones of OCs produce effects in the body similar to those caused by the natural sex hormones produced by the ovaries, but they enter the bloodstream differently and may react differently than the natural hormones. OCs enter through the liver via the gastrointestinal track while the natural hormones from the ovaries enter directly into the circulation and do not go through the liver. Therefore, OCs affect liver function and metabolism of carbohydrates, fats, and proteins; thus, vitamin and mineral absorption is affected. To compensate for those effects, women on the pill should take a vitamin-mineral supplement that is high in vitamins B_1, B_2, B_6, and B_{12}, folic acid, vitamin C, calcium, magnesium, and zinc. High doses of vitamin A, copper, and iron should not be taken because OCs increase absorption of these three substances.

Some women who use the pill gain weight because of fluid retention or increased appetite. An increase of ten pounds or more is a sign that the birth-control pills should be changed or discontinued. When they first start taking the pill, some women experience minor discomfort such as breast tenderness, nausea, vomiting, and spotting between periods. These symptoms usually go away after two or three months of use.

"Side effects occur when the hormone activity of an OC is either much greater or much less than the hormone effect of a woman's own ovarian steroids,"[11] Symptoms that are serious and require that the pill be stopped include affected vision; numbness, weakness, or tingling on one side of your body; severe pains in your chest, left arm, or neck; spitting up of blood; symptoms of thrombophlebitis (severe leg pain, tenderness, and swelling); slurring of speech; and tenderness on the right side just below the diaphragm a possible indication of problems with the liver. If you are having any symptoms, see your physician immediately.

If your symptoms are not indicative of a potentially serious illness, you can control these side effects by identifying whether they are due to estrogen excess or deficiency, progesterone excess or deficiency, or androgen excess. For example, if you have excessive flow with pain and clotting, increased breast size, and urinary-tract infections, you are getting too much estrogen in the pill you are taking. You need to get Dickey's book and find a pill or ask your physician for one that has lower estrogenic activity than the one you now take.

On the other hand, if you are having increased nervousness, are not bleeding after you stop the pill each month, are spotting during the first through ninth days that you take the pill, or you have continuous spotting, then you are not getting enough estrogen. You should find a pill with higher estrogen activity.

If you have experienced an increase in appetite, fatigue, depression, hypoglycemia symptoms, and noncyclic weight gain, you are getting too much progesterone. However, if you have breakthrough bleeding during days ten to twenty-one of taking the pill and suffer from premenstrual symptoms, you are likely not getting enough progesterone.

Most pills also produce some androgen (male hormone) activity. An excess of that activity results in acne, increased hair growth on the mustache area, fluid retention, oily skin and scalp, and an increase in the sex drive.[12]

If you are experiencing some of the symptoms described here, schedule an appointment with your physician, bring the information with you to your appointment, and tell him or her that you would like to try the particular OC you believe would work best for you. If your physician is not cooperative, get a second opinion.

In addition to side effects, using the pill for contraception also has some risks. The FDA package-insert that comes with the pill and lists possible risks and side effects can look scary. Remember, though, that no medication has been studied as thoroughly as oral contraceptives, and any medication, even Tylenol, comes with a list of risks that could lead one to believe it is a deadly drug.

The most common and lasting risk is cardiovascular disease, but this risk can be reduced greatly by careful identification of those women who would be susceptible to cardiovascular effects. These are women older than thirty who smoke cigarettes or have other health factors that are known to put them at high risk. Make certain your physician deals with all of these issues; do not take OCs if you have a high risk for possible cardiovascular complications.

You should be aware that certain medications will interfere with the effectiveness of the pill. Some antibiotics, antifungals, sedatives and hypnotics, anticonvulsants, cholesterol-lowering agents, and other substances may interfere with the pill's ability to prevent pregnancy. This was demonstrated when a granny-to-be wrote a well-known advice columnist saying that her son and daughter-in-law were about to have their first baby. She said the pregnancy was due to the daughter-in-law's ear infection that was treated with antibiotics while she was trusting the pill for pregnancy prevention. If you are on the pill, check with your physician and consult Dr. Dickey's *Oral Contraceptive User Guide* before taking any medication. Ask how it interacts with and changes the effectiveness of your hormonal contraceptive.

Benefits. There are other benefits from the pill besides contraception. Premenstrual tension lessons for some women, menstrual cramps may decrease, the duration and amount of blood loss may be reduced, and the time of menstruation becomes totally predictable. Sometimes acne declines, there is less susceptibility to pelvic inflammatory disease, and the risk of ovarian and endometrial cancer is reduced by 40 to 50 percent. The chance of breast cysts and noncancerous breast tumors is lessened by 50 to 75 percent, endometriosis and rheumatoid arthritis are reduced by 50 percent, growth of excessive body hair often diminishes because the OC suppresses androgen activity, and ovarian cysts are reduced by 65 percent.

The pill can also affect a woman's sexuality; about-equal numbers of women report an increase or decrease in sexual desire. Some women find the physical changes with their periods and the reduction of acne enhance their sexual desire and body image. Many women using oral contraceptives do not experience any significant change in sexual behavior, sexual interest, or sexual enjoyment.

Risks versus Benefits. For women in the high-risk categories, the risks outweigh the benefits, but for the majority of women who are of childbearing age and do not want to get pregnant, the benefits far outweigh the risks. The anticancer benefit mentioned previously should be seriously considered when choosing your method of contraception. The 40 to 50 percent reduction in ovarian and endometrial cancer lasts as long as fifteen years after going off the pill and may last indefinitely. The greatest benefit of the pill is not risking the complications of pregnancy. Ironically, many of the same conditions that put women at risk for taking OCs are the same conditions that would put them at risk if they got pregnant. For these high-risk women, an alternative, highly effective contraceptive method should be used.

What is our conclusion? You are probably better off taking oral contraceptives than not taking them if you meet the following criteria:

- You are a woman in your twenties or thirties.

- You do not weigh more than one-third above your ideal weight.

- You do not smoke.

- You do not have high blood pressure.

- You are not an insulin-controlled diabetic, do not have an elevated cholesterol level or a high LDL/HDL cholesterol ratio, and you have not had any female in your extended family develop diabetes or have a heart attack before age fifty.

- You do not have a history of liver, heart, or vascular disease.

Maximizing Effectiveness. To get the highest effectiveness in pregnancy prevention from oral contraceptives, follow these instructions summarized from *Contraceptive Technology:*[13]

1. Take the pill at the same time every day. Associate taking your pill with something else you do at the same time every day such as brushing your teeth.

2. Choose a backup method of contraception to use—
   a. During your first month of using the pill for protection.
   b. In case you run out of pills.
   c. In case you forget to take your pills.
   d. If you have to discontinue the pill because of serious side effects.
   e. If you need protection from sexually transmitted diseases.
   f. If you have repeated bleeding between cycles.
   g. If you have to take antibiotics or other medications that interfere with the pill's effectiveness.

3. Start your pills according to your physician's instructions and take one pill a day until you finish the pack. If you have a twenty-eight-day pack, begin a new pack immediately. If you are using a twenty-one-day pack, start your new pack one week after you stopped the last pack.

4. Check your pack of birth-control bills each morning to make sure you took your pill the day before.

5. "If you forget to take your birth-control pill or you start your pack late follow the instructions below:

    "If you miss one pill, take that table as soon as you remember it. Take your next tablet at the regular time. You probably will not get pregnant but just to be sure, you may want to use a backup method for seven days after the missed pill.

    "If you miss two pills in a row, then take two tablets as soon as you remember and take two tablets the next day. Then return to your regular schedule but use a backup method of birth control for seven days after two missed tablets.

    "If you miss three pills in a row you will probably begin your period. Whether or not you are menstruating throw away the rest of your pack and begin your next pack as you did when you first started the method. For example, if you are a Sunday starter begin your next pack on Sunday. If you started on any other day, you may simply start your next pack immediately. Use a backup method of birth control until you have been back on pills for seven days.

    "If the only pills you miss are from the fourth week of a 28-day pill pack, simply throw away the missed pills. Then continue taking pills from your current package of pills on schedule. The pills in this fourth week do not contain hormones. So missing these pills does not increase your risk for pregnancy at all."[14]

6. "If you have diarrhea or vomiting, use your backup method of birth control until your next period."[15]

7. If you do not have a menstrual period when expected while taking oral contraceptives consult your physician.

8. Read and follow the instructions on the pill package insert.

Progestin-Only Contraception

Norplant. Norplant, a progesterone-only implant, was approved in December 1990 by the Food and Drug Administration for use in the United States. This was a much-needed new option for women. In one skillful surgical procedure, six rubber-like capsules the size of small matchsticks are inserted under the skin of the inner, upper arm in a fan-shaped configuration. Within twenty-four hours of insertion the woman has virtually 100 percent protection for pregnancy for up to five years. Norplant failures are extremely rare. Some failures after the second year have occurred in women who are significantly over-weight, but in the first year only 0.09 percent of the women who used Norplant got pregnant. Another benefit is that the contra-ceptive effect can be reversed at any time by having the capsules removed. The difficulties some women have experienced with the removal of the capsules can be minimized if they are inserted by a physician who does this procedure frequently.

The six match-sized capsules contain thirty-six milligrams of levonorgestrel (a progesterone that is released at a slow, steady rate over the five-year period). Effectiveness is decreased after that time. Norplant's effectiveness decreases significantly if used with anticonvulsant medications.

Norplant is ideal for women who desire long-term protection from pregnancy and cannot tolerate estrogen, or who have not been reliable in using other birth-control measures. Norplant is not recommended for women with unexplained vaginal bleeding, blood clots, or breast cancer.

The possible side effects and benefits of Norplant are similar to those of other hormonal contraceptives, but the negative symptoms may be more extreme because of some women's re-actions to progesterone. Symptoms such as continuous dull headaches, irregular bleeding, and weight gain are the primary reasons for having the implants removed by the end of the first year. One advantage it has over OCs is that it is not processed through the liver.

Although the five-year cost of the pill would be significantly more than the cost of Norplant, the five-hundred- to six-hundred-dollar fee for implanting Norplant is prohibitive for many women. It is this cost and the current concern with difficult removal that may limit its use despite its safety, convenience, and effectiveness.

Depro-Provera. Depro-Provera is a deep injection of progestins given every three months to inhibit ovulation. It has some of the same advantages as Norplant in that it is not absorbed and processed through the liver and gives moderately

long protection. It is not quite as effective in preventing pregnancy as Norplant or the combined pill, and its contraceptive
effects may take six months to reverse.

Mini Pills. "The effectiveness of progestin-only pills is highest if ovulation is consistently inhibited. When this happens a
woman tends not to have periods of menstrual bleeding."[16] So
if you decide to use the mini pill (progestin-only pill) because
you react to estrogen, you will know that it is most effective in
preventing pregnancy if your bleeding pattern is most changed.

Disadvantages include the warning that mini pills must
never be missed, even by three hours. Also, ovarian cysts are
a frequent complication of mini pills.

All progestin-only contraceptive methods—whether they
are implants, oral medication, or injections—affect menstruation by decreasing it or eliminating it completely. All may be
used by breast-feeding women without affecting lactation.
Some women gain weight from progestin-only contraceptives.
This weight gain is due to increased appetite rather than the
fluid-retention weight gain that comes from estrogen-containing
OCs. Breast tenderness and reduced bone density are two other
side effects that are possible with progestin-only contraceptives.

Hormonal methods of contraception are constantly being
researched. So new products and current information regarding
their effectiveness, risks, and benefits are continually becoming available. Keep yourself informed so your choice is based on
fact rather than fear.

Natural Methods

More and more couples today are considering "natural"
methods of family planning because they fear the potential
risks and side effects of contraceptives. These methods are
based on the principle of avoiding sexual intercourse during the
woman's fertile phase of the menstrual cycle. "Rhythm," or
"Billings," method may be terms you've used to describe natural family planning. The Roman Catholic Church has helpers
trained to teach natural methods, and most family services

offer a thorough training program. Other excellent resources also are available. The Couple to Couple League, P.O. Box 111184, Cincinnati, Ohio 45211, 513-661-7612, is a nonprofit organization that provides natural-family-planning services throughout the world. *The Ovulation Method of Natural Family Planning* details every dimension of planning pregnancies without using contraceptives or sterilization.

While we cannot provide enough information here to train you to effectively practice natural family planning, we will summarize the key techniques to help you determine if this is the method you would prefer.

The traditional rhythm method developed in 1930 was based purely on calculations determined by biological averages, which obviously offers an element of risk because a woman's cycle can vary. Effective, natural family planning requires mucus charting, tabulating the resting-body temperature upon awakening, and inspecting the cervix to determine your fertile days. There are four days of the menstrual cycle, during menstruation, when the woman is absolutely infertile. After that she is considered 97 to 99 percent infertile until she sees that her vaginal mucus has become more abundant, stretchier, thicker, and the consistency of raw egg white. At that time, she can start checking her cervix to detect a change.

After menstruation, the cervix feels hard, and the opening into the vagina is closed. As the cycle moves toward ovulation, the cervix loosens and softens until, about the time of ovulation, it feels soft and the opening actually gapes slightly. After ovulation it returns to its firm, closed state. To prevent pregnancy, total abstinence is necessary from the time of seeing the mucus and noting the softened, open cervix until your temperature has been elevated for three days.

Your waking temperature is lower before ovulation and rises after ovulation. Elevation of your temperature for three days will ensure that the egg is no longer fertilizable. The egg lives twelve to twenty-four hours, but sperm live three to five days.

More training than we can provide here is required to safely use this method. For disciplined, determined, well-trained couples, natural family planning has been successful and enjoyable. One of the benefits is increased awareness of your hormonal cycle. You can enhance your sexual relational by exploring total-body pleasure without intercourse during your fertile or questionable days.

Surgical Sterilization

The opposite extreme of natural family planning is sterilization, a final form of contraception. It ends one's capacity to reproduce.

Male vasectomy is the simplest and safest form of surgical sterilization; this procedure prevents the live sperm from reaching the penis. The sperm normally travel from the testes, where they are produced, through the vas deferens, a tube that leads through the prostate gland to the urethra. During a vasectomy, a small portion of the vas deferens is removed and the cut ends are tied off and sometimes cauterized. This procedure interrupts the sperm's journey so sperm will not be released when a man ejaculates during a sexual experience. He will still produce seminal fluid since some of that is produced in the portion of the duct system above the cut.

One caution: After a vasectomy, a man may have to ejaculate twenty-five times or more before all live sperm are cleared from the duct system above the cut. Several seminal fluid specimens should be taken to the laboratory for confirmation that the sterilization process is complete.

Even though a man's sterilization may be reversed in about 75 percent of the cases, it needs to be thought of as a final, not temporary, method of contraception.

For the woman, sterilization is referred to as tubal ligation. Simple tubal ligation, the tying of the fallopian tubes to prevent the sperm and egg from meeting, is rarely done today because of its ineffectiveness. In addition to the tubes' being tied, to ensure sterilization they need to be crushed, divided and buried, have a section removed, or have a combination of the last two procedures. These procedures do not require major abdominal surgery; the instrument is passed through a small incision in the abdominal wall or through the vagina or the uterus. Many times hospitalization is not necessary.

Reversible methods of tubal ligation are being explored with high effectiveness. Clips or bands are used to shut the tubes, or plugs are inserted to block the end of the tubes. When the woman wants to get pregnant, these obstacles are removed.

When tubal methods fail, which is only 1 percent of the time, it is because the procedure itself failed due to the surgeon's misjudgment; there are some other surgical risks involved as well.

Even though reversibility can be successfully performed, women should think of the tubal-ligation methods as permanent. If you are considering sterilization, gather all the data you can about the specific method your physician will use, the success rate, and any complications and possible aftereffects. Some methods are thought to interfere with pelvic blood flow and produce symptoms of premenstrual tension. Ask questions. It's your body!

Sterilization should not be taken lightly. Even though the results bring incredible freedom, the unforeseen can happen. A child or spouse may die, the couple can divorce, or other great tragedies can wipe out a family. That is why we recommend that the one who is absolutely certain he or she does not want any more children, no matter what the circumstances, is the one who is sterilized. If both spouses are certain, the vasectomy is the recommended choice because of its ease and safety.

Neither male nor female sterilization changes the person's sexuality in any way. The woman will still produce eggs, and the man will still produce sperm. These eggs and sperm disintegrate and are absorbed. The woman continues to menstruate. The man does not usually notice a change in his ejaculation. Hormonal production remains normal for both. Sexual responsiveness and behavior are unaffected except for feeling greater freedom and not having to use contraceptives.

Family planning is a very personal matter. Personal feelings, as well as the technical facts, are important parts of your choice of planned conception. Talk openly with each other about this issue and take responsibility for your sexuality with a focus on the long-term benefits. Choosing a birth-control method is not an easy decision because no method is perfect in both effectiveness and safety. Yet everything has risk, including life itself. Remember that no known contraceptive has a death rate as high as pregnancy—and the death rate from pregnancy is very low.

PART II

Behind Closed Doors

10

••••••

Your Wedding Night

I t is in the sexual experience that we have the possibility of reaching the highest peaks of ecstasy. Because of the powerful potential of sex, the wedding night is an anniversary event, the significant turning point in every couple's relationship. You now are each other's. You have a whole life of togetherness to look forward to. What happens between the two of you that night will be imprinted on your memory forever. In those moments all by yourselves, after the many days of preparation and anticipation, you are free to abandon all previous restrictions. You will no longer have to leave each other and go to your separate living places. You can relinquish all physical boundaries. However the two of you have functioned sexually thus far, this is a first!

What can you do to make your wedding night a special time that leaves you with warm, wonderful feelings? The two of you bring to this night your own unique needs and desires. Your wedding, the reception, the travel to where you will be staying, and the actual setting of that first night will also affect your time together. Whatever your specific circumstances are, we believe there are some basic criteria to a "successful" wedding night for every bridal couple. We'll share those suggestions in this chapter.

Realistic Expectations

As you read and worked through chapter 4, you discussed your expectations. Now you might look back at that chapter and review your discussion, then compare your expectations with the following suggestions.

Timing

Allow plenty of time. Think through the wedding, the reception, the time you anticipate leaving the reception and your expected arrival time at the motel or hotel. If you will be leaving the first-night hotel to travel to a different location for the rest of your honeymoon, what time do you have to check out of the hotel? Do you have to catch a flight the next day? Can you extend your checkout time or find a late-enough flight time so that your first night together is not rushed? We recommend you allow at least twelve hours between arrival at the hotel and your departure. The ideal would be between twelve and eighteen hours.

Feelings

Expect a wide range of possible feelings. You may be excited to be alone together, or you may be sad because you are leaving your home and family. You may be eager to enjoy each other's body sexually and may have no sense of reservation about sharing yourself completely and openly, or you may be hesitant and fearful. You may be energized, or you may be exhausted. You may feel like being tender and close, or you may feel intensely erotic. There is no ideal; the only "requirement" is that the two of you let each other know what you feel and accept each other's needs for that night. Success means you connect and enjoy where you are rather than try to measure up to some false expectation of how you *should* feel the first night.

Preparation

Allow for bodily preparation. If it has been a long time since you showered, shaved, and brushed your teeth, taking time to freshen your bodies for your time together may refresh you and increase your desirability to your spouse. Prepare any contraceptive measures you plan to use. Make sure you have all the necessary supplies and are very familiar with their use.

Connection

Allow for emotional and spiritual connection. This is often more important for the woman than it is for the man. The wife may be eager to talk through all the details of the wedding and reception. She may need to feel valued as a person. She may need to know her husband responds to her beauty. We were taught that we were to start our first sexual intercourse with a time of Bible reading and prayer. That can be a very important way to connect and invite God into your married sex life. We actually were rather legalistic about that "rule," so Joyce read a passage to Cliff in the car on the way to the motel, and we prayed as we drove. We were both very eager!

Sexual Activity

Allow for pleasure without any goal-oriented demands. Remember lovemaking is just that. It is a time of delighting in your bodies without any need for arousal, orgasm, or intercourse. You may want to prepare your bodies and then just enjoy falling asleep in each other's arms. You may enjoy a time of passionate kissing and fondling and then fall asleep and continue later that night or in the morning when you wake up. Or you may enjoy the pleasure of each other's body and a full sexual experience.

What is most important is that you don't go further than both of you desire. Let the most tired, conservative, or hesitant one set the pace and the boundaries. One spouse's pushing for more than the other desires will be remembered negatively for years to come. The consequences are not worth getting what you want at that moment! Limit sexual activity the first night to what both of you would freely desire.

Success

Define success for your first night so that there is no way you can fail. If your only expectation for your wedding night is that you both enjoy being together without any demands to do more than the most hesitant of you desires, then you will surely succeed and have no regrets. Many first nights are made less than ideal by comparison with some external standard, but if you don't set such a standard, your wedding night can be ideal for you.

Expect to feel many emotions as you experience the realities of fatigue, adjustment to each other, being newly married, the newness of your setting, and for some, the "firsts" of your sexual activity. Recognize that you have the honeymoon and many years following it to get to know each other totally. You will grow in your sexual enjoyment as you become more comfortable communicating clearly exactly what touch and sexual activities you find most exciting.

Your Model

The Song of Solomon is the most beautiful model of a wedding night's first sexual experience. Joseph Dillow's book *Solomon on Sex* interprets that passage so vividly.

Dillow assumes by the text that the bride and groom retire to the bridal chambers around twilight. Solomon begins their time together by raving on and on about the beauty of his wife. His enjoyment of her body is evident—not as a means to his own gratification, but as a deep appreciation of her. Solomon mentions her eyes, hair, teeth, lips, and neck, and he praises her body separately from a sexual focus. It would seem that he is enjoying caressing those parts as he fondly talks about them.

Solomon has connected with his new wife's personhood before he delights in the rest of her body. He uses beautiful symbolism to describe her breasts and nipples. It is clear that he not only enjoys the appearance of her breasts, but he also "feeds" among them. He refers to her genitals as a garden. The frankincense, or scent, of her genitals arouses him. A woman needs to know that her body arouses her husband, especially if her body can be enjoyed for his pleasure without any demand being placed on her. Solomon concludes his response to Shulamith's body with these words: "You are altogether beautiful, my darling,/And there is no blemish in you" (Song of Sol. 4:7).

After Solomon affirms her beauty, he creates a fantasy for her of their traveling to her home to make love in the countryside. His excitement builds with intensity as he talks about his heart beating fast, her garden, or genitals, being locked up (those of a virgin), and their genital secretions (symbolically referred to as streams of water and a cistern of water) flowing.

Just as we recommend that the wife initiate entry, Shulamith invites genital contact (often interpreted as an invitation for oral sex). "May my beloved come into his garden/And eat its choice fruits!" (Song of Sol. 4:16). Never does he seem to push himself on her or demand from her. He just affirms and enjoys her until she begs him to come to her genitals. They consummate their relationship as they eat and drink in the sexual pleasure of one another's body. What a beautiful model God has given us for the sexual relationship between a husband and wife!

The Sexual Experience

It is not important whether you consummate your marriage (have your first married sexual intercourse) on the wedding night, the next day, or later during your honeymoon. It *is* important that you do not avoid each other. After a while, if you have not had sex and one of you is getting concerned about that, call time out. Find out what is going on and how you might help.

Whenever you have sex for the first time after your wedding, *GO SLOWLY!* So many times, couples who have waited for marriage to have sexual intercourse are so eager (just as we were) that they bypass all the wonderful caressing, kissing, and fondling that were such a vital part of their physical interaction before. Now that they can do the "real thing," couples often forget about caressing, or they think the caressing and kissing are not necessary. But that is what made their bodies so hungry for the real thing; when they skip all that intense connecting, the sexual experience can be very quick and leave both feeling disappointed.

We recommend that you spend at least as much time enjoying the pleasure of each other's body as you would have on any date or time together before marriage. You might begin with your clothes on. As arousal and desire for more builds, gradually take off each other's clothes. Again, let the more hesitant one lead.

Generally this is where the man needs to slow down. We like how Popenoe says it:

> Coming to the consummation of the marriage, few women will respond to "cave-man tactics" with anything but revulsion. Patience, self-control, and unselfishness on the part of the husband, always necessary, are never more important than during these first days and nights. A determination to place his own feelings second and to think first of the feeling of his wife, is the key to success.[1]

This reinforces the biblical teaching that the husband is to love his wife as Christ loved the church. That love is described this way in Philippians 2:3: "Do nothing from selfishness or empty conceit, but with humility of mind let each of you regard one another as more important than himself."

For the woman, the way you can regard your husband as more important than yourself is to be an active participant. Just as your husband will need to focus more on the slowing-down part, you may need to attend to the second criterion for your first sexual experience: *GET ACTIVE!* Your own frame of mind will greatly affect your first time together as husband and wife. If you can free yourself from all fears, false modesty, girlishness, and resistances, you will be able to listen to your body and communicate both verbally and physically what you would like. It is not your "duty" to please your husband; it is your "duty" to enjoy his body and go after your pleasure with gusto! You may be surprised to find that he is pleased by this enthusiasm.

Sometimes roles are reversed. It is the husband who is hesitant and fearful and the wife who is impatient. If that is likely to be the case for you, apply the opposite roles discussed above to your situation.

Connect with each other! We often recommend that married couples begin their sexual times by bathing or showering together. That is a way to relax, connect, and prepare your bodies for each other. In *Solomon on Sex,* Dillow refers to a Christian counselor friend, Don Meredith, who recommends this for the first night's experience:

> When they get to the motel, they are to draw a deep, relaxing bubble bath. Let the new bride get into the bath first while the husband is in the other room. A candle lit in the bathroom, being the only light, will produce a warm, romantic atmosphere. As they relax together in the bathtub, they can discuss the day, talk, and even pray, thanking the Lord for the gift of each other. As they communicate and share, the warm water drains away the tensions of the day, and the bubbles sufficiently hide the wife's body so she is not immediately embarrassed.[2]

He goes on to recommend that they stimulate each other under the water as a way of reducing inhibitions. If this idea sounds good to both of you, try it. Remember to pack a candle and some matches.

You may not anticipate bathing together as a relaxing, connecting, and romantic event at all. Continue to talk about and create your own first night. You may want to add a touch of surprise for each other, or you may not like any element of surprise, even if it is romantic and meant to be positive. If you do not like to be taken by surprise, let your fiancé know that immediately.

Pleasure each other. The only negative part of the bathtub scenario is that connection leads directly to stimulation. We would modify that slightly by recommending playful genital touching under the water and plenty of time before and/or after to really be passionate with each other before pursuing direct, erotic stimulation. Touch, talk, kiss, and explore every inch of one another's body to the degree that you both feel free to do that. Soak in the good feelings of being touched and touching. Have fun as you do. Nibble on each other. Let each other know how much you enjoy the other. As you enjoy yourselves, if anything you do is negative for the other, positively invite a different touch or activity. For example, if a touch is too light and ticklish, ask for a heavier touch. Or if kissing gets too intense or forceful, invite softer lips.

As you become ready for direct genital stimulation, invite that by guiding your partner's hand to your genitals or rubbing your genitals against your partner's body. Explore and learn together what feels good. Do not expect that you will automatically know how to touch each other in the way that feels best. Accept your spouse's guidance as a loving desire to enhance the experience for both of you and take away demand for you to automatically know what feels right to him or her.

Allow the arousal to build in waves, enjoying the genital stimulation and then moving to other parts of the body. You want to keep each other hungry for more touch, not saturated so that you get irritated with the stimulation. This is particularly true for women. Direct clitoral stimulation is often more irritating than it is arousing. Most women prefer a flat hand over the clitoral area or fingers on either side of the clitoris to stroke the shaft rather than the tip of the clitoris. Pain and pleasure are closely connected in the body, so if no pleasure is being stimulated you are furthest from triggering pain. The following graph illustrates how quickly direct stimulation can, with a slight shift in its intensity or location, change from causing peak arousal to instant pain. That is why it is so important for you, the woman, to signal your husband to let him know what you desire—because there is no other way he can know what you need and know when the stimulation gets too intense. You, the man, would do better to vary the stimulation automatically and keep your wife wanting more rather than pursuing orgasm too intensely. If you, as the woman, want to be stimulated to orgasm before entry and that is not a demand for performance but comes from the level of your arousal, go for it!

Entry should be attempted only at the woman's invitation. It is her body that is being entered; therefore, she should guide the penis into her vagina. When you, the woman, feel ready to allow entry, let your husband know that you desire him. It might be easiest for you to get on top of him while he is on his back. He or you can apply lubricant to his penis and separate your labia (lips) and apply lubricant to the opening of your vagina. Use his penis as a paintbrush over the opening of your vagina and on your clitoris. Poke the penis into your vagina just a little. Tighten and relax your PC muscle as you do. Intentionally relax your vaginal muscle as you guide his penis in. You may

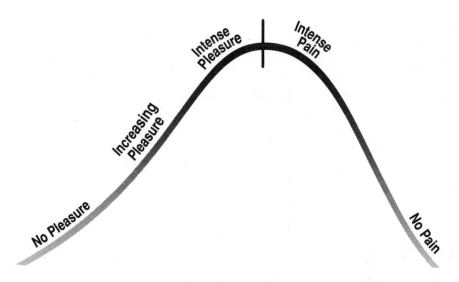

No Pleasure · Increasing Pleasure · Intense Pleasure · Intense Pain · No Pain

FIGURE 10–1

need to push against his penis to push through your hymen and vaginal muscle.

If you experience resistance, it is usually because the labia are stuck together, you're pushing at the wrong place (that is, you are not quite at the opening or do not have the penis at quite the right angle to enter the vagina), your hymen is a little tough to break, or your vaginal muscle is not relaxed. The latter is the most likely. Remember you are both new at this; just enjoy the process of trying. Play around with different positions if one doesn't work. Stretch or dilate the vagina and try again. Get a hand mirror and together try to figure out what is happening. Do not keep trying until you are frustrated. Stop while the attempts are fun, get some sleep, and pursue pleasure again when you have time to do so leisurely and are not tired. Don't rush to try entry, but continue to pleasure one another. Play with attempts at entry in the process of enjoying each other. If frustration ensues, seek help.

When the penis actually enters the vagina, you may want to stop, withdraw, celebrate, and try entry again later. Or you may just lie quietly together and enjoy the closeness of this special moment. Then gradually build rhythmic thrusting. Rest every now and then to slow down the process and enjoy every sensation. Engage in kissing, breast stimulation, and clitoral stimulation while you are resting together. When you both decide you are ready to thrust to ejaculation, build the frequency and intensity of the thrusting gradually. Think of trying to enjoy every moment and make it last as long as possible, like licking your favorite ice cream cone. Resist the urge to thrust or to pursue ejaculation. That will end your time quickly and may be disappointing. If that should happen by mistake, don't get down on yourselves. You have years to learn to extend intercourse. You may have some regrets about this first time, but if your expectations were realistic you know that is normal. Savor the good feelings of being together and stay connected. If you, the woman, need more stimulation, ask for that. The husband can also offer that.

Spend time talking and cuddling when you finish. Affirm each other. Let each other know what you enjoyed. Share fantasies of other possibilities for sexual play if those ideas don't intimidate. Have tissue, washcloths, a small towel, or some type of wipes at the bedside to catch the seminal fluid and vaginal secretions after sex. There will be a bit of a mess, but the woman can easily handle that by putting tissue or a washcloth between her legs to catch the secretions as they seep out of her vagina. The man can wipe off his penis as necessary.

It would be quite common, if this is your first sexual experience and you have not been bringing yourselves or each other to orgasm, for the woman not to be orgasmic. When we got married, we didn't really even understand about orgasm so Joyce probably wasn't orgasmic at first, but it wasn't an issue for us. We don't even know whether she was or wasn't. We both loved our times together and remember them, including the wedding night, with great fondness. Now those initial experiences would seem disappointing for us, but they were not disappointing then! And that is appropriate. Our accurate knowledge, lack of unrealistic TV and movie-star models, and our naiveté prevented us from having any real goals. That was a perfect start for our sexual life together. You, too, need not be disappointed if the orgasmic reflex doesn't happen for you initially. If you are allowing arousal, enjoy that and let it build and extend. Eventually, the reflex of orgasm is likely to get triggered, especially if you are active and uninhibited. If you feel frustrated or feel like crying because you have not had release, recognize that as one way your body may be letting down and releasing the tension buildup of the sexual arousal in your body. Hold each other and share the crying. Do not take it as a sign of failure and avoid each other. Bring that release into your connected feelings.

Even though it lacks the moral guidelines we would associate with sex, a sexual book, *The First Time,* has some excellent input for enhancing your first sexual experience. We would like to summarize these for you here, changing some of the conditions to fit our values: Your first sexual experience will be enhanced if your spouse is a sensitive, informed partner who is willing to talk about feelings, if it occurs in a safe location and is not rushed, if you use adequate birth control and protection against sexually transmitted diseases (if either of you is a potential carrier), and if you are ready emotionally to risk that level of intimacy and vulnerability.[3]

Questions and Answers

How do we cope with "morning breath" without breaking spontaneity by jumping out of bed to brush our teeth?

Couples are affected differently by nighttime or morning breath. Some are not bothered at all; it's just not an issue for them. In the most challenging situation, one spouse is extremely sensitive to breath and the other is not. That can cause conflict because the insensitive one feels criticized by the sensitive one, and the sensitive one feels disregarded by the insensitive one. Whether one or both spouses are aware of bad-breath issues, they can work out a plan that easily takes care of stale breath: keep breath mints or breath spray at the bedside.

How important is it for both of us to have clean hands and bodies to protect the other from developing irritations or infections?

It is very important to be clean. Nails should be filed and smooth, hands should be freshly washed, teeth should be brushed and flossed, and genitals should be clean. The hands

and genitals are especially important—the hands because they
fondle the genital openings, which are a clean part of the body
that become infected when exposed to germs, and the genitals
because they can easily become contaminated by feces from the
rectum. When freshly washed and free of infection, the genitals
are clean.

**What techniques can be used to tell the other person
that what they are doing is pleasurable?**

Nonverbal or verbal responsiveness is a strong reinforcer
and very contagious. You can moan, groan, or let your spouse
know that right at this moment you feel like you could do what
you're doing forever.

**How does a woman stimulate a man so he is prepared for
entry by her invitation?**

The woman's invitation for entry should not be a demand
that the man must be ready at that moment. It just means that
whenever he is ready, she is. Often, if the woman is ready, her
arousal will have gotten the man eager too. The woman par-
ticipates in preparing the man for entry, not only by her own
involvement and responsiveness, but also by enjoying her
husband's genitals. Stroking the shaft of the penis, in addition to enjoying his entire body, will usually get a man ready
for entry.

**Do most women experience bleeding and pain when the
hymen breaks during the first entry?**

The response can range from absolutely no pain and no
bleeding to such severe pain that entry is impossible and there
is noticeable bleeding. The last two possibilities are rare. When
the vaginal opening has been stretched and a lubricant is used,
and when the women guides the penis in at her own pace, there
is often no bleeding and only a momentary "Ouch!"

**What can I do to reduce my fear of the pain of intercourse?
I am a virgin and I am dreading the wedding night. I have
always avoided pain at any cost.**

Unfortunately, your *fear* is likely to cause pain unless you
work past it. The fear will not go away by ignoring it. Talk about

it, and prepare, prepare, prepare! Stretch your vaginal opening at least twenty minutes daily. Get a gynecological examination, and ask your physician for dilators. Learn to control your PC muscle so you can voluntarily relax it. Learn visualization and relaxation techniques. Every day when you stretch your vagina, picture your first sexual intercourse. Note when your fear sets in. Replace the fear with positive thoughts and feelings. Imagine the penis in your vagina feeling like a warm, soft, moist, loving sensation. Take charge of when and how entry happens. Use lots of lubricant. Let your husband know as soon as you feel afraid. Stop pursuing entry at that point and just hold and affirm one another, then try again. Often anticipation is the biggest hurdle. Once you actually pursue entry, the fears may dissipate. If you cannot get beyond your fear, get help from a sexual therapist.

Is "quiet vagina" for newly marrieds only?

No. Quiet vagina (resting without thrusting after entry) is used by couples throughout their married lives as a means to extend sexual pleasure after entry and to delay ejaculation for men.

Does the woman's expanding her vagina before intercourse take away from God's plan for the women to be a virgin?

No. A virgin is a woman who has not had sexual intercourse. She has not had a penis in her vagina. She has not become one with a man. She is still a virgin!

What can I do to relax the muscle during intercourse so that my vagina isn't so tight?

Practice the PC muscle exercises described on pages 90–91 so you can control that muscle when you choose to relax it. Learn total-body relaxation techniques. When you notice the vaginal muscle is tight, try bearing down like you do when you are having a bowel movement, but now you are pretending you are pushing something out of your vagina.

What if my wife is initially aroused and them loses lubrication before entry?

This is very common. That is why we recommend using a lubricant every time until you notice you have forgotten to use it. Lubrication occurs within ten to twenty seconds of any genital stimulation. During prolonged love play, lubrication is likely to dry.

What if the man wants sex two to three times per day? Should the woman submit?

It is interesting that the question states, "the man *wants* sex," not that he desires his wife. Usually the man who wants sex that often is not responding to an urge that is growing out of his closeness and enjoyment of his wife. Rather, he is an insecure person who is using sex to get affirmation. This will kill the woman's sexual desire by the end of the honeymoon, if not sooner. So our answer to this question would be: not if he wants to enjoy an involved sexual partner for the rest of life!

Must a woman have an orgasm every time?

Some women feel a need for an orgasm every time; others do not. There is no right or wrong. The woman's enjoyment of the sexual experience may have nothing to do with having an orgasm. For her it may be the closeness and connection that is most satisfying. This varies greatly from woman to woman. A successful sexual experience is not dependent upon arousal, orgasm, ejaculation, or intercourse.

Isn't it uncomfortable for the woman to lead?

It depends so much on how she leads. If she is controlling, demeaning, or demanding, it is very uncomfortable. If she sets the pace by being open about what she is feeling and desiring and her husband sensitively responds to her, it can be wonderful for both. The woman is more variable and complex in her need for emotional readiness, in her physical responsiveness, and her sexual desires than the man is. Because of this, it usually works best if the man delights in the woman but lets her set the pace, as Solomon did in the Old Testament.

If a woman is experienced and her husband is not, it will be very important for her to lead until they are equally comfortable with the sexual activity.

It seems like after waiting so long for sex, we're going to want to go right to sexual intercourse on our wedding night.

Is it detrimental to go right from foreplay to intercourse without getting acquainted with each other's genitals?

Getting acquainted with each other's genitals, even though it seems like that would be beneficial to do before pursuing sexual intercourse, is likely to feel rather clinical and exposing for a newly married couple. Even couples who have been married for years sometimes have difficulty being that vulnerable with each other. We don't think that would be a necessary step to consummating your marriage. It is natural on the wedding night to just let down all restrictions and go for it. Do be sure to include the conditions described previously for a "successful" wedding-night experience so you don't move too quickly from foreplay to intercourse and feel let down.

How do you avoid getting into a sexual rut?

You probably don't have to worry about that quite yet, but it's wise to be aware of that possibility. Joyce had been taught in her premarital class before our wedding that a couple should not get into a sexual rut. Being a good student she thought we had to try a new position every time we had sex on our honeymoon, when we had not even mastered the basics!

The best way not to get into a rut is to allow quality time for your sex life and to learn to guide each other in the sexual experience. If each of you takes responsibility to listen to each other's needs and desires and communicate them to one another without demand, you won't have to keep trying to figure out what works and then keep doing over and over what worked once. Rote repetition of what worked once is a sure way to get into a rut and diminish the spark of your sexual relationship.

11
◆◆◆◆◆◆

Keeping Sex
for Pleasure

So often couples ask us, "What sexual activities are okay for a married couple?" As best we understand Scripture's teaching and what happens in the body during a sexual response, God designed sex for two purposes: procreation and pleasure. Thus, within the context of Christ's two commandments—to love the Lord your God with all your being and to love your neighbor as yourself (Matt. 22:37–39)—you, as a married couple, are free to engage in any sexual activity intended for procreation or pleasure that does not in any way violate your relationship with God or with each other.

Never should any activity take away from your closeness with God or be something that is negative for one of you. There are enough ways that you, as a couple, can enjoy ingenuity, zest, and vitality in your sex life without interfering with either of these primary commitments.

Establish Positive Sexual Patterns

To shift from your initial romantic or passion-driven sexual energy to a deeper, more intimate and affectionate sexual relationship may take some work. First, you will need to counteract the myth that satisfying sex just happens naturally. Popenoe wrote about this more than fifty years ago:

> The love-life of intelligent human beings is not a "natural" thing—no more so than is one of Chopin's Preludes or Beethoven's Symphonies. The mating impulse is biological, but the ways in which it is expressed are part of our social background and cultural heritage. No one can afford to rely on mere instinct as a guide to the unfolding of two personalities in marriage.[1]

It is not true that you will either have a good sex life or you will not. The quality of your sexual relationship is not dependent upon fate; it is dependent upon *you*. You can be among the 50 percent of couples who do not have difficulties in their sexual relationship rather than aligning with those who continually struggle sexually. In this section we will share some principles we believe are basic to establishing positive sexual patterns in your married sex life.

Develop a Positive Sexual Confidence

Sexual self-confidence has to be learned. The general self-confidence you gained or lacked during your childhood years will either help or hinder your sexual self-confidence. If you lack general self-confidence, you will need to develop good feelings about yourself as a person before you will be able to enjoy sex with confidence.

Knowledge, practice, and positive sexual experiences will lead you to a positive sexual confidence that will allow you to know your sexual needs and desires without being demanding or insecure in pursuing those needs with your spouse. Sexual self-confidence is a quiet, inner sexual awareness that can let you enjoy the giving and receiving of sexual pleasure, without insisting on sex for satisfaction. If you are secure in your sexuality, you will accept each other's sexual differences and not take them as a personal assault of your sexual attractiveness. Thus, your sexual self-confidence will enable you to keep sex for mutual pleasure in your marriage.

Nurture Individual and Relationship Growth

A relationship is only as strong as the individuals who join together to form it. A sexual relationship is only as dynamic as the general relationship of the two who are sharing their bodies with each other. The two of you will need to allow separateness, as well as plan for quality togetherness. Attend to personal and relationship needs as they arise. If you don't, those issues will eventually spill over into the bedroom. As the two of you learn to bring out the best in each other, you will each become better individuals, and your relationship will grow deeper in love and in sexual enjoyment.

Learn to Pleasure Each Other for the Sake of Pleasure

If you are familiar with our writing and teaching, you know this is our theme. To focus on pleasure in your sexual relationship, you will need to bring to your marriage or develop the attitude that you have the *right* to pleasure, and so does your spouse. Both of you are worthy of sexual pleasure, but you will only be able to give and receive pleasure freely if each of you feels free from sexual demands. Anxiety due to demands you give yourselves or each other will interfere with every phase of the sexual experience.

To keep your sexual experiences focused on pleasure and free of demands, begin each sexual time with the reminder that you are there to enjoy yourselves and each other without any demand to have to get aroused, to have to perform for each other in any certain way, to have to be orgasmic, or to have to have intercourse. Lovemaking is the time for the two of you to pull away from all the demands and responsibilities of life and just delight in each other without any expectations—never by violating the other person. The only expectation is that you give your bodies to each other for mutual pleasure. Pleasure cannot be demanded from each other, but rather, is freely pursued.

The involuntary responses of sexual arousal and release may occur when you are relaxed and soaking in sexual pleasure, but they cannot be the goal. When you *try* to get aroused or *try* to have an orgasm, your trying will interfere with those natural bodily responses. If you find yourself trying, distract yourself by telling your spouse that you are demanding a response of yourself. Verbalizing your mental demands and anxieties will distract you from them and help you refocus on the good sensations of touching and being touched.

Focusing on pleasure enhances your bodily awareness by letting you soak in the sensuous touch and skin-to-skin contact of each other's body. This works best when each of you is able to give your body to each other to enjoy and able to enjoy each other's body.

Kissing is the most intimate and challenging form of pleasuring; make sure it is a positive part of lovemaking for both of you. That may be difficult to talk about, especially if one of you is not pleased with how the other kisses. To express corrections can be very hurtful, yet it is vital that the two of you learn to mutually enjoy passionate kissing. To do that, we recommend that you first talk about any past negative experiences either of you have had with kissing. If kissing was ever forced on you abusively, it will be important that you lead in all kissing until you are able to invite kisses from your spouse. Then we recommend that you proceed with the kissing exercise described below. Kissing is an indicator of a sexual relationship. It is rare for a couple with sexual difficulties to say they enjoy their kissing. If you can keep kissing alive and well between you, your sexual relationship is likely to also do well.

Kissing

Step 1: The man will take responsibility to see that the experience happens. Prepare a comfortable setting with low lights and soft music.

Step 2: Brush teeth, use dental floss, and gargle.

Step 3: Read and discuss these instructions.

Step 4: Sitting on the couch, fully clothed, each of you describe to the other how you like to kiss and be kissed. Use positive descriptions rather than listing what you don't like. Reflect back to each other what you understand from the other.

Step 5: The woman will use her lips to experiment with kissing her spouse's lips. Pucker your lips and gently peck across your spouse's lips and cheeks from one side to the other, from top to bottom lip, etc. Take time to nibble on your spouse's lips, taking the upper or lower lip between your lips. The man will follow her lead. Be passive, but responsive.

Step 6: Reverse roles. The man will follow Step 5 to discover how he likes to kiss. The woman will follow his lead. Be passive, but responsive.

Step 7: Take turns leading in experimenting with the use of your lips and tongue to find ways that you both enjoy: pecking, nibbling, licking, sucking, and in any other way interacting with each other's lips and tongues. Keep it soft and experimental.

Step 8: Allow the involvement with each other's mouth to become mutual, simultaneous enjoyment, if that is comfortable for both of you. Take turns inserting your tongue in and out of each other's mouth. If one of you becomes too intense or forceful for the other, gently remind the intense one that you'd like to keep it soft, safe, and experimental.

Step 9: Talk about the experience. What felt especially good? What barriers did you encounter? How would you like to enhance your kissing?

Reprinted from Penner and Penner *Restoring the Pleasure* (Dallas: Word, 1993). Used by permission.

You can learn to focus on giving and receiving pleasure before marriage and continue to progress in your involvement with each other after marriage. You can start with a foot and hand caress and then proceed to a facial caress and on to a back caress. After marriage, you may wish to continue with total-body caressing, first excluding breasts and genitals then including them in a general sense and eventually including them for the purpose of pursuing stimulation and then entry. Step-by-step descriptions of these exercises will be included at the end of this chapter. The caressing is to be sensuous stroking, not a muscle rub; the focus is on skin-to-skin pleasure for both the giver and the receiver. The exercises are not only a way for beginners to learn to give and receive pleasure; they are for sexual retraining for couples who have developed ineffective sexual habits.

Pursue Sexual Pleasure Responsibly

Not only do each of you have equal rights to sexual pleasure in marriage, you also have equal responsibility. Enjoying each other's body and letting each event take on its own character is easiest when each of you feels comfortable pursuing your own desire for touch. As both pleasurer and receiver, you must take responsibility for discovering, communicating, and going after your sexual feelings and needs, but that must be done without demand and not at the other's expense.

Demand is actually reduced when you can count on your spouse to go after his or her needs and desires rather than expecting you to produce a response in him or her. You, in turn, will please your spouse most when you are not preoccupied with pleasing but are fully enjoying yourself sexually both as the pleasurer and the receiver. As the receiver of touch, your only task is to soak in the pleasure and to redirect your spouse when the touch is not pleasing. You can check with your spouse if at any time you think your pleasure may be interfering with his or her pleasure. As the pleasurer, your only responsibility is to lovingly touch your spouse in a way that feels good to you, enjoying his or her body for your pleasure. Caress slowly. Take time to radiate warmth through your fingertips and to take in the sensation and pulsation of your spouse's body. You cannot expect your spouse to know when, how, and where you want to be pleasured; you are responsible to let each other know your needs and desires. This only works if that is a mutual commitment.

Anticipate and Time Your Sexual Interaction Carefully

As with anything else in life, *timing* and *anticipation* are important ingredients to the sexual patterns you establish. They will be most natural when you make your sexual relationship a priority. If you have set aside blocks of time to be available to each other physically, you will be able to mentally picture and prepare yourselves for your times together. If quality time has not been predetermined, you can anticipate and find time for your sexual relationship by constantly picturing the two of you together and enjoying bodily pleasure. Your ongoing positive expectation of having time together will work well if *both* of you exercise that anticipation. If not, your constant readiness may be experienced as pressure by your spouse.

Cultivate Romance

Pay attention to those little details of your sexual relationship that will add romance. Refer to chapter 2 for specific suggestions. Romance will help you shift from initial passion to an ongoing life of sexual fulfillment. Continue to woo, court, and seduce each other. Pay attention to your spouse. Touch each other when you pass by. Take a moment to give your spouse a positive message of regard and care. Write notes of affection and appreciation to each other, and withhold unkind thoughts and feelings.

Create a romantic atmosphere that appeals to all the senses: sight, smell, touch, sound, and even taste. If your living situation will allow for it, design your bedroom or your most common lovemaking location to have a sense of separateness to which you can escape. Enhance your lovemaking atmosphere by keeping it free of clutter and add touches that each of you enjoy. Music is often a great addition. You may enjoy moving your bodies together to the rhythm of the music. Dancing in the nude in the privacy of your bedroom can be a romantic beginning to sharing your bodies with each other. A dimmer switch on the light, a colored light bulb, or candle light all are possible visual variations. Privacy is a necessity, especially for most women. The first item of repair when you move into a new home should be a lock on the bedroom door!

Romance does not have to be fervent or serious; it can also be fun. Lighten up in the ways you express romance. Be adventurous and childlike. A little tease can add spark to your romantic life. You both need to have a sense of humor for teasing to work effectively, and the teasing must not be hurtful or degrading in any way. It has to be fun and uplifting for both of you. Romance will slip away if you do not consciously decide to keep it alive.

Keep the Lines of Communication Open

Bernie Zibergeld, in *The New Male Sexuality*, gives a delightful description of how couples can establish openness about their sexual relationship:

This is what I think of as oral sex: opening one's mouth and saying something. Every survey I'm aware of has found a strong positive correlation between this and sexual satisfaction. It's not that people who have good sex over time always talk about it or even that they talk about it a lot. It's simply that they have the option of talking about sex when there's something to be said.[2]

Your ability and willingness to talk about sex will depend upon the naturalness and ease with which you are able to share your thoughts, desires, feelings, and fantasies about your sexual relationship as they arise. Some couples need to schedule times to talk, sort of like you schedule a six-month checkup for your car.

Eliminate Hindrances to Success

Throughout this book, we've referred directly or indirectly to the hindrances to a positive, fulfilling sexual relationship in marriage. As a review, we'll provide a summary here. We believe the items on this list are self-explanatory. Getting your sex life off to a great start means you are aware of these possible problems and you know how to avoid them.

Sex is too quick.

Sex is functional and for physical release only.

Sex is a substitute for intimacy rather than an expression of intimacy.

Either or both of the spouses are trying to please each other rather than delight in each other.

Either or both have come to the marriage with unresolved sexual issues from the past.

Either or both come with unrealistic sexual expectations.

Relationship conflicts need to be resolved.

Sex becomes mechanical and a matter of routine.

Sex only happens when both or one is fatigued; quality time is not allowed for sex.

Sex means simply arousal, release, and/or intercourse.

Sex is one-sided rather than a mutual expression designed for mutual fulfillment.

Establish the Emotional-Relationship Dimension of Sex

The key ingredients of your sexual relationship must be attended to if you are going to keep sex for pleasure in your marriage. These ingredients are sexual desire, initiation, pleasuring, entry, enjoying the process, letting go, and affirming. In chapter 4, "Clarifying Expectations," we had you talk about your sexual pattern before marriage and your expectations for after your marriage. Now we want to suggest how you can positively develop these critical emotional-relationship dimensions of your sexual life.

Sexual Desire

Sexual desire is the urge to be touched, to be close, or it is the urge for sexual arousal, orgasm, or intercourse. Sexual desire is God-given and innate in every one, even though that desire is experienced differently by different people.

For some, sexual interest has a very natural ebb and flow throughout life that may occur spontaneously and automatically. If that is true for you, your desire may surface somewhat regularly according to the buildup of sexual energy, or it may occur as you exercise or pamper your body. It may be set off by a certain expression, look, activity, or talent, or by seeing or touching each other. Sexual desire may get started by something sensuous, like music, the sound of ocean waves, a romantic setting, a scent, a story, or a picture.

Others do not seem to have that automatic awareness of sexual desire. You may need certain conditions to make you aware of those needs. You may become aware of sexual urges when you are away from the pressures of life—your work, your children, or social obligations.

Having a special time for each other may trigger your sexual desire: a private time at home in your bedroom, a special meal together, a time of talking together, or a time of physical, emotional, or spiritual connection.

There may be very specific behaviors that ignite your sexual urges, actions you do yourself or behaviors you need from your spouse. You may need a hug, a kiss, help with the chores, or an action that says, "I care about you." It may be that you need to take time to prepare yourself mentally by thinking about being together sexually (that positive mental anticipation we talked about earlier in this chapter) or by reading something romantic. Reading the Song of Solomon may get you in touch with your sexual needs.

When you need a specific behavior from your spouse to spark your sexual interest, getting what you need becomes more complicated. Sex works best in all dimensions when each of you takes responsibility for your own needs. Therefore, when your need requires action by your spouse, you must communicate that need. Avoid the game of thinking *If he loves me, he'll know what I need. I've told him before, so he should remember. If I have to tell him, it won't work.* If you convince yourself it won't work, it surely won't. So take responsibility to know and communicate clearly, openly, and consistently what you need to activate your sexual urges.

Initiation

Acting on your sexual desire with one another is initiation. You may initiate sexual contact before any arousal or as the result of being turned on or sexually excited. Initiation may be the expression of your desire to just be close and warm or for intense sexual play that will lead to intercourse and release. It may grow mutually between the two of you, or it may come from one of you to the other. Mutual initiation often grows out of physical contact like a hug, kiss, or crawling into bed together. Spending time working, playing, talking, or just being together may also spark desire that triggers mutual pursuit of sexual behavior.

More often initiation occurs when one sexually desirous spouse expresses desire for the other. This interest may be communicated in words, by reaching out physically, or in more subtle ways. The message may be a direct, verbal invitation or a more symbolic message. You will likely develop your own love language to express desire to be with one another sexually. Many women need their husbands to express their desire as positive messages about them or as messages of their value to the husbands. All women respond much more favorably to, "You are gorgeous. I'd love to spend some time with you," than to, "I need sex" or "You haven't met my sexual needs in a long time." The last two requests make the woman feel like she could be anyone, as long as she gives him an ejaculation. She feels like she is servicing him. A physical approach works great if it is positive for both, but if one of you feels that hugs or kisses are given only to "get sex," that can cause you to avoid those connecting behaviors. Physical initiation must be an expression of care and connection with each other without a demand from one spouse to the other. Subtle initiation is fun if the other one catches the subtleties. Preparing your body, the setting, or a special treat are all possible subtle ways to initiate sex.

Initiation flows best and causes the least amount of tension when both of you are free to express your desires without putting pressure on the other to feel the same as you do or to respond with enthusiasm. If the other does not feel open to a sexual encounter, another option other than "No" should be offered. You make yourselves vulnerable when you express your desire for each other. Getting a "no" as a response can hurt. A more positive response might be, "Boy, you caught me off-guard. Give me a little time to see if I can get with that possibility." You could also offer other options: "I'm exhausted, but what if I get to bed early and we set the alarm to have some time tomorrow morning?" or "I don't have the energy to get aroused, but I would love some pleasuring, and I wouldn't mind bringing you as far as you'd like." The possibilities are endless. They could include a later time, a different physical activity, or a different focus. Almost anything is better than "no."

Variation and open communication without demand are essential to the spontaneous, ongoing expression of each of your desires for physical closeness.

Pleasuring

Becoming one—totally—takes time. It takes time to mesh your worlds, communicate with one another, and delight in the stimulation of each other's body. Pleasuring begins with the process of getting into each other's world and bringing together your emotions, spirits, sensations, and bodies. It includes a focus on all of the senses. You must both appeal to each other's needs for sight, smell, touch, sound, and taste. Meshing will occur more naturally when you have spent time together; it will take more effort if your worlds have been separate and consuming.

Two types of communication are necessary to enjoy pleasuring: verbal and nonverbal. Talking about what you like, don't like, or would like should be done apart from the sexual experience. Verbal messages during sex should indicate your enjoyment and express positive invitations for the touch you would enjoy. Nonverbal communication lets you signal each other during sex without interrupting the flow of the pleasure. These nonverbal signals can be taught apart from the sexual experience.

Delighting in the erotic touching of each other's body is vital to the giving and receiving of pleasure and will likely trigger some arousal and possibly release. To maximize the pleasure each of you receives, acknowledge your body's hunger for touch and go after that, enjoy touching each other in ways that are pleasurable to you, and agree to let each other know if any activity is negative by inviting some other touch that would feel better. Since women are more complex and sensitive, it usually works best if the woman sets the pace for sexual stimulation. As one woman explained to her husband, "It's like when we ride bikes together. Since you can go faster than I can, it works best if you always keep your front tire right behind mine." Sex often works best if the husband thinks of keeping his wife hungry for more; rather than pushing her for more than she wants, he needs to keep just a little behind her. A sexually satisfied woman is usually one who has taught her husband how and when she wants to be stimulated sexually. That requires a husband who is willing to learn from his wife and allow her to be the expert on her body.

Being able to love each other and enjoy erotic touching without feeling the need to please, without demanding performance, and without feeling failure is vital to sexual pleasure.

Entry

Total sexual union is not necessary to have total sexual fulfillment or the intimacy of bodily pleasure. As we have said repeatedly, when entry of the penis into the vagina is desired, it is best if it is initiated by the woman since it is her body that is being entered. We all feel threatened or violated when someone enters our "territory" without being invited. Thus, it will relax you, the woman, to know that your husband will wait for you to signal him when you are ready for entry. It will also take the pressure off him to magically know when you want entry.

Enjoying the Process

Entry of the penis into the vagina does not have to be the beginning of the end. When the focus is on pleasuring rather than climax, there can be a time of resting together and enjoying the penetration of the penis into the vagina without thrusting. There can be freedom to withdraw, reenter, and "play around," allowing the turned-on feelings to ebb and flow in intensity. This is the time in the sexual experience to abandon all fears and inhibitions so you are free to intensify the heavy breathing, rhythmic movement, noises, and grimaces that are a natural part of the body's sexual response to pleasure.

When you are both free to enjoy the process and let sex flow freely, the moods of your sexual experiences will tend to vary from tenderness to passion to fun and games. Sometimes the mood may be intensely erotic and at other times functional. Either can be a pleasurable way to meet your sexual needs.

Letting Go

When you are not controlled or inhibited and you are receiving adequate stimulation, letting go will occur somewhere in the process of lovemaking. Letting go is obvious in men but may be a struggle or a source of confusion for many women.

To help women understand the sensation of letting go, we compare it to a sneeze. The buildup of tension in the pelvis is due to vasocongestion—blood and fluid filling the genitals—just like the nasal passages get congested before a sneeze. There is that tingling sensation both in the nose before a sneeze and in the pelvis before an orgasm. You can stop an orgasm just like you can stop a sneeze, but you cannot "will" either to happen. If those pelvic, tingling sensations are pursued with stimulation and activity, the contractions in the passageways will release the tension and fullness—that is an orgasm, a pelvic sneeze!

Affirmation

When you allow yourselves to be vulnerable and let go sexually—to be out of control and release all of your sexual intensity with one another—a closeness and a deep sense of warmth follows. This is an important time of sharing. When you have not been able to let go of all the intensity that built up during sexual arousal, you may feel tense or frustrated or disappointed. We encourage you to continue your closeness during the crying, if that happens. Hold each other rather than pulling away. Affirm your love, care, and commitment to each other.

Learning to keep sex for pleasure is vital to making the transition from a passion-driven sexual relationship to an ongoing sexual relationship. Once two people can have each other every day and there are no restrictions on their being together sexually, sex changes. There is something that happens when two individuals become one and commit themselves to each other for a lifetime. That can bring incredible freedom, but it can also bring demands, anxieties, or expectations that interfere with sexual pleasure.

As you establish positive sexual patterns, eliminate hindrances to success, and attend to the emotional-relationship dimensions of sex early in your married sex life, you will set a positive tone for years of sexual enjoyment with each other.

Foot and Hand Caress

(Read out loud together and follow the steps.)

Step 1: The woman will take responsibility to initiate this experience and set the atmosphere. Choose a location in which the receiver can be seated or reclined in a comfortable, upholstered, high-backed chair or couch. The pleasurer should be positioned to be able to comfortably caress the receiver's feet and hands.

Step 2: Bathe or shower individually. Wear comfortable clothes or robes. You may bring a pan of warm, soapy water to soak each other's feet if you both desire.

Step 3: The man will be the first pleasurer; the woman will be the first receiver.

Step 4: *Receiver:* Get comfortable in the chair or couch. Lie back and close your eyes. Breathe in deeply and exhale slowly several times, letting your body sink into the chair or couch. Soak in the gift of your spouse's touch. If your feet should feel ticklish, this is a positive sign of intense responsiveness. To relieve the ticklishness and help you receive the sensuous touch, focus on the sensations of the skin contact. You may need to direct your spouse to touch more firmly and/or move to a different part of your foot.

Pleasurer: You may or may not use a lotion. If you do, warm it in your hands first. With or without lotion, start caressing your spouse's foot. Get to know his or her foot through touch. *Slowly* explore the toes, arch, top of foot, ankle, and even the lower leg. Always maintain contact with the body part being caressed and inform your spouse before you move to the next part. Caress one foot and then the other. In the same manner, caress one hand and then the other. Enjoy all surfaces and parts of each hand and lower arm. Inform your spouse when you are finished.

Step 5: You may want to take a rest or break before you reverse roles and repeat Step 4. The woman will be the pleasurer; the man will be the receiver.

Step 6: Write your reactions: What did you enjoy most? What was difficult? Discuss your written reactions with each other.

These exercises are reprinted from Penner and Penner, *Restoring the Pleasure* (Dallas: Word, 1993). Used by permission.

Facial Caress

Read out loud together and follow the steps.)

Step 1: The man will take responsibility to initiate this experience and set the environment, making certain to provide comfort for both of you.

Step 2: Bathe or shower individually. Have hair clean, dry, and away from the face. Man should be cleanly shaven.

Step 3: The woman will be the first pleasurer, and the man will be the first receiver.

Step 4: *Receiver:* Position yourself comfortably on a bed or couch, with or without a pillow, with your head near the unobstructed edge of the bed or couch. Let yourself relax with eyes closed. Breathe in deeply and exhale slowly a few times, letting your body sink into the bed or couch.

Pleasurer: Sit in a comfortable chair, positioned so that you have easy access to your partner's face. You may or may not use a facial lotion or cream (Allercreme is great). Close your eyes and focus on the sensation of the touch as you explore your partner's face. Pleasure and explore as if you are a blind person getting to know your spouse through touch. Find eyebrows, eyes, all aspects of the nose, cheeks, forehead, chin, lips. Gently, sensuously, and lovingly enjoy the warmth of your partner's face. Inform your partner when you finish.

Step 5: You may want to take a rest or break before you reverse roles and repeat Step 4. The man will be the pleasurer, and the woman will be the receiver.

Step 6: Write your reactions here. What did you enjoy most? What was difficult? Discuss your written reactions with each other.

Back Caress

(Read out loud together and follow the steps).

Step 1: The woman will take responsibility to initiate this experience and set the atmosphere, making certain the temperature of the room is comfortable and there is privacy.

Step 2: Bathe or shower individually. If possible, you will be nude for this experience. If nudity is too difficult, use the minimal covering to provide the safety needed.

Step 3: The man will be the first pleasurer; the woman will be the first receiver.

Step 4: *Receiver:* Get comfortable lying front down on the bed or location chosen. Focus on the enjoyment, relaxation, and gift of your spouse's touch.

Pleasurer: Position yourself so that you can comfortably enjoy your spouse's back. Start by putting your hands flat on his or her back and just feeling the pulsation and warmth of the other's skin. Move your hands over his or her back at a slow sensuous rhythm that comes from inside you. If you want to add lotion, inform your spouse and warm the lotion in your hands before you apply it to his or her back. Do not violate the boundaries and move your hands farther than your spouse's back.

Step 5: You may want to take a rest or break before you reverse roles and repeat Step 4. The woman will be the pleasurer, and the man will be the receiver.

Step 6: Write your reaction here or on the back. Give your feelings and what you learned about yourself. Discuss your written reactions with each other.

Total-Body Pleasuring Excluding Breasts and Genitals

(Spouses: Read out loud together and follow the steps.)

Step 1: The husband will take responsibility to initiate this experience and set the atmosphere. The room temperature should be set so both of you will be comfortable without clothes or covers. Prepare a room that is softly lit and has a relaxed, uncluttered environment.

Step 2: Bathe or shower together. You may wash each other's non-sexual body parts.

Step 3: The wife will be the first pleasurer, and the husband will be the first receiver.

Step 4: As more of the body is included in the pleasuring, it is important to remember that sexual arousal is an involuntary response and not the goal or purpose of this experience. *Do not become concerned if there is or is not arousal; the purpose of this experience is body awareness.* Discuss these instructions before proceeding.

Step 5: *Receiver:* Lie on abdomen in a comfortable position.

Pleasurer: Place your hands on your spouse's back. With your eyes closed, focus on the sensations of your spouse's body: warmth, pulsation, vibrations, etc. Begin to move over his or her entire back with sensuous touch, radiating your warmth and care. Proceed in the same manner to neck, arms, and legs. Inform your spouse when you are ready for him or her to turn over.

Receiver: Turn onto your back.

Pleasurer: Sitting with your spouse's head in your lap (if it is more comfortable for you or your spouse, cover your genitals), proceed with a facial caress. Then continue down his or her neck, shoulders, arms, and hands. Move to the side of your spouse to enjoy his or her abdomen, legs, and feet. Do not touch breasts or genitals. It is important that you not violate that boundary.

Step 6: You may want to rest or take a break before you reverse roles and repeat Step 5. The husband will be the pleasurer; the wife will be the receiver.

Step 7: Write your reactions. Were there uncomfortable movements? What anxieties or demands slipped through your minds? What was most relaxing? Most pleasurable? Discuss your written reactions with each other.

Total-Body Pleasuring Including Breasts and Genitals without Purposeful Stimulation

(Spouses: Read out loud together and follow the steps.)

Step 1: The wife will take responsibility to initiate this experience and set the atmosphere with attention to temperature, privacy, and mood.

Step 2: Bathe or shower together. You may wash each other's body totally.

Step 3: The husband will be the first pleasurer, and the wife will be the first receiver.

Step 4: Continue to remember that sexual arousal is an involuntary response and not the goal or purpose of this experience. *Do not become concerned if there is or is not arousal; the purpose of this experience is body awareness.*

Step 5: *Receiver:* Lie on your abdomen in a comfortable position.

Pleasurer: Place your hands on your spouse's back and proceed to pleasure, taking in the warmth and sensations of your spouse's back, buttocks, arms, and legs. Take time to enjoy each part as you have in previous pleasuring exercises. Inform your spouse when you are ready for him or her to turn over.

Receiver: Turn onto your back. Positively redirect your spouse if anything he or she does is negative or demanding.

Pleasurer: Sitting with your spouse's head in your lap (with your genitals covered) proceed with a facial caress. Then continue down his or her neck, shoulders, chest, arms, and hands. Do not focus on the breasts. Just go over them as you have every other part of the body. Move to the side of your spouse (or between his or her legs) to pleasure his or her abdomen, genitals, legs, and feet. Include the genitals only in a general stroking over the top briefly. Inform your spouse when you are finished. *Do not pursue specific stimulation.*

Step 6: You may want to rest or take a break before you reverse roles and repeat Step 5. The wife will be the pleasurer; the husband will be the receiver.

Step 7: Write your reactions. Particularly attend to any demands that are arising and any enjoyment that is flowing. Discuss your written reactions with each other.

Total-Body Pleasuring Including Breast and Genital Stimulation

(Spouses: Read out loud together and follow the steps.)

Step 1: The husband will take responsibility to initiate the experience and set the atmosphere with attention to temperature, privacy, and mood.

Step 2: Bathe or shower together. You may wash each other totally.

Step 3: The wife will be the first pleasurer; the husband will be the first receiver.

Step 4: Even though stimulation is added to this exercise, arousal should neither be expected nor stopped. Sexual arousal is an involuntary response. *Do not become concerned if there is or is not arousal.* Enjoy whatever happens.

Step 5: *Receiver:* Lie on your abdomen in a comfortable position.

Pleasurer: Place your hands on your spouse's back. Enjoy pleasuring the back of your spouse's body in any way that is positive to you, giving and receiving warmth through your hands. Rely on your spouse to redirect you if anything you do becomes negative or demanding. Inform your spouse when you are ready for him or her to turn over.

Receiver: Turn onto your back. Soak in the pleasure.

Pleasurer: Sitting with your spouse's head in your lap (if that is comfortable for both of you) proceed with a facial caress. Then continue down his or her neck, shoulders, chest, arms, and hands. Enjoy stimulating his or her breasts for your pleasure, not for the result it produces. Incorporate the type of touch your spouse enjoys. Move to the side or between the legs of your spouse to pleasure his or her abdomen, legs, and genitals. Again, enjoy stimulating his or her genitals for your pleasure, incorporating what you have learned about the type of stimulation your spouse prefers. Never touch in a way that is negative to your spouse. Inform your spouse when you are finished.

Step 6: You may want to rest or take a break before you reverse roles and repeat Step 5, but you are free to continue. The husband will be the pleasurer. The wife will be the receiver.

Step 7: Discuss the experience. Write your reactions.

Total-Body Pleasuring with Entry

(Spouses: Read out loud together and follow the steps.)

Step 1: The wife will take responsibility to initiate the experience and set the atmosphere. It will be important for this exercise to not only provide for mood, temperature, and privacy, but also contraceptive, if needed.

Step 2: Bathe or shower together. Enjoy each other's body in any way that is positive for both of you.

Step 3: Talk about your feelings of being able to proceed to intercourse. Adjust for any concerns or demands that might arise.

Step 4: The husband will begin by giving the wife a facial, hand, and foot caress. Then spend some time mutually hugging, kissing, and enjoying the pleasure of each other's body in any way that is positive for both of you. Include breast and genital stimulation and using the penis as a paintbrush to stimulate the wife's genitals. She may invite the husband to do some poking of the penis into the vagina by adding a lubricant to the penis and between the labia, separating them as she does. With the woman in the top position, poke in a little at a time. Enter all the way when that is comfortable for both of you.

Step 5: Rest together quietly without thrusting. Enjoy the closeness of each other's body. Kiss and pleasure as you desire. Then begin gentle thrusting. The woman should control the thrusting. Stop to rest every few minutes. Move around in any way you desire. When it is desirable for both of you, allow the intensity of the thrusting to build. Continue as long as that is pleasurable for both of you. If there is release for either or both of you, that is fine, but it is not necessary. Ejaculation and orgasm are reflex responses to the intense buildup of sexual arousal. When your body is ready for that and you can allow it, it will happen. That is not an expectation of this exercise.

Step 6: Write your reaction. Talk about the experience from start to finish. What was most positive? What got in the way? Was there any pain, anxiety, demand?

12
••••••
Getting Past Disappointments

exual union is designed to bring delight and pleasure. Sometimes that pleasure comes easily to sexual beginners. With patience, openness, and a willingness to learn, all couples have the ability to discover joy and fulfillment in their sexual relationship. For some couples, though, sexual disappointments during the honeymoon continue on into the marriage. This is not likely for you, since you have been reading and doing your homework thus far!

We hope the preparation you have done will bring you to a joyful wedding night, a wonderful honeymoon, and many years of a fulfilling sexual relationship. However, if that is not the case, we want to briefly acquaint you with the various disappointments that are possible and direct you to some help for resolving those quickly. Should you need an additional reference, please refer to our book, *Restoring the Pleasure*.

Sexual disappointments are apt to occur if your sexual experiences do not get started as you envisioned. You may have come to your married life with a history of negative input or experiences that make it difficult for you to enjoy the fullness of your sexual relationship. You may have false expectations of what sex in marriage is to be. You may lack knowledge or openness with each other. You may have a high fear of failure or such an intense need to please that you approach your sexual times with anxiety. Either you or your spouse may be avoiding sex, approaching each other in a way that is uncomfortable for the spouse, or have unrealistic expectations of how sex gets started. Possibly your response to sex has surprised you. Maybe you were very desirous before marriage, but you became afraid when the time actually arrived to consummate your relationship. Maybe when you attempted intercourse you could not make entry happen. Maybe you found intercourse to be very painful.

Sexual problems fall into five primary categories: problems of desire, problems with arousal, and problems with release, pain, and addiction. When you are engaged and anticipating marriage, it is difficult to imagine that you might have a problem in one of these areas. We trust you will not. Yet it is helpful to be able to identify when a disappointment you are experiencing is actually a sexual problem that might require some help.

Problems of Desire

Differing Desires

You, as a couple, may find that you have differing sexual interests. This may come as a surprise to you, or you may have had some indications of these differences before marriage. Most often, differing sexual needs don't emerge until some time after the wedding.

No two people are exactly the same. Just as the two of you will vary in your need for food, you will probably vary some in your need or desire for sex also. Such basic differences are normal.

One of you may be a high-energy person who could have sex almost anytime. That can put pressure on the lower-desire person. Although there's nothing wrong with either of you in this situation, the one with lower desire may begin to feel that all the other spouse wants is sex or that there is something wrong with him or her because of his or her lower desire. As the higher-energy person, you would help your sexual relationship by letting the lower-energy person determine the frequency of your sexual encounters. If you pursue sex when *you* want it, it will tend to discourage your spouse and decrease his or her desire even more. Eventually, resistance will set in, and you will end up having sex less frequently than you would have if you had allowed your spouse to be in control of initiating sex.

On the contrary, one of you may have a much higher energy drain than the other. If one of you is getting a new business started and working long hours, you may not have as much energy left for sex. You may want your spouse to initiate sex, or you may prefer to select certain times to be together when you are less strained. After children are born, the wife often has less energy for sex. That reality will need to be adjusted to.

Differences in sexual desire may be the result of your differing levels of sexual fulfillment. If you are not being satisfied sexually, you will find that with time your sexual desire will lessen. You can revive your energy for sex by increasing your level of fulfillment.

You will need to work at adjusting to your sexual differences so they do not negatively impact your relationship. Start by talking about those differences. As clearly as you can, define how much you actually do differ. Frequently, when we ask spouses how often they would like to be together sexually, their answers are not as far apart as they expected. Once you have clarified your differences, work out ways to reduce them. For example, if the person with more energy handles some of the home responsibilities so the one with less energy can get a nap; that may increase the sexual availability of the one with lower energy. Also, a full sexual experience is not always necessary. It might be that the one with a higher need could be brought to orgasm when the other one does not have the energy to pursue orgasm for himself or herself.

Lack of Sexual Desire

If you lack sexual desire, that means your natural urge to be physically close, to be touched, to be aroused, and to have release is in some way blocked so you are not sexually drawn to your spouse.

Some people with inhibited sexual desire are not aware of any sexual feelings at all, not even a flickering. Others masturbate but have no desire for the intimacy of sex with their spouses. Others desire sex with their spouses, but only when that is not possible! Finally, there are some who so connect their sexuality with risk and guilt that they only desire sex before marriage or outside of marriage when they believe it to be wrong.

Perhaps you blocked your desire for sex as a way of controlling your level of sexual involvement before marriage. This is particularly true for individuals who were sexually active before marriage and then decided not to be. But it can happen to any couple who did not learn to separate their natural sexual desires from their behaviors. They did not control their actions by managing their "external circumstances" and deciding together on their physical boundaries. For example, some couples sleep together but decide not to do anything but kiss. Sharing the same bed is the external circumstance designed for sex. To engage in that behavior (of sleeping together) but not allow any physical intimacy will require turning off sexual desires even when asleep. That desire cannot be turned on by simply saying "I do" at the altar.

A woman may lack desire for sex because she does not feel valued or cared for by her husband. She may feel he is only interested in her when he wants to have sex. Trust may have been violated in their relationship, so she does not desire him sexually. He may be insensitive to her needs. If there are relationship issues that need to be resolved, marital counseling can help revitalize the woman's sexual interest in her husband.

Sexual conflict due to past sexual abuse, religious antisexual teaching, or having been raised in an alcoholic home are deeper reasons why women lack sexual desire.

If you experienced any sexual input or had a sexual encounter as a child, adolescent, or adult that left you feeling confused, guilty, or traumatized, your sexual desire may have shut down as you approached marriage or shortly thereafter. Women who have experienced inappropriate sexual associations in their past usually had a heightened awareness of sexuality as children;

as adolescents and adults they typically have intense sexual desire outside of marriage and then turn off those feelings once sex is expected within marriage. If that is true for you, you may have kept your past a secret. You would serve yourself and your marriage well to get professional help to undo the sex-related conflict of your past. You will need to grieve the loss of your innocence and develop a positive view of your sexual self. It will take deliberate, guided steps for you to disconnect shame, guilt, and trauma from your sexual experiences in marriage and learn to connect positive feelings with your married sexual life.

Rigid antisexual teaching during childhood will interfere with your adult ability to express yourself sexually in your marriage. You will need to be given permission to enjoy your sexuality and receive sexual pleasure with your husband. You may need to get that permission from studying the Bible or from your spiritual mentor.

If you were raised in an alcoholic or emotionally out-of-control home, your conflict about sexuality will show up as intense resistance to sex, not just a passive lack of desire. You will have ambivalence about being sexual. You will have difficulty losing control even though you certainly know how to be out of control. Because of your dislike of what you saw in your home, you will persistently avoid sex so you don't have to let go; yet when you finally give in and sexual arousal takes over, you have great sex. This can be very confusing to your husband. He wonders why you would resist giving in to something you seem to enjoy so intensely. It is because you struggle with control issues, and letting go sexually is to be out of control.

What can be done to reverse the pattern of the daughter of an alcoholic home? Since your resistance is now in control of your sexual relationship, use your need for control to work for you rather than against you. Take positive, active control, becoming sexual by decision, not by desire. This will not be an easy decision; you will have to *decide* to be sexual, even though you have intense conflict about it. Start by behaving sexually. Kiss passionately every day, and enjoy total-body pleasuring at least once or twice a week. Set aside time on your calendar and make sure these things happen. The success of changing your pattern of resistance will depend both on your determination to follow through with your decisions and your husband's ability to not pursue sex at all. He will need to allow you to be in control. It will be better for both of you if he does.

Men also struggle with lack of sexual desire. The same issues that lead to women's lack of desire can also affect men. Some issues *only* affect men's dilemma with desire, however.

The sexually naive male may lack desire because of feelings of inadequacy and underdeveloped emotional expression. He may have been raised in an overprotective home and missed many of the developmental expressions of childhood sexual curiosity. Because of these developmental gaps, he is awkward in a physical relationship. If this should describe you, be encouraged. You will be very responsive to education and training. With the help of a loving wife and the exercises and information provided here and in our book *Restoring the Pleasure,* you will find that full, confident sexual functioning is only steps away. As you gain competence, your desire to be together with your wife sexually will increase rapidly.

Emotional-sexual blocks are not so easily reversed. These deeper barriers are a more difficult challenge and usually require psychotherapy. You may avoid sex with your wife due to a fear of intimacy caused by a lack of bonding with your primary caretaker during your first year of life. Sexual trauma can cause the same phobic reaction to sex in men as in women. Men also develop aversive feelings toward sex as the result of religious antisexual training just as women do. If you were raised by a controlling, male-depreciating mother, you will have difficulty wanting to be open and vulnerable sexually with a woman. You may also lack confidence in your maleness and, as a result, have difficulty pursuing sex with your wife. Undoing these deeper sexual barriers will require an understanding of why they exist as well as a guided process to establish a sexual pattern that does not provoke your anxiety, avoidance, or resistance to being sexually intimate with the woman you love.

Left untreated, problems of sexual desire can destroy a marriage. It is difficult to accept the problem objectively and separate it from the person and the relationship. You will tend to feel your spouse's lowered desire as a personal message about you. Get help early to reverse the difficulty and work out a system of sexual functioning that affirms the needs of the one with higher desire without putting pressure on the one with less desire.

Problems with Arousal

Sexual arousal is an involuntary bodily response controlled by the passive branch of the autonomic nervous system, the parasympathetic branch. That's why arousal occurs automatically and regularly during sleep in both men and women. When these responses *do not occur* during sleep, there is a *physical* problem that needs to be corrected medically. When the responses *do* occur during sleep but *not* during sexual play, anxiety is usually the culprit that is interfering with the natural, involuntary response of sexual excitement.

Lack of Feeling Aroused

Women are rarely unable to lubricate vaginally except for hormonal reasons. Lack of lubrication is common for the postmenopausal women who are not taking hormonal replacement therapy. The best solution is to use a vaginal lubricant. Much more commonly, women struggle with not feeling aroused. It is as if their emotions are not connecting with their bodies. If you lack feelings of arousal even though you are getting lubricated and showing other signs of sexual excitement, you need to give yourself permission to be a sexual person and enjoy those sexual feelings. You and your husband can then work together to remove any sexual demands and the need to please. Begin actively listening to your body and vigorously going after sexual pleasure. To do that, you will need to intentionally connect your sexual feelings with your bodily responses. Both you and your husband can note and affirm the signs of arousal your body gives you. Focus on the sensations in your breasts and your genitals, the involuntary responses of nipple erection and vaginal lubrication. Enjoy these responses, even if you do not feel aroused. As you learn to pay attention to and enjoy your bodily responses, the feelings will come alive.

Erectile Dysfunction

Men's difficulty with arousal shows itself physically as erectile dysfunction, or impotence—the difficulty in getting or keeping erections. All men experience times of difficulty with erection, and it is normal for the intensity of the erection to increase and decrease during a long lovemaking time. That is not erectile dysfunction. When difficulty with getting or keeping an erection becomes a regular concern, however, help is needed. First, medical causes must be explored. If there is absolutely no physical basis for the problem, then the anxiety factor will need to be eliminated. That will require a systematic sexual-retraining process. If you worry about getting or keeping erections, learn to distract yourself from constantly watching the state of your penis. The best distraction is a wife who enjoys your body for her pleasure without a need for your erection. To get the focus off your erection, rule out any attempts at intercourse and learn to enjoy pleasuring each other for the sake of those good feelings of touch and closeness without attending to the state of your penis. Tell your wife *every* time you catch yourself thinking about how your penis is responding or not responding. At first, expressing your feelings of anxiety or self-awareness may be difficult because you may be telling her constantly. But expressing your worries and distracting yourself from your performance anxiety will reduce the frequency of its occurrence as well as its negative effect on your penis.

Problems with Release

The most frequent difficulty among couples who are newly sexually active is one of release. Men and women encounter opposite dilemmas with release. Men come too soon while women have difficulty allowing themselves to let go. That is partly because letting go is controlled by the active branch of the involuntary nervous system, and men tend to be active while women tend to be passive. Therefore, the best solution to reversing both of these difficulties—premature ejaculation and orgasmic inhibition—is to reverse roles. The woman should become more active and the man more passive.

Premature Ejaculation. When the man does not have control over when he ejaculates, he will often ejaculate before either he or his wife is ready for that to happen. This is premature ejaculation.

If you are concerned about your lack of control, the first thing you must do is tell your wife. Because a woman can stop her orgasm at any point, the wife of a husband who ejaculates prematurely naturally tends to think her husband does this because he only cares about getting his release and does not care about her. Rarely is that the case. The husband usually feels very badly about his early ejaculation but does not know how to stop or delay it. Take heart. Ejaculatory control can be learned!

There are three methods that can be learned to control ejaculation. The "stop-start" method is described by Helen Singer Kaplan in her book *PE: How to Overcome Premature Ejaculation*.[1] Whatever method you choose, Kaplan's book is an excellent resource for teaching you helpful attitudes and ways to increase full sensual awareness as a means to gaining ejaculatory control. The "squeeze technique" was originally introduced to the professional community by Masters and Johnson. Since then, many sexual therapists have taught that approach and perfected its use. You will find a detailed instruction process for learning the squeeze technique in our book *Restoring the Pleasure*. Another method, the scrotal pull, is not as widely used, but is also effective. It uses the fact that both testes elevate and pull up close to the body as a man gets excited and nears ejaculation. By keeping the testes pulled down, ejaculation can be delayed.

Ejaculatory control *can* be learned. Many couples use the steps taught in self-help books to learn it by themselves. The couples who try self-help and do not find success fail either because they have false expectations or they don't follow the instructions as directed. One common false expectation is that manual stimulation of the man can be stopped and/or the woman can apply the squeeze and then he can enter the vagina and thrust vigorously without ejaculating. That usually doesn't happen. Instead, there is a period when the couple needs to rest, perhaps quietly caressing and holding each other, allowing the arousal to dissipate. Then stimulation can be resumed until there is a full erection. Again, the stimulation must be stopped and/or the squeeze applied and a rest period allowed. This is practiced repeatedly without entry until the man has control outside of the vagina. Once control is learned without intercourse, entry can be attempted after several stops and/or squeezes followed by rest periods. After entry, the man will continue to need to rest and/or squeeze and allow his arousal to dip before he can resume thrusting.

Both men and women need to learn to allow their arousal to build in waves. Most men will ejaculate quickly after entry if there is intense thrusting. Couples have difficulty following the instructions, which direct them to apply the squeeze or stop the stimulation as soon as there is a full erection. Instead, they proceed with stimulation or thrusting until the warning signs are felt. But then it's too late to delay the ejaculation; the man has reached the point of no return.

Another common error that keeps a man from gaining control is that he wants to keep himself aroused rather than allowing his arousal to dissipate after the squeeze or the stop. He has difficulty changing his mind-set and instead rushes to arousal. The most difficult change for the man to make is to be totally passive and soak in pleasure without pursuing release.

Orgasmic Inhibition. Even though the reflex of orgasm is as natural as the foot jerk in response to a tap on the knee, many women have never experienced, rarely experience, do not know if they have experienced, or believe they have to work hard to experience that peak of physical release. Women who have difficulty allowing an orgasm find that their arousal builds and then levels out when they are about to make it over the hill. That is the exact point at which the involuntary control shifts from the passive branch to the active branch of the nervous system.

If you have difficulty being overtly sexual or letting go of control, you may unknowingly stop this switch from happening by resisting your body's natural changes. This is the point at which the heart rate increases, breathing becomes heavy and noisy, facial grimaces occur, involuntary thrusting takes over, and sexual noises are most natural. If you inhibit any of these bodily responses, you block the orgasmic response. If you exaggerate any of these natural responses, you encourage your orgasmic release. There is a distinct difference between *simulating* or *exaggerating* the natural bodily responses and *faking* an orgasm. Never fake, but *do encourage* your body. The primary difference is that you let your husband know what you are doing and why.

You *can* learn to let go. Whether you learn it through self-stimulation or with your husband, here are the steps you need to follow: (1) Stop mentally focusing on the goal of orgasm and refocus on the pleasurable sensations of touch and arousal, (2) Reduce your self-consciousness about your natural sexual response, and (3) Take responsibility to actively go after your own sexual needs and desires. As you are able to make these changes, you will be able to enjoy longer and higher peaks of arousal. Eventually, the reflex of the orgasmic response will be triggered.

Pain Interrupts Pleasure

Sex is meant to feel good. When sex hurts, its purpose is interrupted. Thus, pain during intercourse must be taken very seriously and relief sought with diligence.

First-Intercourse Pain. Other than the slight pain of breaking the hymen, the pain of first intercourse can be prevented. In chapter 11 we discussed specific steps you can take to prepare for first intercourse; we will review a few of the basic essentials here:

1. Begin stretching your hymen and the opening of your vagina by using graduated dilators or inserting first one finger, then two, and then three.

2. Practice the PC muscle exercises described on pages 91–92.

3. Have a gynecological examination to verify that the opening of your vagina is free of infection or irritation and able to accommodate an erect penis.

4. Complete the genital self-examination in chapter 6 to learn to know your genitals and be in charge of them.

5. Buy and use a genital lubricant for all sexual intercourse until you realize afterward that you forgot to use it.

6. Proceed to entry slowly. Take time to enjoy all the pleasure you allowed before marriage.

7. You, the woman, invite and guide the entry of the penis into the vagina.

8. Pause for a few moments after entry to allow the vagina to relax and to allow the man's arousal to subside.

That first time of consummation will be a memory that lasts forever. Make it a good one!

Vaginismus. The involuntary, spastic contracting of the muscles surrounding the entrance to the vagina can make penetration extremely painful or impossible. This problem results from negative feelings such as fear, pain, and violation that have been connected with vaginal penetration or the anticipation of it.

You can learn to relax the tightened vaginal muscle by working through one or more of the following four tracks: (1) Through reading, writing, and talking, you can free yourself of the emotional conflict and tension associated with entry into the vagina. (2) Through a sexual-retraining process, you can learn to trust the giving and receiving of sexual pleasure. (3) You can engage in an active process to help you gain acceptance of and voluntary control over your genitals. (4) You can achieve entry into the vagina through a gradual process of reducing fear and relaxing the vaginal opening. The last step is the most unique to this particular problem; vaginal dilation exercises are the key to successful treatment of vaginismus.

Entry into the vagina without pain can be achieved without surgery or other intrusive procedures. You *can* learn to control that muscle so that entry does not cause pain.

Physically Based Pain. An increasing number of women, particularly young women, are reporting pain during intercourse. Pain does not have to be tolerated, In fact, pain cannot be allowed to continue if you are going to enjoy sexual pleasure. Several physical problems can cause pain during intercourse: Infections, irritations, tears or fissures, childbirth trauma, or a tipped uterus are some of the most common. To reduce physically based pain, follow these guidelines:

1. Talk with your husband about the pain. Develop a signal to let him know when you are feeling pain so you can change your activity to relieve it. Any sexual activity associated with pain should never be continued.

2. Identify exactly *when* in your sexual experience the pain

is triggered and *how long* it lasts. Note specifically *where* the pain is located. It is helpful if you can describe *what type of pain* you experience: stinging, burning, stabbing, dull, rubbing, or sharp.

3. Take charge of getting relief from your pain. Seek medical help and describe in detail what you have already discovered about your pain. Boldly inform your physician that the pain is interrupting your sexual pleasure, and you want treatment to relieve that pain. If the physician minimizes your pain or tells you to just keep trying, change physicians!

4. Enjoy and focus on the sexual activities that do not elicit pain.

Addictions Interfere with Intimacy

One of the most perplexing of all sexual dilemmas is sexual addiction. Simply stated, if some sexual behavior controls you and your life, you are struggling with a sexual addiction. The sexual addict feels controlled by the urge in the same way an overeater is mastered by the desire to eat or an alcoholic is driven by the urge to drink.

An addict's preoccupation with sex will interfere with his marriage by either pulling him away from his wife or causing him to act out the addiction with his wife. The wife who complains about her husband's lack of desire for her will often discover that he has difficulty being intimate and physically close with her so he will find release in response to pornography, cross-dressing, peeping, picking up prostitutes, homosexual encounters, exhibiting, obscene phone calls, child molestation, or incest. A man who acts out his addiction with his wife may want to bring other women or objects into their sex life. Or he may persistently pursue sex with his wife, making her feel like a sex object rather than a partner with whom he is sharing romantic, intimate, physical expressions of love.

Patrick Carnes of Del Amo Hospital in Torrance, California, has been a pioneer in the study and treatment of sexual addictions. Dr. Carnes first brought the subject into public awareness with his best-selling book, *Out of the Shadows.* Since then, he has lectured extensively throughout the country, trained many professionals, and further defined sexual addiction in a later book, *Contrary to Love: Helping the Sexual Addict.* Much of what we understand about sexual addictions is borrowed from Carnes's work. His formulations fit quite accurately with our clinical experience.

Addiction often begins with what sexual therapists call a precipitating event. If someone at a critical stage of development was exposed to a sexual stimulus that led to arousal and release, the person may have become hooked on that particular input. Frequently, this event occurs at a time of emotional turmoil or neediness. The person's response to the stimulus, the sexual acting out, offers the person an escape from the emotional pain and problems of life. Once this habit of dealing with stress has developed, the sexually addicted person will handle stressful periods in life by turning to the addiction for relief. This, in turn, worsens his pain, and the negative vicious circle continues.

Carnes describes four stages of the addiction cycle that follow the initial acting out: preoccupation, ritualization, the addictive behavior, and the reaction of despair. The four stages occur in this distinct sequential pattern. It is the predictableness of this sequence that makes an addiction an addiction, even though the timing of the cycle is unique for every addict.

The stage of **preoccupation** is characterized by the addict's obsession with the desire to act. This urge begins gradually and builds until the desire to act overtakes all of his resolve not to act. That is when the **ritual** stage sets in.

Predictable patterns develop for each addict that precede the actual behavior. Rationalization, denial, and intellectualization are ways the addict modifies his thinking to diminish the blame he feels and to avoid facing the reality of his actions. The child abuser convinces himself that the children really like what he is doing to them or that this is his way of teaching them about sex. Or the husband justifies his visit to the prostitute or his enmeshment in his tenth affair by convincing himself that he deserves this because of how his wife has been "holding out on him lately." The addict's thinking becomes impaired in order to justify what he is preparing to do.

The process of "zoning out" of reality prepares the addict for the third stage, **the addictive behavior.** The addict is compelled to act until he feels his needs have been met. Usually this action includes ejaculation for the man or orgasm for the woman.

After he is satiated, there is immediate relief, but that is quickly followed by **despair.** His remorse includes his resolve never to act in this way again. The resolve may offer control of the cycle for very short or extended periods of time. But unless there is intervention and accountability, the cycle will repeat itself as the desire to act again gets triggered.

If you suspect that you or your spouse may be a sexual addict, seek professional help from an expert in this field immediately. If you need a reference, call us, or call the Carnes group. Patrick Carnes has developed a Sexual Addiction Screening Test that professionals can use to evaluate the likelihood that you or your spouse may be suffering from an addiction.

If this is your situation, please understand that sexual addictions can be controlled. But in addition to stopping your addictive pattern of behavior, you will also need help to shift your core beliefs that led to the behavior. Those two changes will reduce the obsession and the cycle that follows. If you are a sexual addict, you will need to work with a professional and commit yourself to working with a group of sexual addicts in a Twelve-Step program. To find a local self-help group, contact Sexaholics Anonymous at 805-581-3343, or Sexual Addicts Anonymous at 612-339-0217, and Co-Sexual Addicts, referred to as Co-S.A., at 612-537-6904.

As you begin to manage your addiction, you will finally be able to live without secrets and enjoy a sense of control instead of chaos. Addictive tendencies may be a life-long struggle, but you do not have to succumb to them. Recovery is possible. Your task is to face the true reality of your situation: that you are helpless and that you can recover with God's help and a daily commitment to manage your life in the way you have learned from your therapy and your group.

Many married couples struggle with some aspect of their sexual relationship, but that struggle can be relieved. The sexual response pattern is easily conditioned. So if your sexual response was set into motion in a way that is causing you trouble, you can change it through a process of sexual retraining. You *can* get past sexual disappointments!

13

••••••

Keeping the Spark Alive

A couple came to us for sexual therapy when he was eighty-seven and she was eighty-four; they had enjoyed a delightful sexual relationship for sixty years, but now he was having some difficulty keeping an erection. With a little correction, they were merrily on their way.

When we asked them how they had kept the sexual spark alive in their marriage for many years, they told us they took time for themselves sexually. They talked freely with each other about their sex life. They both were physically fit. Throughout their marriage they had read sexual guides and had fun experimenting and teaching each other.

They also said little surprises and treats were a common part of their sexual times (she was more likely to bring these to their experiences than was he). They were both able to soak in sexual pleasure—a positive sort of selfishness, but not really selfish in that each spouse's ability to enjoy pleasure brought delight to the other.

He had developed a style of allowing her to lead sexually, and both took responsibility for their own sexuality. They had a successful pattern of working out their differences and had always had lots of fun playing together. They were an ideal example of how to keep the spark alive over a lifetime.

At this early stage of your relationship, keeping the spark alive in your marriage over your lifetime probably is not your most eminent concern. Yet it is important to tend to even now. Elaine Hatfield, who did a survey of six hundred couples, reported that the feeling of "being in love" usually lasts from six to thirty months. That does not mean love dies after that but that the romantic, passionate love of your initial attachment and excitement has grown into a more mature, caring, committed love. Other researchers agree: "Research by the Yale psychologist Robert Sternberg indicated that, although passion wanes with time, intimacy and commitment may continue to grow. That quiet kind of love gives us what we needed all along: a friend, confidant and partner to share life with."[1]

To delight the same person sexually day after day, month after month, year after year, will take attending to the following recommendations.

Schedule Time

Time to Be Physical

We are not talking about scheduling intercourse or arousal or release. Nor are we suggesting that you have to feel any sexual urge to be together physically. Many of life's circumstances will interfere with your sexual desires, but you can still maintain a satisfying sexual relationship. You will be surprised at how frequently feelings will follow behaviors. If you wait for feelings, your sex life could be very sporadic! Remember, *you* can make sex happen; you do not have to wait for it to happen to you.

Having a time of physical intimacy without any of the "Big Three"—arousal, release, and intercourse—can actually be delightful. It is much like dating or like your relationship before you became more physically involved. Learning to enjoy one another's body without any of the demands for arousal, release, or intercourse allows for your individual differences from day to day and provides for more variety in lovemaking.

But you may say, "This chapter isn't for me. How unromantic to schedule sex. It's not fun if you don't feel like it!" The myth that spontaneity is an essential ingredient to a passionate sexual experience hinders hundreds of married couples' sex life. It is common to expect that those feelings will just happen like they do in television soap operas and in the movies. The sex that "just happens" on TV or in the movies is not between married couples. For the most part, married couples do not tend to catch the glance of their spouse across a crowded room and get so turned on to each other that they slip off into a bathroom at the host's home and passionately "do it." That kind of sex is driven by the adrenaline of desiring something that you cannot or should not have. Some individuals become addicted to that adrenaline urge, and it keeps them from being deliberate about building the intimacy of their sexual life in marriage. If that is the case, professional guidance will be necessary to help make the transition from a "zap-type" sexual desire to a deep, loving desire for closeness and intimacy.

Spontaneity does work for some married couples throughout their lifetime; they make the transition from a passion-driven sexual urge to an ongoing physical awareness of desire. This awareness keeps them together on an intimate level sexually without scheduling. Our observation is that spontaneity is most successful when the woman is aware of her sexual needs and free to communicate them to her husband without creating pressure or demands. Her physical expression of desire is more likely to get her husband to want to have sex with her than his physical expression of desire is apt to elicit a positive response from her. However, her complaining that he is not having sex with her as often as she would like will push him away. A turned-on woman is likely to turn on a man. An unhappy woman is likely to make the man distance himself because he interprets her unhappiness as a message that something is wrong with him that needs to be fixed. To put it bluntly,

**A turned-on woman usually turns on a man;
a turned on man is often a demand to a woman.**

This principle may not seem "fair," but wise couples accept it as a fact of life that can greatly enhance their sexual times together.

For most of us, scheduling is eventually necessary to keep our sexual spark alive. Every other commitment in life is scheduled. If we don't block out time for sex, the only time we get for it is the leftovers, usually five- to seven-minute sexual experiences after the eleven o'clock news. This is the most common lovemaking scenario between married couples in America. No wonder so many married people look for sex outside of their marriages!

The contrast to the typical spontaneous sexual scenario in America is a special time of connecting and romance that happens because you planned it. You scheduled quality time to be together when you were not both exhausted, distracted by the tasks of life, or feeling a demand to respond sexually. When you schedule times to be physical, you must be sure that these times allow for physical, emotional, and spiritual connection without any sexual expectations of what is going to happen between the two of you. Many times you will take time to pleasure each other, hug and kiss, cuddle, share your thoughts and feelings. Sometimes this may trigger desire for arousal, which may then lead to genital stimulation if that is comfortable for both of you. Remember:

**Never engage in sexual activity
that is negative for one of you.**

If you both desire or would not be violated by pursuing arousal, release, and/or intercourse, that is great, as long as it is not *expected.* Arousal, release, and intercourse should not be pursued during every scheduled time for physical intimacy or they will become expected. And you should never engage in sexual activity that is negative for one of you.

Time to Talk

Just as you will need to keep your sex life alive by scheduling time to be physical, you will also need to schedule time to talk about your sexual relationship. This talk time should be away from the bedroom and not when one of you is aroused or pursuing sex. It is best if it occurs when you are rested and will not be interrupted.

Talk about what you enjoy about your sexual relationship. Talk about what you have discovered works for you. You might each keep an ongoing list of new discoveries of conditions you need for a fulfilling sexual time. These conditions might include restedness, privacy, freedom from outside pressures, the temperature of the room, the state of your relationship, security from interruptions, the process of initiation, the way you get connected, and many others.

Talk about what you would like to change. Keep updating how you feel about all the areas of your sexual relationship. As your bodily responses change and you become aware of different needs and desires for pleasuring and stimulation, communicate them to your spouse. Once you have defined a need for change, make a plan for how you will make that change, specifying when and how you can do it. When one of you desires a change, the other spouse should not interpret that desire as a message of inadequacy. Change should be an ongoing expectation.

Now, talking about sex is not natural for many people. If it is a difficult topic for you, try reading this book out loud to each other. That will break down barriers of discomfort and familiarize both of you with sexual terminology.

Sex talk may not only be difficult because of your discomfort with the topic; it may also be that the two of you are typical of many men and women and you use different language to express your desires and feelings about sex. It might be helpful to read Gary Chapman's book, *The Five Love Languages* and pursue in more detail the ways you each communicate love. What is your love language? Are you receiving each other's messages accurately? Some husbands and wives need to think of each other as foreigners speaking a different language. John Gray's book, *Men Are from Mars, Women Are from Venus: A Practical Guide for Improving Communication and Getting What*

You Want in Your Relationship, even includes an entire chapter on "Speaking Different Languages." In that chapter, Gray states, "The Martian and Venusian languages had the same words, but the way they were used gave different meanings."[2] Dr. Gray goes on to explain that because women use words to express feelings, they take the liberty to use generalizations such as "never" and "always." In contrast, because men use words to convey facts and information, they take the woman's generalizations literally. Thus, the man will argue with the woman to try to convince her that he doesn't "always" and he has "sometimes." Consequently, the woman complains that she does not feel heard. This is just one of the many differences between men's and women's communication that can cause so much stress between husbands and wives. The two of you would do yourselves a big service by starting immediately to clarify your messages to each other, especially those messages about sex.

Then there is bedroom talk. Solomon and Shulamith were very explicit in describing the positive physical attributes of each other in Song of Solomon 1:15–16. They also talked openly about the sexual pleasure the other was giving (see Song of Solomon 2:3–5). Then they continued with a clear expression of what they wanted each other to do to stimulate them (2:6). They expressed themselves in beautifully symbolic love language. Today you are unlikely to use such poetic expressions, but the two of you can develop your own private sexual vocabulary. Don't hesitate to be explicit in using words that enhance excitement, but do not offend one another. The bedroom is your private lovemaking chamber. Your love talk can be unique to the two of you.

Times to Keep in Shape

We have often said that couples would enhance their sexual relationship greatly if they started walking together instead of watching TV together. In fact, the best thing you can do for your sexual relationship is to turn off the TV (or at least drastically reduce your TV time). Don't turn it on unless you want to purposefully watch something. Having a TV on all the time is like having another person living in your home with you. Controlling the TV now will not only help your sex life, it will also greatly benefit your family when children come along.

Keeping physically fit will improve your attractiveness to each other, increase your sex drive, and enhance your responsiveness. In addition to working out or walking, your eating habits also affect your physical fitness. Reducing fats, sugars, alcohol, and additives (like preservatives and other chemicals) in your diet will increase your general physical well-being. Eating plenty of fresh fruits and vegetables, whole grains, and low-fat proteins, and drinking eight to ten glasses of water a day will increase your stamina, brighten you skin and hair, and generally enhance your physical condition.

Managing your schedule to reduce stress and allow adequate sleep also will help you stay in shape. We have already addressed the importance of grooming before your first married sexual experience. That is not something you should slack off on once you are married. Keep your bodies well tended for yourselves and for each other.

What to Plan into Your Scheduled Times

Time to Experiment

As a newly married couple, you may need to get the basics working smoothly before you are ready to start any experimentation. But once you are feeling pretty secure with each other sexually, you may want to follow the once-a-week suggestions in our book, *52 Ways to Have Fun, Fantastic Sex*.[3] Varying the activities you enjoy during your sexual experiences will add a great deal of newness to your sexual times. You might also consult a book that shows various positions and have fun getting into these positions without being aroused and without having entry.

You can add spark to your sex life by experimenting with new places to have sex. Sometimes a different room than your bedroom adds a whole new perspective. Varying the lighting is important, and adding sound can be great. Play your favorite music, or try a sound-effect tape. You might like ocean waves, rain, or rhythmic beating of drums. Experiment to see how various background sounds affect each of you. The texture of what you wear, what surface you make love on, and what you use to pleasure each other can be varied. Odors are important; eliminate all negative odors from the sexual experience and add

positive scents if you like. Wearing your husband's favorite per-
fume or your wife's favorite cologne can be a turn-on.

If you came to your marriage with inhibitions, experiment
methodically to reduce them. Define your inhibition as clearly
as you can, then write out how you would be sexually if you did
not feel inhibited. Identify the smallest steps possible that you
could take to move from where you are to where you would like
to be sexually. Try functioning according to the first small step.
When you get comfortable at that level, move to the next
step. Keep pushing yourself step by step until you are free of
your inhibition. Use the following form to record the steps you
need to take.

Experimentation is natural for some couples; they try new
ways of being together without even thinking about it. For others, it has to be deliberate. And for still others, experimentation
requires outside ideas.

Teaching Times

In order to grow in your lovemaking you will need to teach
each other about your bodies, about what feels good and about
the sexual experience per se. To teach each other about what
kind of touch you enjoy sexually and when and where you like

to be touched, try a talking/teaching experience. Begin by talking to each other about what works best for you, then show each other and guide each other's hands in pleasuring your bodies as you talk about what you are feeling. As you become freer to responsibly and sensitively teach one another sexually you will find more and more delight in your sexual life.

Our book *Restoring the Pleasure* has an entire section that describes "The Sexual Retraining Process," a set of detailed teaching exercises. Couples can work through these exercises one by one or pick and choose the exercises that would be most helpful to them.

Special Treats

Special treats can range from remembering to dim the light in the bedroom to enjoying an elaborate weekend away at your favorite resort.

Remembering to do special things that you each enjoy will add distinctiveness to your lovemaking. We recommend that you anticipate your scheduled times together by taking responsibility to do one small action that will make your time more interesting. Bring creative ideas to your sexual times, rather than just hoping your spouse will do that for you. If you have an idea of a treat that you would enjoy, do it! Do not get into playing the game of, "If he loved me, he would know what makes sex special for me, and he would remember to do that." *You* are the one who remembers because *you* are the one who is affected. So make it happen!

Things to Learn for Your Times Together

Pleasure for the Sake of Pleasure

When you have sex for other reasons other than for pleasure and enjoyment of each other's body, sexual apathy or performance anxiety sets in. The most common example of this is the man or woman who is complaining about his or her spouse's lack of sexual desire. As we assess the situation, we discover that the one who wants more frequent sex is pursuing it out of an anxious need for affirmation rather than an urge to be close and enjoy physical pleasure. The overly desirous spouse is communicating a demand to have the other spouse meet his or her needs rather than a desire *for* the other person. There is a huge difference in delighting in one another's body for your pleasure or demanding that your spouse meet your needs.

You may have difficulty consciously accepting your responsibility to pursue bodily pleasure. You may block your own awareness of your desire for pleasure or feel shy about being sexually overt. You might actually turn yourself off and then wait for the magic wand to trigger your sexual urge. Then, when that instant turnon does not happen, you will be disappointed.

Take Responsibility for Your Own Sexuality

When you learn to take responsibility for your own sexuality, you will not be disappointed. You will not wait for sex to happen to you. You will start behaving in the way you imagine is best for you and the feelings will follow. You will start kissing passionately on a daily basis. You will plan sex into your lives. You will prepare yourselves mentally and physically for your times together. You will make certain that the conditions for good sex are present for your sexual times. You will take responsibility for your own sexual response by listening to your body, going after what your body desires, and communicating what you would enjoy.

To take responsibility for your sexuality, you need to know your body. If you have not completed the exercises in chapter 2, be sure to do that. You also need to be free to enjoy your spouse's body for your pleasure, incorporating what you know is enjoyable to him or her. This is not a one-sided, selfish enjoyment, but a mutually enjoyed pleasure. As you both freely go after sexual pleasure responsibly with deep love, care, and consideration of each other, you will enjoy a long life of sexual fulfillment and delight.

Keep in Touch with Sexual Feelings

To keep your sexual feelings for each other alive, those feelings need to be nurtured. Protect and pursue your feelings for each other. Light that pilot light regularly. Fan the flames of your passion, as we discussed in the introduction to this book. Make sure you do not use up all of your sexual drive energy with the tasks of life. Take a nap on the days you plan to be together in the evening. Do everything you know how to do to keep sex alive in your relationship.

Keep in touch with your body by caring for it, knowing it, and exercising it. Women, exercise your PC muscle that controls the opening of your vagina; do at least twenty-five to fifty contractions per day. You may say, "I'm just not a disciplined person." But if your relationship is important to you, you will find time to keep your feelings alive. Plan cues into your life that remind you to do the things you need to do to keep your sexuality alive.

Keep in touch with your sexual thoughts; don't fight them. If sometime during your past you developed fantasies that cause you to feel guilty, you may have stopped all sexual thinking. Our minds were designed by God with the capacity for imagery. That is one way we are sexually different than the animals. What we put into our minds is important. You may need to replace your past images with healthy images. You may need to read the Song of Solomon every day in a modern paraphrase. You might write out your ideal sexual fantasy experience with your husband, then picture that often throughout the day. Imagine you and your spouse in some unusual romantic or exotic setting. Encourage positive sexual feelings and pictures.

What if you find yourself having sexual feelings for someone other than your spouse? Unfortunately sexual *feelings* are not monogamous. What you *do* with those feelings is your responsibility and must be monogamous. Whenever you have a sexual thought or response to someone other than your spouse, immediately replace the image of that person with the image of your spouse. Do not shut off the feelings; bring that energy and spark home to bed. Use those feelings to benefit your relationship. Keep your sexual vitality alive by directing those feelings appropriately rather than either depressing them or pursuing them. Sexual feelings are not selective, but sexual behaviors must be selective, and sexual thoughts can be controlled and directed.

Have Fun and Play Together

Sex does not have to be serious. Some sexual times will be warm and passionate; others will be intensely erotic. Still others will be fun and games. Laughter can help a sexual relationship greatly. Have gentle pillow fights in the nude. If ticklishness is not a negative sensation for one of you, tickle each other. Kiss each other all over playfully. Enjoy teasing touch that is just for fun, not to produce a response. Learn to laugh together.

Negotiate Differences

Maybe one of you needs more touching while the other needs more release. Plan some time when the one that desires touching can be pleasured without pursuing arousal and release. Then participate in pursuing release for the other if that is not aversive to you. Most couples negotiate their differences in all other areas of life, but it is amazing how hesitant couples are to objectively talk about and plan for their differences in their sexual relationship. Let us address some of the most common sexual differences that need to be negotiated.

What do you do if one of you is a morning person and the other is a night person? Maybe you are active and alive at six in the morning, but can hardly keep your eyes open by ten at night. On the contrary, your spouse cannot be awakened until he or she has had a cup of coffee sometime between eight and ten in the morning but is up and going until midnight or after. You may need to schedule "nooners." Actually there are a number of possible ways of negotiating sexual times around your personal sleeping habits. The "early bird" might come in and awaken the late riser with breakfast in bed, some breath mints, and a warm washcloth. This might be a special time for the two of you to talk or read something inspirational and pray together and then snuggle. If that leads to sex, fine; if it doesn't that's great too. Other times the night person might come and "tuck in" the early-to-bed spouse. You might even fall asleep together and get up later to pursue your nighttime tasks. In the long term, the two of you would do well to work on adjusting your conditioned sleep patterns to be more compatible. If each of you tries working toward the other's time schedule by half an hour at a time, before long you will be going to bed together and getting up together.

Another typical difference that we often receive letters about is that the woman wants more spiritual involvement from her husband, and she feels all he wants is sex. She has difficulty sharing herself sexually because of his lack of spiritual connection with her. That is a great one to negotiate. Make a deal that every time he takes time to read and pray with you or share your spiritual concerns, you will have a time of physical intimacy.

Invite God into Your Sex Life

If you grew up associating sex with sin, it is time to undo that false connection. Actively recognize your sexuality as a gift from God. Thank Him for your sexual feelings. Ask him to enrich and bless your sexual times together. Realize that He delights in your having a wonderful sexual time as husband and wife.

As you actively preserve and enhance your sexual relationship, you will keep your sexual spark alive throughout your lifetime. There is no need to become less sexual as you become parents or as you age. You can enjoy sex until the day you die. And that would be our hope for you. May your affection, love, and enjoyment of each other's body last well into your eighties and nineties.

Epilogue

♦♦♦♦♦♦

Two Become One: A Symbol of Christ and the Church

For this cause a man shall leave his father and mother, and shall cleave to his wife; and the two shall become one flesh. This mystery is great; but I am speaking with reference to Christ and the church.
Ephesians 5:31–32

he final message we want to leave you with is one that we have taught in our seminars for twenty years, and that is the connection that Scripture makes between sexuality and spiritually. Becoming one sexually is more than a physical act. It is also a beautiful symbol of our becoming one with God. Let's look at the similarities between the sexual relationship of a husband and wife and our relationship with God.

231

Desire

Becoming one sexually begins with sexual desire, which is experienced as that urge to be touched, to be close, to be aroused, or to have release. All of you have been created with that urge, but sometimes barriers from your past may block you from feeling that desire. Other times your sexual energy may get used up by responding to the demands of life. Still other times, you may not desire sexual togetherness because sexual experiences have been negative.

Likewise, the Bible teaches that you have been designed to seek union with God. "Seek the LORD and His strength; / Seek His face continually" (Ps. 105:4). "How blessed are those who observe His testimonies, / Who seek Him with all their heart" (Ps. 119:2). "And without faith it is impossible to please Him, for he who comes to God must believe that He is, and that He is a rewarder of those who seek Him" (Heb. 11:6).

God's desire to be in a relationship with you is clearly demonstrated throughout Scripture. "For thus says the Lord GOD, 'Behold, I Myself will search for My sheep and seek them out'" (Ezek. 34:11).

Even though you are designed to desire God and even though His desire for you is constant, sin can keep you from experiencing that urge for God. Similarly, desire for one another sexually can be blocked, and desire for oneness with God can be interrupted. Nevertheless, just as your need for God does not go away when you do not feel it, neither will your need for sexual oneness in marriage disappear when that urge is blocked. Both spiritual and sexual oneness is a constant desire for all of mankind, whether or not that need is felt.

Initiation

Initiation is acting upon your desire. It is the process of connecting two desires. You will not always experience sexual desire at the same time. Just as initiation will often begin with one of you expressing your desire for the other, God initiated a relationship with you by giving his Son, Jesus Christ, as a mediator so you can become one with God. You have access to

God's presence through Christ. "But God demonstrates His own love toward us, in that while we were yet sinners Christ died for us" (Rom. 5:8). He initiated a relationship with you long before you were aware of a desire for Him. "Behold, I stand at the door and knock; if any one hears My voice and opens the door, I will come in to him, and will dine with him, and he with Me" (Rev. 3:20). He calls for a response to His initiation: "Seek the LORD while He may be found;/Call upon Him while He is near" (Isa. 55:6). His invitation to become one with Him is always available to us, but it never comes with a demand for a response. Similarly, when the two of you are free to express your desire for one another without pressure or demand, initiation can flow freely without eliciting resistance.

Pleasuring

Pleasuring is that total process of enjoying being together sexually. It is becoming one physically, emotionally, and spiritually. This includes the meshing of each other's worlds, communicating with each other, and stimulating each other. You will enjoy each other most and be most open and vulnerable with each other when you feel connected. To be connected takes time. If you spend much of your time being together, that connection or meshing may happen naturally. When you have been apart most of the day, living your separate roles, you will need time to bring your worlds back together, communicate with each other, and delight in one another before you will be free and open with one another sexually.

Comparably, it takes time to develop a sense of oneness, openness, and vulnerability with God. Time is needed to communicate with Him and allow Him to reveal Himself through His Word. You must *learn* to bring God into your world, just as you will need to learn to get into each other's worlds. Sometimes you will feel an urge to talk with God and have time with Him, but often you will develop a sense of oneness and openness with God because you have taken time to be with Him whether or not you felt like it. This is also true of your sexual relationship. If you are going to openly and freely enjoy the pleasure of each other's body, you will need to design time to connect, communicate, and touch each other. You will need to learn to be in each other's presence sexually without demand and with total abandonment.

Entry

Entry is that total and complete sexual union; it is becoming one. Just as a husband is to love his wife sexually as Christ loved the church, so it works best if the husband waits for the wife to initiate entry. God has offered Himself to you through Christ, yet He waits for you to invite Him into your life. You, the husband, can follow Christ's model by allowing your wife to initiate entry. God does not enter your life without being invited; likewise, don't enter your wife sexually without being invited.

Enjoying the Process

The sexual relationship is most enjoyable if entry is not the beginning of the end. Once entry occurs, if the man thrusts until he ejaculates, the experience will feel rushed and incomplete. It is important to learn to rest quietly together, to allow a slow rhythmic building, to be free to withdraw and reenter, to roll around, and to allow the sexual union to be different each time. Sometimes you will feel intensely erotic; other times you will feel soft and tender. Sometimes you will be playful and silly; other times you will have sex just to meet your physical needs. This variation will happen as both of you are free to let the process of enjoyment evolve.

Your relationship with God is very similar to this process. Entry into the presence of God is essential to total union and communion with Him, yet sometimes we don't learn to *enjoy* our relationship with God. Instead, entry becomes the beginning of the end; once you invite Him into your life, that is it. When that is the case, you miss so much of what God has to offer. As you learn to enjoy the process of your relationship with Him, you will find your feelings varying. Sometimes your relationship with Him will be intense; other times it will be warm and tender. Sometimes you will enjoy the humor in it, and there will also be times when it is just there to meet your needs—it is functional.

Allow yourselves to enjoy the process of being one with God just as you learn to enjoy the process of being one with each other.

Letting Go

When you allow yourselves to let go sexually, there is a deep sense of warmth, satisfaction, and fulfillment. To let go requires being out of control and releasing all of your sexual intensity. With that release comes the peak, orgasmic experience.

To relinquish the control of your life to God and allow Him to be Lord of your life requires you to let go and allow yourself to be totally vulnerable and open with God. You cannot hold back; all of who you are is released with Him. With that letting go comes that peak spiritual awareness and a deep sense of satisfaction and fulfillment. You experience true warmth.

Affirmation

Your need for affirmation will vary depending on how totally you are able to allow yourself to let go. When both of you feel sexually fulfilled, affirmation will flow readily between you. Similarly, when you have been in the presence of God, have given yourselves openly to Him, and have known oneness with Him, you will rest in that quiet peace and security that flows easily. "'I love Thee, O Lord, my strength.'/The Lord is my rock and my fortress and my deliverer,/My God, my rock, in whom I take refuge;/My shield and the horn of my salvation, my stronghold" (Ps. 18:1–2). "Let my meditation be pleasing to Him;/As for me, I shall be glad in the Lord" (Ps. 104:34).

May you continue to grow in your knowledge and experience of becoming one with God and with each other as you delight in a lifelong sexual relationship. May the joy of your marriage shine as a light to those around you as it reflects your love of God and of others. Here's to many, many happy years!

Notes

◆ ◆ ◆ ◆ ◆ ◆

So You've Found the Love of Your Life

1. James C. Dobson, *Love for a Lifetime: Building a Marriage That Will Go the Distance* (Portland: Multnomah, 1987), 57.

2. Lewis B. Smedes, *Forgive and Forget: Healing the Hurts We Don't Deserve* (San Francisco: Harper & Row, 1984), 94.

3. Gregory J. P. Godek, *1001 Ways to Be Romantic* (Weymouth, Mass.: Casablanca, 1991).

4. David M. Schnarch, Ph.D. *Constructing the Sexual Crucible: An Integration of Sexual and Marital Therapy* (New York: Norton, 1991).

5. Neil Clark Warren, *Finding the Love of Your Life* (Colorado Springs: Focus on the Family, 1992), 133.

6. *Los Angeles Times* View section, 2 February 1994, E1.

Chapter 1 Dispelling Myths

1. William H. Masters and Virginia E. Johnson, *Human Sexual Inadequacy* (Boston: Little, Brown, 1970), 87.

2. Warwick Williams, *Rekindling Desire* (Oakland: New Harbinger, 1988), 19.

Chapter 3 Getting to Know Each Other

1. Sidney M. Jourard, *The Transparent Self* (New York: B. Von Nostrand, 1964).

2. Harville Hendrix, *Getting the Love You Want* (New York: Harper & Row, 1990), 143–44.

3. David Keirsey and Marilyn Bates, *Please Understand Me* (Del Mar, Calif.: Prometheus Nemesis Book Co., 1984).

Chapter 4 Clarifying Expectations

1. *Family Policy*, a publication of the Family Research Council, Washington, D.C., William R. Mattox, Jr., editor, vol. 6, 6 (February 1994): 1.

2. Ibid., 2.

3. Ibid., 4.

4. Ibid.

5. Nowval Geldenhuys, B.A., B.D., Th.M., *The Intimate Life* (Grand Rapids: Erdmans, 1957), 36.

6. Dobson, *Love for a Lifetime*, 44.

7. Reported by Tina Adler, staff writer, in a recent issue of the *American Psychiatric Association Monitor.*

8. John Gray, *Men Are from Mars, Women Are from Venus* (New York: HarperCollins, 1992).

Chapter 5 Pursuing Biblical Passion

1. Joseph C. Dillow, *Solomon on Sex* (Nashville: Thomas Nelson, 1977).

2. Louis H. Evans Jr., *Hebrews,* The Communicator's Commentary Series (Waco, Tex.: Word, 1985), 243.

3. "Sexually Explicit Movies May Impede Sexual Intimacy," *Contemporary Sexuality,* December 1990.

Chapter 6 Discovering and Enjoying Your Bodies

1. Alan P. Brauer and Donna J. Brauer, *ESO* (New York: Warner, 1963).

2. A. K. Ladas, B. Whipple, and I. D. Perry *The G Spot* (New York: Holt, Rinehart and Winston, 1982).

3. Julia R. Heiman and Joseph LoPiccolo, *Becoming Orgasmic* (New York: Prentice Hall, 1988).

4. Clifford Penner and Joyce Penner, *Restoring the Pleasure* (Dallas: Word, 1993).

5. Brauer and Brauer, *ESO,* chapter 6.

Chapter 8 Preparing for Your First Time

1. Paul Popenoe, Sc.D., *Preparing for Marriage* (Los Angeles: American Institute of Family Relations, 1938; reprint 1961).

2. Ibid., 5.

Chapter 9 Choosing and Using Family-Planning Options

1. *Time* magazine, 3 December 1984.

2. *Contraceptive Technology*, 17th ed. (New York: Irvington Publishers, 1994), 113, 154.

3. Ibid., 113.

4. Ibid.

5. Ibid.

6. Ibid.

7. Ibid.

8. Ibid., 348.

9. Ibid., 113.

10. Richard P. Dickey, M.D., Ph.D., *Managing Contraceptive Pill Patients*, 8th ed. (Durant, Okla.: Essential Medical Systems, 1994).

11. Ibid., 35.

12. Ibid., 148–49.

13. *Contraceptive Technology*, 272–75.

14. Ibid., 274.

15. Ibid.

16. Ibid., 288.

Chapter 10 Your Wedding Night

1. Paul Popenoe, *Preparing for Marriage*, 4–5.

2. Dillow, *Solomon on Sex*, 13.

3. Karen Bouris, *The First Time* (Berkeley, Calif.: Conari Press, 1993).

Chapter 11 Keeping Sex for Pleasure

1. Popenoe, *Preparing for Marriage*, 22.

2. Bernie Zibergeld, *The New Male Sexuality* (New York: Bantam, 1992), 353.

Chapter 12 Getting Past Disappointments

1. Helen Singer Kaplan, *PE: How to Overcome Premature Ejaculation* (New York: Brunner/Mazel, 1979).

Chapter 13 Keeping the Spark Alive

1. Morton Hunt, "Does Love Really Make the World Go Round?" *Parade* magazine, 8 February 1987, 16.

2. John Gray, *Men Are from Mars, Women Are from Venus*, 59.

3. Clifford Penner and Joyce Pener, *52 Ways to Have Fun, Fantastic Sex* (Nashville: Thomas Nelson, 1993).

Additional References

◆ ◆ ◆ ◆ ◆ ◆

Chapman, Gary. *The Five Love Languages*. Chicago: Northfield Publishing, 1992.

Hilliard, Marion. *A Woman Doctor Looks at Love and Life*. New York: Permabook, 1957.

McCarthy, Barry, and Emily McCarthy. *Female Sexual Awareness*. New York: Carroll and Graf, 1989.

McCarthy, Barry. *Male Sexual Awareness*. New York: Carroll and Graf, 1988.

McIlhaney, Joe S. Jr., M.D. *1250 Health-Care Questions Women Ask*. Grand Rapids: Baker, 1985.

Miles, Herbert J., Ph.D. *Sexual Happiness in Marriage*. Grand Rapids: Zondervan, 1969.

Pearsal, Paul, Ph.D. *Super Marital Sex: Loving for Life*. New York: Doubleday, 1987.

Penner, Clifford, and Joyce Penner. *The Gift of Sex*. Dallas: Word, 1981.

————. *Sex Facts for the Family*. Dallas: Word, 1992.

Smalley, Gary, and John Trent, Ph.D. *The Language of Love*. Colorado Springs, Col.: Focus on the Family, 1988.

Smedes, Lewis B. *Sex for Christians*. Grand Rapids: Eerdmans, 1976.

Wright, Norman H. *So You're Getting Married*. Ventura, Calif.: Regal Books, 1985.